D1483385

VIOLENCE

Violence, Alimut (אלימות) in Hebrew stems from the same root as silence, non communication, Elem (אלם), Hence the alternative to dialogue is verbal and physical violence.

Martin Buber

Violence

An Integrated Multivariate Study of Human Aggression

S. GIORA SHOHAM, *Faculties of Law and Fine Arts, Tel Aviv University, Israel*
J.J.M. ASHKENASY, *Sackler School of Medicine, Tel Aviv University, Israel*
G. RAHAV, *Faculty of Social Sciences, Tel Aviv University, Israel*
F. CHARD, *Faculty of Social Sciences, Tel Aviv University, Israel*
A. ADDI, *School of Education, Tel Aviv University, Israel*
M. ADDAD, *Department of Criminology, Bar Ilan University, Ramat Gan, Israel*

Dartmouth
Aldershot • Brookfield USA • Singapore • Sydney

Published by
Dartmouth Publishing Company Limited
Gower House
Croft Road
Aldershot
Hants GU11 3HR
England

Dartmouth Publishing Company
Old Post Road
Brookfield
Vermont 05036
USA

British Library Cataloguing in Publication Data
Shoham, S. Giora
   Violence : Integrated Multivariate Study of Human Aggression
   I.Title
   302.54

Library of Congress Cataloging-in-Publication Data
Violence : an integrated multivariate study of human aggression / by
   S. Giora Shoham ... [et al.].
      p. cm.
   ISBN 1-85521-432-6
   1. Violence–Psychological aspects. 2. Violence–Physiological
aspects. 3. Violence–Social aspects. I. Shoham, S. Giora, 1929-
RC569.5.V55V53   1995
616.85'82–dc20   95-13057
                                               CIP

ISBN 1 85521 432 6

Printed and bound in Great Britain by Ipswich Book Co. Ltd., Ipswich, Suffolk

Contents

Preliminary Word

The present volume incorporates empirical and theoretical studies from all realms of human violence. The first part presents a unique bio-psycho-social study of violent prisoners. Since recent legislation in most countries no longer allows the collection of data of the kind we had succeeded in compiling, the chances of replicating this type of study are quite remote. The probabilistic research on the violence of the prisoners is supplemented by a situational analysis of a 'Danse-Macabre' which leads to the act of violence or the violence avoidance cues which lead away from the violent act. Sexual violence is then analysed within the context of the rapist-victim dyad. Violent drivers are presented as a special case of non-normative recklessness. Inner-directed violence is presented in a study of suicide. Finally, a model of macro-violence is presented examining the Holocaust as a symbiotic entanglement between Nazis and Jews.

This study was partially supported by a research grant
from the Israel Ministry of Police.

1 The Many Faces of Violence

Why has the First Temple been destroyed? Because of three things: idolatry, incest and bloodshed. But the Second Temple in which the Jews were studying the Torah, obeying the Commandments and giving charity, why has it been destroyed? Because of unfounded hatred. This means that unfounded hatred weighs like all the three transgressions of idolatry, incest and bloodshed together.

Talmud Yoma 9

INTRODUCTION

Impulsiveness and violence are types of behaviour which may be linked to criminality, whereas aggression is recognised as a fundamental human drive or instinct (Singer, 1971). A discharge of destructive energy transforms aggression into violence.

We assume a rather strict determinism of human behaviour, which ranges within a configuration of somatic and environmental factors, and envisages three levels of interaction involved in the genesis of human behaviour: biological, psycho-personal and socio-cultural. The aetiology of violence is related to all three of these levels of human functioning.

The flow from one level to another is continuous and gradual, not discrete or compartmentalised. Our hypothetical model suggests that impulses or stimuli are received by the nervous system through our senses, and generate neuro-endocrinological responses. These are sifted through and processed by the psychological-personality parameters of the individual, and are finally structured by his or her socio-cultural patterns of experience. The aetiological hierarchy envisages a complex configuration of factors inherent in human behaviour, so that at any given moment, the behavioural pattern of a given individual is unique and not reproducible. The probability that the configuration of factors within each level and between the three levels would be identical to the corresponding configuration of another person is so remote that it can be assumed to be non-existent.

1

The relationship between the various levels in generating behaviour is dynamic. Moreover, a multiphasic relationship exists between each level and the others, with every level linked simultaneously to the others and receiving feed-back from them.

The notion of a behavioural hierarchy entails the idea that for each pattern of behaviour, the relative contributions of the different levels are not equal. Yet, the relative preponderance and intensity of each level in the generation of a given pattern of behaviour determines the nature and form of this behaviour. Consequently, if we are able to grade the relative contribution of each level to the resultant behaviour, we shall have the framework for understanding the contents and form of a given case.

However, even if one level contributes more to the genesis of a given type of behaviour, the others, nevertheless, always leave their imprint. In the case of violent behaviour, one person may be predisposed towards it more than another, due to a high level of testosterone. A predisposition to violence on the personality level might be related to a person's need for stimuli, as measured by the Sensation Seeking Scale (SSS) (Zuckerman, 1964); field dependency, as measured by the Rod and Frame Test (Witkin et al., 1962); a high tendency to take risks, as measured by an instrument developed by Shoham et al. (Shoham et al., 1976); and other parameters indicating stimulus-seeking activist behaviour (Shoham, 1979).

Social and cultural factors may raise the probability of violent behaviour, e.g., the killing of an adulterous wife in southern Italy, or the killing of a sister who is pregnant but unmarried in the Middle East. Faulty socialisation may also increase the probability of violation of both norms and laws which proscribe violent behaviour in a given context (Shoham, 1964). All these are predisposing factors, which interact with situational factors, i.e. the exchange of words and acts, *in situ*, and lead to the eruption of violence on a biological level (Shoham, 1968).

The aetiological hierarchy relates to the predisposing factors in the following manner. A person who is allergic to alcohol is given a glass of laced fruit juice at a party. After drinking it, he takes a Jeep and drives it at full speed into a shop, killing two people. If his violence is taken as the dependent variable and we relate it to the independent variables in the aetiological hierarchy by multiple regression analysis, we would conclude that in his case, the interaction of alcohol with his biological structure would explain most of the variance. However, we still have to ascertain the role of the person's personality parameters in raising or lowering the chances of the actual eruption of violence. Furthermore, how did his socialisation influence his ability to restrain himself, even in the extreme biochemical upheaval into which his allergy had pushed him?

In the case of the 'crazy psychopath' who is always looking for trouble, most violence would be explained by stimulus-seeking low sensitivity to pain. Even in this case, we would still need to measure the autonomic nervous system by the low GSR (galvanic skin response) rates, the level of testosterone and cortisol in the blood, as well as the internalisation of specific norms which impede or enhance the eruption of violence. However, the subject's stimulus-seeking personality would be the predominant factor in the aetiological hierarchy.

Finally, if an Arab kills his sister, who became pregnant out of wedlock, most of the explanation would lie in the socio-cultural realm. Yet, we should still have to answer the question of why this specific person, rather than another member of his family, undertook to carry out the ritualistic killing.

Our approach is synthetical and holistic, for we see the individual as an operational unit, not as a mere configuration of parts. The research therefore, presents the interrelationship of biological, psychological and cultural factors in violent prisoners.

Theories of property and professional crime stress the socially learnt component, following the approach advanced by Sutherland, which states that most criminality, whose prime motive is profit, is considered 'normal' behaviour. This is a negative determination, because it does not stress the personality deficiencies amongst these criminals, as opposed to the general population. Violence, inasmuch as it has no professional criminal correlates, such as 'settling scores' in the underworld or mercenary violence, is usually accompanied by a lack of internal conflicts. If we accept this assumption, then violence is related to structural dynamics entailing the lack of a preventive barrier against uncontrolled behaviour. This lack of control is usually structural and therefore related to the violent offender's personality. Thus, the measuring system presented here places more of an emphasis on personality analysis than on general criminological variables.

PERSONALITY AND VIOLENCE

The most widespread explanations of violence indicate a significant connection between biological and personality components. Megargee (1982) denotes those internal factors which motivate an individual to commit an aggressive violent act, in a given situation, as 'instigation to aggression'.

One of the factors that separate violent criminals from the rest of the population stems from the access of the latter to legitimate channels for the discharge of anger and hatred. Megargee (1966) and Lane (1978) revealed that individuals whose personality structures do not allow for the release of aggression, accumulate violence to the point where they must perform an extremely violent act.

According to Eysenck (1967), a dimension of the introvert-extrovert can be found in the personality of the violent criminal. Introversion is related to a high cortical excitability level and quick conditioning in the slow building up of inhibitions.

3

Extraversion, on the other hand, relates to a low cortical excitability level, slow conditioning and the building up of inhibitions at a rapid rate. The quality of conditioning dictates the way in which social norms are acquired.

Many researchers equate psychopathy with extraversion. Zuckerman (1964) claims that psychopaths need a high level of stimulation in order to perform optimally their roles. Based on similar findings, Quay (1965) suggests that the quest for stimulants, which characterises psychopaths, is one of the factors contributing to their criminal behaviour. Allsop's (1965) findings regarding antisocial children indicate a linearity, or at least an increase in antisocial behaviour, parallel to an increase in psychopathy, extraversion and neuroticism.

We summarise, in chart form, our proposed typology of behaviour, based upon hypothetical variables and corresponding traits, thus:

Personality
Types, Dimensions and Traits

Separant		*Participant*

	Interactive Dimension	
Activist		*Quietist*
'Stimulus Hunger'		'Stimulus Aversion'
'Reducer'		'Augmentor
	Ontological Dimension	
Object-inclusion		*Self-Exclusion*
'Field dependence'-		'Field independence'-
'Sharpener'		'Leveller'
	Normative Dimension	
Outwardly aggressive		*Inner Castigation*
'Extrapunitive'		'Intropunitive'
Sanction orientation		Moral orientation
Outer control		Inner control
High risk taker		Low risk taker

We propose to denote the high violence probability profile as 'separant'. Its dimensions appear on the left hand side of the chart, whereas the low violence probability profile which we may denote as 'participant', appears on the right hand side. The separant aims to contain, or 'swallow', the object, whereas the participant wishes to be contained or merged with the object. The description and proposed measurements of each individual dimension in the profile are as follows:

In the interactive dimension, the first parameter is 'stimulus hunger', which characterises the separant, whereas 'stimulus aversion' is related to the participant. This conceptualisation is based on Eysenck's research findings concerning his extrovert-introvert personality continuum. His extrovert is characterised by sociability, impulsiveness, activity, liveliness and excitability, whereas the introvert is marked by diametrically opposite traits (Eysenck, 1967). The more violence-prone separant would therefore be stimulus-hungry, whereas the more quietist participant, striving for inaction, i.e., a state of non-stimulation, would be less likely to resort to violence. This might be linked to Eysenck's findings that the introvert reacts favourably to sensory deprivation. He also found that the extrovert is relatively insensitive to pain, but suffers acutely when in a state of sensory deprivation. This finding could be linked to the separant need for activity and the stimulation of the object, whereas the participant seems to suffer from stimuli which catapult him away from the coveted state of inaction. Stimulus-hunger and stimulus-aversion are readily measured by Eysenck's M.P.I. and other instruments (Eysenck, 1967).

Another character trait relating to the interactive dimension of the personality is revealed by Petrie's ingenious experiments on those who subjectively increase the size of the stimuli (augmenters) and those who decrease it (reducers) (Petrie, 1980).

Petrie's instruments consist of a block of wood divided at measured intervals and an elongated piece of wood which widens towards the end (Petrie, 1980). The subject first rubs the piece of wood while blindfolded, and then the block. He then has to point out the place on the widening piece of wood which seems to him to have the width of the block. The reducer points out the width at a point on the piece of wood which is narrower than the block, whereas the augmenter tends to point out a place that is wider (Petrie, 1980). This test is extremely simple, because the main components of the instruments are two pieces of wood and anyone, even a non-professional, can be trained to administer it.

The second, ontological, dimension relates to the 'object inclusion' of the separant and the 'object exclusion' of the participant. The separant displays a higher 'field-dependence' than the participant, who tends to be 'field-independent'. These two concepts, as well as Witkin's later study on 'psychological differentiation', relate to the object, setting an environmental perception while performing the task (Witkin et al, 1962). The field-dependent displays a low psychological differentiation, because he is dependent for his performance on cues stemming from the overall gestalt and the background set of a situation. In other words, performance is dependent on the configuration of the surrounding object. On the other hand, those who are field-independent and display higher psychological differentiation rely on their own cognitive cues, rather than on the outward gestalt of objects (Klein and Schlesinger, 1950). Field-dependence or independence is measured by the Rod and Frame Test (Witkin et al., 1962). A somewhat related test is George Klein's 'Sharpener' and 'Leveller' Dichotomy (Klein and Schlesinger, 1950). The separant would tend to be more of a sharpener, trying to pinpoint details of the object, thus displaying an intolerance of objective ambiguity; whereas, the leveller of objective details would tend be more of a participant type displaying tolerance of objective ambiguity. The leveller-

5

sharpener personality traits may be measured by instruments developed by Klein (Klein and Schlesinger, 1950).

The third normative dimension deals with the self-object relationship. The 'intropunitive type' is the guilt-ridden self-accuser, who rarely tends to solve disputes by violence, whereas the separant tends to be more outwardly aggressive, blaming others in an 'extrapunitive' manner. This trait could be measured by Rosenzweig's test (Rosenzweig, 1965).

The participant also tends to legitimise social norms, i.e., he is 'morally oriented'. He has deeply internalised social norms, so that external repressive sanctions are unnecessary to secure compliance. This trait is based on Rommetveit's theory on the internalisation of social norms (Thibaut and Kelly, 1959). We have developed a scale to measure the internalisation of norms (Shoham, et al., 1976), based on the hypotheses that the sanction-oriented, i.e., those who comply with norms only through fear of sanctions, would tend to be more violent. Rotter imputes to his 'internal controller' a belief in his ability to manipulate the external world (Rotter et al., 1962).

Finally, we have the high and the low risk takers. The more violence-prone high risk takers can be measured both by the scale which we have developed as well as by Shoham (Shoham et al., 1985).

The final outcome is a tri-dimensional model that incorporates seven basic character traits. These traits are *continua* rather than dichotomies, combining the separant's inclination towards violence, and the participant's avoidance of violence. After testing this model, we have built a scale and instrument to measure proneness to violence on the personality level (Shoham, 1964).

The psychological parameters of violence are naturally linked to personality formation, which is related to socialisation within the family. Hence, our next section will deal with the family parameters of violent prisoners.

FAMILY PARAMETERS OF VIOLENCE

The nuclear family is one of the major social institutions, so that many changes in social structure are correlated with changes in such a family. It is not surprising therefore, that a large number of theories have tried to explain delinquent and criminal behaviour as consequences of problems in the structure and processes of the offender's family. As Wilkinson (1974) has noted, the notion that a broken or malfunctioning family is the cause of criminal behaviour has often been mingled with moralistic overtones (Shoham et al., 1985). Consequently, it is rather difficult to distinguish between those elements of the conclusions of various authors which are based on competent measurements and those deductions which are largely based upon ideological and ethical convictions.

All major theoretical orientations in the socio-psychological approach to criminal behaviour (Kornhauser, 1978) are consistent with the idea that pathologies in the structure and functioning of the family are likely to be significant. From the perspective of strain, or anomie orientation, problems within the family unit reduce the individual's opportunities to cope successfully with societal demands and hence, operate as a crime-and deviance-inducing mechanism.

The effect of problems in the family is clearer according to the subcultural approach. Delinquency, it is claimed, is essentially the outcome of a differential association process. Therefore, as the broken or malfunctioning family fails to socialise the child into acceptable social norms, it contributes to his socialisation into alternative, deviant norms (Sutherland and Cressey, 1960; Shoham, 1964). According to another approach suggested by control theory (Hirschi, 1969), delinquent behaviour emerges whenever the controls over the individual's behaviour are lowered. The family serves as a major control agent. Any process which reduces its ability to react consistently to transgressions, or which lowers the juvenile's attachment to it, may be considered a delinquency or deviance-inducing process.

These theoretical approaches do not necessarily contradict each other. Indeed, in many cases, they may be considered complementary (Rahav, 1983), as they lead to the same conclusions. A survey of research findings concerning the family and delinquency indicates that, despite a few arguments to the contrary (Rosen, 1950; Wilkinson, 1974), the overwhelming majority of the findings are consistent with the hypothesis that broken, or conflict-ridden, families have higher rates of delinquent children than those that are intact or without conflict (Gove and Crutchfield, 1982).

Hence, we propose the hypothesis that violent and aggressive behaviour are related to unstable, conflict-ridden relationships within the nuclear family, and to weak or non-existent relationships with members of the family of origin. More specifically, our hypothesis is that violent prisoners will come from tension-ridden families, and families in which at least one of the parents manifests role-inadequacy. Moreover, following Parson's (1947) masculine protest hypothesis, we expect that maternal dominance will be associated with violence. On the other hand, attachment to both family and peers would be expected to correlate negatively to violent behaviour (Hirschi, 1969).

Following the family parameters of violence, we shall now devote our attention to some sociological manifestations of violent prisoners.

SOCIETAL CORRELATES OF VIOLENCE AS RELATED TO PRISONERS' ATTITUDES TOWARDS SOCIAL NORMS

After the pioneering work of Parsons and others in the 1940s on the social model of prisons, researchers have begun to regard the behaviour of the prisoner as enmeshed in social norms. This approach envisages that compliance or infringment of the norms within prison, the structure of the prison, the nature of the custodial staff, and the prisoners' subculture determine the framework of the normative system in which the prisoner lives (Irwin, 1970). Irwin and Cressey (1962) showed that many prisoners bring an adherence to a criminal subculture with them to prison, which prepares them for life 'inside'. Moreover, many prisoners identify with the criminal world and adjust their behaviour in prison accordingly. In this study, we intend to incorporate the link between the accepted and deviant perception of social norms of the prisoner and his violence. There is evidence of a link between the prisoner's attitude towards law enforcement agencies and his violence. Violent prisoners display a more negative attitude towards the police and lawyers than non-violent prisoners do (Cleaver, Mylonas and Reckless, 1968). The subculture of prisoners has been found to be related to their violence as well as to overcrowding within prisons. Megargee (1976) lodged groups of subjects in rooms of different sizes and studied their behaviour for three years. He found a significant link between room space and the number of normative infringements and their gravity. The link between discipline and overcrowding was found to be curvilinear, meaning that overcrowding is a sufficient, but not a necessary correlate of normative infringement.

Having surveyed the psychological parameters, the family parameters and the societal attitudes of prisoners, we shall proceed to examine their biological correlates, which concern neural and endocrinological structures.

THE NEUROBIOLOGY OF VIOLENCE

Impulsiveness seems to be linked to the high-probability-of-violence profile. It involves a mental state of excitement, linked to the arousal of the autonomic nervous system. Impulsiveness creates a favourable condition for the transformation of human aggressiveness into violence. There are four stages of impulsive behaviour: a provocative stimulus, a feeling response, visceral changes, and non-rational outbursts (Adam, 1982). The impulsive person 'overreacts', since the impulsive outbreak (fourth stage) is not logically or proportionately related to the provocative stimulus. Sometimes, the provoking stimulus is lacking altogether. Then, one faces a three step mechanism of impulsiveness, as manifested by anger, fury and rage. Impulsiveness may last for minutes, hours or weeks, during which period, individuals are unable to evaluate behaviour and actions logically. Impulsiveness may also be accompanied by cognitive incoherence. Psychologists and psychiatrists relate psychopathy to spontaneous impulsive violence (Henderson, 1939).

The region of the brain most principally involved with emotions is the limbic system, represented by cortical areas and subcortical nuclei.

Figure 1. *The Limbic System and its Related Areas in the Brain*

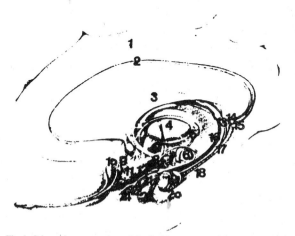

Fig. 1. Schematic presentation of the limbic system – (the emotional brain) (with author's permission). 1 Gyrus cinguli; 2 indusium griseum; 3 stria terminalis; 4 nucleus medialis thalami; 5 nuclei habenulae; 6 nucleus ruber; 7 fasciculus telencephalicus medialis; 8 corpus mamillare; 9 septum verum; 10 area subcallosa; 11 girus diagonalis; 12 fibrae amygdalofugales ventrales; 13 crus fornicis; 14 gyrus fasciolaris; 15 fasciola cinerea; 16 fissura choroidea; 17 gyrus dentatus; 18 subiculum; 19 cornu ammonis; 20 limbus Giacomini; 21 nucleus corticalis amygdalae; 22 nucleus anterior amygdalae; 23 nuclei basalis + lateralis amygdalae; 24 cortex praepiriformis

As the limbic system also controls autonomic functions through its subcortical nuclei, namely the amygdaloid complex, the septal region, the preoptic area, the hypothalamus, the anterior thalamus, the habenula and the central midbrain tegmentum, it has been named the 'visceral brain'. Anatomical correlation of violent behaviour has mainly been observed in animal studies. Aggressive-violent behaviour occurs in animals under natural conditions (Leyhausen, 1956) but can also be elicited by electrical stimulation (Bandler et al., 1972: Berntson, 1973). It has been found that when the hypothalamus and the brain stem are stimulated electrically, violent behaviour occurs (Wasman and Flynn, 1962). An interesting effect was observed when the stimulation of the dorsal hippocampus suppressed attacks of violence caused by the stimulation of the ventral hippocampus, leading to the discovery of an arousing and inhibiting area in the hippocampus (Watson et al., 1983). In the Macaque monkey, a normally aggressive animal, bilateral removal of the amygdaloid nuclei greatly reduced the reaction of fear and anger (Berntson, 1973).

Despite these obvious relationships between anatomic regions of the animal's brain and violence, animal functions and features cannot be automatically transposed to humans. We shall therefore review some of the relevant literature on the neurobiological bases of human violent behaviour. One of the earliest associations between impulsive violence in humans and the limbic system was the observation of co-existence of intra-nuclear inclusion bodies in the hippocampus cells of patients afflicted with rabies and those with violent behaviour towards their environment (Viets, 1926). Teratoma of the third ventricle with damage to the hypothalamus resulted in non-rational behaviour after alcohol consumption (Alpers, 1937), since the hypothalamic region has a function in controlling behaviour and its damage may result in irrational violence. In a similar manner, tumours of the diencephalo-hypothalamus and hypophysis resulted in impulsive violence (Reeves and Plum, 1969; Leslie, 1940). Defects in the septum pellucidum and temporal lobe tumours were found to be associated with rape (Reeves and Plum, 1969; Malamud, 1967). This is because both the temporal lobe and the septum pellucidum regulate emotions and an injury of these regions of the brain is associated with violence. Temporal lesions due to haemorrhage, aneurysma or sclerosis were also found to be associated with impulsive violence (Zeman and King, 1958; Poeck, 1969).

Temporal epilepsy of a psycho-motor type was sometimes found to be associated with impulsiveness, aggression and epileptic fits manifesting themselves at times in uncontrolled violence (Bingley, 1958; Falconer and Serafentinides, 1963). Episodic behaviour dyscontrol, an epileptoid type of brain activity detectable by electroencephalography, has also been associated with violence (Boch Rita, et al., 1971; Monroe, 1970; Maletzky, 1973). Askenasy et al. (1983) found episodic behaviour dyscontrol to be associated with a confined environment for both violent and non-violent prisoners.

A link between temporal lobe lesions and violence should be related to brain-hemisphere dominance, i.e., violence is more likely if the temporal lobe lesions are located in the dominant hemisphere of the brain (Hill, 1944; Mark and Ervin, 1970).

In a number of patients whose aggressive actions were related to homicide, depth electrodes implanted in the amygdaloid nuclear complex recorded epileptic discharges during violent behaviour (Narabayasi et al., 1963). In experimental conditions, the amygdaloid complex was stimulated electrically and violent behaviour occurred. When the stimulation ceased, the violence also subsided (Narabayashi et al., 1963). Moreover, when the amygdala was destroyed or extracted, violence was no longer obtainable by excitation (Narabayashi et al., 1963).

The idea that violent behaviour has an epileptic basis led to several clinical experiments using anticonvulsant drugs to treat impulsive violence, with ambiguous results (Tunks and Dermer, 1977). Narabayashi reported of 60 aggressive patients whose amygdala had been removed, that 29 of them were 'greatly improved', i.e. became calm and socially adaptable, 22 were 'moderately improved', 7 'slightly improved' and 2 showed no change (Narabayashi et al., 1963). Other results from partial amygdalectomised patients were less optimistic (Memple, 1971; Hitchcock and Cainus, 1973). Neurosurgery of the posterior hypothalamus was performed in a series of 44 aggressive patients with good results in attenuating their violence (Mark et al., 1975).

A review of the side effects of neurosurgery on violent patients showed that in cases where neurosurgery stopped violence, pseudocoma or an autism-like, 'locked-in-syndrome' appeared (Adams, 1982). It was suggested that the section of associative pathways to the frontal brain is the cause of placidity and apathy, which sometimes appear following neurosurgery for violence (Bear, 1983). Bilateral temporal lobe excisions performed on violent patients resulted in the Kluver-Bucy syndrome, consisting of visual agnosia, hypersexuality and bulimia (Marlowe et al., 1975; Pillien, 1967; Kluver and Bucy, 1938).

The following conclusions can be drawn from this short review of the literature of the neurobiology of violence. There is no single aggression or violence centre, just as there is no anti-aggression or anti-violence centre in the brain; rather, there are many centres and regions in the brain which are associated with violence (Siegel and Edinger, 1983; Kleist, 1931). It is obvious that impulsive violence does not always reflect a disease or a pathology of the limbic system (Andy, 1970; Kim and Umbach, 1973). Modern criminology has to disagree with the idea that pathological medical causes determine violence. But it is evident that impulsive violent behaviour has a neurobiological potential.

The neurobiologic potential of Shoham's separant violence-prone types involves a dynamic interrelationship of many regions of the nervous system. Eysenck's hypothesis, adopted by Shoham, suggests the existence of a cortex hungry for stimuli in the separant, as opposed to a cortex averse to stimuli in the participant (Eysenck, 1967). The separant type, due to his sensation and impulse-seeking, easily establishes the circuitry needed to establish a violent behaviour pattern. The participant reacts favourably to sensory deprivation, which is related to his tendency to isolation, passivity and quietism. Hence, his predisposition to violence is lower.

The interest in the relationship between EEG and violence was initiated by a subject who had murdered his mother without apparent motive, and in whom the effect of hypoglycemia on cerebral functioning was detected by electroencephalography (EEG) (Hill and Sargent, 1943). Later, many other studies substantiated the usefulness of EEG in predicting violent behaviour (Hill, 1944; Hill and Sargent, 1943). Aggressive tendencies were found to be related to abundent theta activity (Hill, 1944; Saul et al., 1949; Hill, 1950; Verdeaux, 1970; Gibbs et al., 1945).

The use of EEG to differentiate between personality traits and other behavioural characteristics is controversial. With respect to violence, most authors who report positive results associate violent crime with EEG abnormalities that reflect minimal brain-damage. Since violent persons generally suffer more than their share of head trauma, these EEG changes have been dismissed as an acquired feature of a violent lifestyle. However, a close relationship between aggressiveness and theta rhythm is generally accepted (Sweet et al., 1969; Yarzura-Tobias and Nweziroglu, 1975; Saul et al., 1949; Hill, 1950; Verdeaux, 1970; Gibbs et al., 1945; Ellingson, 1954; Williams, 1941). Williams found up to 65 per cent of violent subjects to have bilateral temporal theta rhythm (Williams, 1941; Williams, 1969). Other studies dedicated to this association found EEG abnormalities in 50 per cent of psychopaths (Lairy, 1964; Hill, 1952). Grossman described the appearance, during spontaneous sleep, of an abnormal finding, i.e. 6-14 cycles per second (c/s) spikes in posterior regions of the brain in aggressive psychopaths (Berntson, 1973). Lairy underlines the importance of recording EEG in aggressive subjects during both wakefulness and sleep, because of the need to monitor theta waves in wakeful subjects and 6/14 of the same subject during sleep (Lairy, 1964).

Of a group of 194 aggressive psychopaths, in repeated EEG recordings, three distinct types of electrographic 'immaturity' were described (Williams, 1969); (1) 22 per cent displayed bilateral theta activity in the temporal and central area, (2) 32 per cent did not display any theta activity, but rather unstable alpha responding to photic stimulation with subharmonics; (3) 14 per cent displayed a slow theta of 3-5 c/s and of a high amplitude in the posterior temporal regions, mostly with a right hemispheric lateralisation. The slow activity was increased by deep breathing and blocked by photic stimuli. All the above-mentioned EEG theta rhythms are considered to be of hippocampal origin, and are related to violent behaviour (Lairy, 1964). This electroencephalographic pattern is explained by the continuous need for higher input of stimuli on the part of aggressive subjects maintained in a permanently alert state. All these studies confirm the hypotheses of Eysenck and Shoham as to the biological potential of human behaviour (Shoham, 1964; Shoham, 1968; Eysenck, 1967).

Significant findings concerning the electroencephalographic correlates of violence have been made in relation to temporal lobe epilepsy. Many cases of organic temporal epilepsy are associated with aggressive behaviour. Nuffield developed an aggression scale, which he applied to 322 children with temporal lobe epilepsy.

Temporal lobe epileptics had aggressive scores nearly four times as high as those of the petit-mal patients (Nuffield, 1969). In another study among 100 children with temporal lobe epilepsy, 36 exhibited outbursts of rage (Ounsted, 1969). On the other hand, a study of 150 temporal lobe epileptics did not reveal a single case of aggressive behaviour (Arthur and Cahoon, 1964). Moreover, among a school population, electrographic signs of epilepsy were found without any features of aggressive behaviour (Keating, 1961). The generally accepted opinion today is that epileptic brain activity does not imply aggressive behaviour. Rather, there is a specific temporal lobe epilepsy originating in the amygdalohippocampic region which is intimately related to aggression and impulsive violence.

Permanently implanted stereotaxic electrodes in medically intractable epileptics offered the unique opportunity to show the electrical correlates of amygdalohippocampic epilepsy and violence (Wieser, 1983). Negatively, this was demonstrated by the removal of the amygdala and hippocampus of these two patients and the subsequent cessation of the rage attacks (see figure 2).

Figure 2.

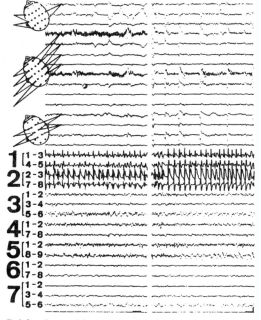

Fig. 2. Stereoelectroencephalogram of an amygdala seizure in a rage attack. Two sections at the beginning of the 2nd and 4th minute of this seizure are shown (with author's permission). Calibration: 1 s; 50 microvolt, TC = 0.3; F = 70

13

The electrical activity of the human cortex, particularly of the occipital cortex, can be aroused and to some extent controlled by photic stimulation (Cohn and Nardini, 1958). Four types of reaction to photic drives have been described in the literature: synchronic, harmonic, nonsynchronic and indifferent. The synchronic photic drive is an imposition of a one-to-one frequency ratio on alpha waves with an energy above the mean electrical activity. The non-synchronic is an imposition of a frequency ratio which is neither the photic stimulus rate nor the harmonic one. Electrical activity of the human cortex, which is indifferent to any photic stimulus, is called the indifferent photic drive. The effect of photic stimulation in impulsive aggressive subjects was found to block slow theta activity, or to effect a synchronic drive with high amplitudes, which is denoted a photomyoclonic reaction (Stafford-Clark et al., 1951). The latter was found to be age-related in aggressive psychopaths, and diminished with age (Cohn and Nardini, 1958; Bonnet, 1957). The photic drive in these studies was related to the occipital waves and not to the temporal ones (Cohn and Nardini, 1958; Bonnet, 1957).

It should be stressed when reviewing electrophysiological correlates of violence that subjects in 'total institutions' in a confined and disciplinary environment have a higher percentage of disturbed EEG recordings (Stafford-Clark, et al., 1951; Levy, 1952).

A survey of the EEG recordings of a group of confined aggressive subjects, when compared with the EEG recordings in an aggressive group of nonconfined subjects, showed approximately 20 per cent more disturbed EEG in the former (Stafford-Clark, 1959). When recording EEG among nonconfined and imprisoned aggressive psychopaths, no differences were found (Levy, 1952). Eight per cent more pathological records of EEG were found among motiveless aggressive murderers (Stafford-Clark, 1959; Levy, 1952). Thirty-four per cent more abnormal EEGs were found when comparing recidivists with individuals who had only one conviction (Levy and Kennard, 1953). In contrast to all these studies, in a sample of 100 convicted prisoners, 30 per cent displayed abnormal EEG records irrespective of their aggressive or non-aggressive behaviour profile (Gunn, 1969).

The comparison of prison personnel with confined subjects showed a percentage of 5 per cent abnormal EEG in the former versus 25 per cent in the latter (Stafford-Clark, 1959). A very large study revealed that 12 per cent of the general population would be expected to display abnormal EEGs (Williams, 1941). From the present review of electrographic correlates of confined subjects, it can be concluded that a significantly high percentage of abnormal EEG recordings characterises this population of 'total institution' inmates. In a more detailed analysis of abnormalities among these subjects, temporal lobe abnormalities found in impulsive aggressives were 74 per cent, as against 59.1 per cent in non-habitually-aggressive prisoners. Frontal lobe abnormalities were found in 57 per cent of aggressive prisoners, versus 19.3 per cent in non-aggressive ones (Williams, 1941). Gunn reported an increased incidence of

14

epilepsy in a British prison population, as compared with national figures for the general population (Gunn, 1969). Williams reported the highest differential percentages between the EEG abnormalities of a normal population, '12 per cent', and a confined population, '65 per cent' (Heath and Mickle, 1960). Lorne et al. (1970) corroborated EEG abnormalities, analysed by means of spectral analysis in a delinquent versus non-delinquent group, and found a highly significant correspondence between neuropsychological test profiles and EEG abnormalities in the delinquent group (Siegel and Edinger, 1983). Additional support for the presence of electroencephalographic abnormalities in socially deviant subjects was offered by various studies (Lorne et al., 1970). We may conclude that in a population confined in institutions, a higher percentage of EEG abnormalities will be found. Hence, we shall have to take this into account when evaluating the results of our studies, which will be presented in chapter two of this volume.

Another conclusion is that the slowing frequency of the cortical activity towards theta waves located mainly in the temporal lobes, characterises violent prisoners. It is suggested that the slowing frequency of cortical activity is also related to a hunger for stimuli, which also characterises the impulsive violent subjects. Because of a high percentage of abnormal EEG records among their relatives, it was assumed that aggressive subjects are genetically predetermined (Heath and Mickle, 1960; Currie et al., 1971). There is evidence of association between human aggression and sex chromosome alterations, such as sex cariotype with supernumerary x or y, such as 47 xxy (Klinefelter's Syndrome) or 47, xyy (Jacobs et al., 1965; Casey's et al., 1966). An extra y chromosome was considered to contribute to aggressive tendencies (Eichelman et al, 1981; Forssman and Hambert, 1967; Parson, 1967; Mednick and Christiansen, 1977).

However, no clear cut conclusion can be drawn from the numerous studies on the relationship between chromosome alterations and aggression. No evidence has been found that humans with supernumerary sex chromosomes, either x or y, were prone to aggressiveness. Hence, it is not worthwhile to carry out cariotype identification for the diagnosis and the prediction of violence. One or more gene defects were related to violence in some studies (Eichelman et al., 1981). However, the evidence was not conclusive and the results could also be explained by environmental factors.

THE ENDOCRINOLOGIC CORRELATES OF VIOLENCE

It is very difficult to define the neuroendocrinal dimension of the violent prisoner population. The few studies of the function of the hypothalamopituitary gonadal axis in men in emotive situations emphasise the inhibition of testosterone and decreased

15

sexual activity. The most frequently studied hormone as related to violence is testosterone. Persky et al. (1971) studied 18 healthy young men and found that the production rate of testosterone was highly correlated to a measure of aggression derived from the Buss-Durkee Hostility Inventory (Persky et al., 1971). A multivariate regression equation was obtained between the testosterone production rate and four psychological measures of aggression and hostility, which accounted for 82 per cent of the variance in the production rate of testosterone in these young men. Rose et al. (1972, 1975), in studies on rhesus monkeys, showed that dominant males, exposed to a sudden and decisive defeat by other males, experienced a decrease in plasma testosterone levels. Plasma testosterone in this primate species seems to be significantly influenced by the outcome of conflict related to alterations in a social group status. Kreuz and Rose (1972) studied plasma testosterone levels and indices of fighting and verbal aggression in 21 young prisoners. While plasma testosterone levels did not differ between fighting and non-fighting individuals and did not correlate with psychological test scores, the ten prisoners with histories of more violent and aggressive crimes in adolescence had a significantly higher level of testosterone than the eleven prisoners without such a history. These investigators hypothesised that, in a population predisposed by social factors to develop antisocial behaviour, levels of testosterone may be an important additional factor in placing individuals at risk of committing more aggressive crimes in adolescence.

Meyer-Balburg et al. (1974) separated four low-aggression male undergraduate college students from six high-aggression students on the basis of the Buss-Durkee Hostility Inventory and found that while the two groups were reasonably differentiated on several aggression scales, they did not show any significant differences in the production rate, plasma levels, or urinary level of testosterone. Ehrenkranz et al. (1974), on the other hand, determined plasma testosterone levels in 36 male prisoners, 12 with chronic aggressive behaviour, 12 socially dominant without physical aggressiveness, and 12 who were neither physically aggressive nor socially dominant. These groups were separated on the basis of a battery of psychological testing; it was found that there was a significantly higher level of plasma testosterone in the aggressive group as compared with their non-aggressive group or the other two groups together. The socially dominant group also had a significantly higher level of testosterone than the non-aggressive group. Doering et al. (1975) performed a longitudinal study of the association between mood and plasma testosterone by sampling 20 normal young men on alternate days for two months with a multiple effect adjective checklist and plasma testosterone concentrations. Inter-subject correlation coefficients between hostility, anxiety, depression and plasma testosterone were all positive, but only the correlation between depression and testosterone was barely significant at the 0.10 level. Between the other two effects and testosterone, the correlations were not significant.

Rada et al. (1976) classified 52 rapists and 12 child molesters, hospitalised in an institution for mentally disordered male offenders, according to the degree of violence expressed during the attack. Plasma testosterone level was measured for each subject. The most violent rapists had a higher mean plasma testosterone than normal subjects, child molesters, or other rapists. Mean Buss-Durkee Hostility Inventory scores for all the rapists were significantly higher than the mean for normal subjects, but individual hostility scores did not correlate with plasma testosterone.

Monti et al. (1977) studied 101 healthy young adult male volunteers by the administration of questionnaires for anxiety, hostility, social desirability and sexual interest and practices, and two daily determinations of serum testosterone concentration.

Individual testosterone levels on the two days correlated significantly ($r = 0.69$, $p < 0.001$), but with only 48 per cent shared variance, indicating a poor correspondence between the two daily testosterone values. Testosterone levels correlated to a significant degree with some of the psychological measures, but because of the large sample size, all correlations were quite low. Thus, in these normal subjects, no major relationship was found between the questionnaire items and testosterone levels.

Persky et al. (1977) studied forty male alcoholics during one week of abstinence and one week of unlimited alcohol intake. Compared to levels during the week of abstinence, plasma testosterone was reduced significantly during the week of alcohol intake. Only low borderline significant correlations occurred between testosterone levels and hostility, as measured by the Buss-Durkee Hostility Inventory and the Multiple affect Adjective Check List.

Relationships between testosterone levels and the psychological dimensions of aggression, social dominance, hostility and depression, remain in some doubt (Shah and Roth, 1974; Rose 1975; Kling, 1975). There is some data in the literature suggesting the way testosterone acts on mental functions. Zimmerman and Isaacs (1975) demonstrated decreased cerebral cortical cyclic-AMP levels in male rats subsequent to the injection of testosterone, showing that at a cellular level, testosterone can significantly affect brain chemistry. Stumpf and Sar (1976) elucidated the distribution in the mammalian brain of neurons in which there is a nuclear concentration of steroid hormones and testosterone, selectively stimulating the somato-motor system. Herrmann and Beach (1976) showed that testosterone is involved in sexuality, aggression, energising systems, psychomotor function, higher mental performance, mood and personality characteristics. All the above data, despite the doubt about the relationship between testosterone and aggression, must be the object of further studies.

17

Testosterone is closely related to two hormones: the luteinising hormone and Prolactin. The pituitary gonadotrophine luteinising hormone secreted by the anterior pituiary gland is essential for the secretion of testosterone. It is under the control of a hypothalamic factor for regulating the luteinising hormone (LH) releasing hormone. Prolactin is secreted by the anterior pituitary gland, under the regulating control of a thyrotrophic releasing factor and under the negative control of a specific Prolactin inhibitory factor (PIF). There is an inverse relationship between the rate of release of Prolactin and the testosterone and LH. For all these reasons, a proper study of the testosterone secretion has to include LH and Prolactin. Another methodologic problem to be solved when determining testosterone is the fact that plasma testosterone levels vary from hour to hour and from day to day within the same subject and among subjects. Goldzieher et al. (1976) emphasised the large fluctuation properties of the plasma level in three hormones: testosterone, pituitary gonadotrophine luteinising hormone (LH), and follicle stimulating hormone (FSH). For this reason, Goldzieher et al. (1976) concluded that three equal samples taken at 15 intervals is a required sampling method. The principle glucocorticosteroid is cortisol or hydrocortisone. It acts on the intermediary metabolism of predominantly anti-insulin and on the regulation of protein, carbohydrate, lipid and nucleur acid metabolism. It is mainly catabolising, but also increases glycogen content and promotes a hepatic storage of glucose.

The integrity of personality is enhanced by cortisol. Emotional disorder such as impulsivity, aggression and violence are common with either excesses or deficits of cortisol.

As a general conclusion of present surveys of the bio-psycho-social correlates of violent prisoners, we may stress that violence cannot be regarded as *sui generis* pathology, but rather as a correlate of the behaviour of the whole human organism. Hence, we have pointed out the need first to study the bio-psycho-social behaviour of the human organism as a hostile entity, and to regard violence as one deviant manifestation of that holistic organism.

References

Adams, R.I. (1982), 'The Limbic Lobes and the Neurology of Emotions', *Textbook of Neurology*, pp.381-92.

Allsop, J.F. (1965), In Eysenck, H.J. (1967), *The Biological Basis of Personality*, Springfield, Ill: Charles C. Thomas, pp.36-7.

Alpers, R.J. (1937),'Relation of the Hypothalamus to Disorders of Personality'. *Arch Neurol*, Vol.38, pp.291-303.

Bach, Rita G., J.R. Lion, C.E. Clement & F.R. Ervin (1971), 'Episodic Dyscontrol: Study of 130 Violent Patients', *Am. J. Psychiatry*, Vol.127, pp.1473-8.

Bear, D.(1983), 'Hemispheric Specialisation and the Neurology of Emotions',*Archives of Neurology*, Vol. 40, pp.195-202.

Bernston, G. G. (1973), 'Attack, Grooming and Threat Elicited by Stimulation of the Pantime Regementum in Cats', *Physical Behaviour*, Vol. 11, pp.81-7.

Bingley, T. (1958), 'Mental Symptoms in Temporal Lobe Epilepsy and Temporal Lobe Gliomas', *Acta Phychiatr. Scand*, (suppl. 120) pp.1-151.

Bonnet, H. (1957), 'La Response Myclonique a la SLI, en Psychiatrie'. *Ann. Med. Psychol*, Vol. 1, pp.865-92.

Brown, G. L., & F.K. Goodwin (1986), 'Human Aggression: A Biological Perspective'. In: W. Reid, D. Dorr, S. L. Walker, J.W. Bonner (Eds.), *Unmasking the Psychopath*, New York: W.W. Norton. pp.132-56.

Casey, M. D., C. E. Blank & D. Street (1966), 'XYY Chromosomes and Antisocial Behaviour', *Lancet*, Vol. 2, pp.859-60.

Cohn, R.& J. E. Nardini (1958-59), 'The Correlation of Bilateral Occipital Slow Activity in the Human E.E.G. with Certain Disorders of Behaviour', *Amer.J. Psychiat*, Vol. 122, p.44.

Currie, S., W. Heatherfield, R. Henson & D. Scott (1971), 'Clinical Course and Prognosis of Temporal Lobe Epilepsy: A survey of 666 Patients', *Brain*, Vol. 94, pp.173-90.

Doering, C.H., H.K.H. Brodie, H.C. Kramer, R.H. Moos, H.B. Becker & D.A. Hamburg (1975), 'Negative Affects and Plasma Testosterone: A Longitudinal Human Study', *Psychosom. Med*, Vol.37, pp.257-68.

Ehrenkranz, J., E. Bliss & M.H. Sheard (1974), 'Plasma Testosterone: Correlation with Aggressive Behaviour and Social Dominance in Man', *Psychosom. Med*, Vol.36, pp.469-75.

Eichelman, B., G.R. Elliot & J.D. Barchas (1981), 'Biochemical Pharmacological and Genetic Aspects of Aggression', D.A. Hamburg & M.B. Tourderau (Eds.), *Biobehavioural Aspects of Aggression*, New York.

Elliot, F.A. (1978), 'Neurological Aspects of Antisocial Behaviour', W.H.Reid (Ed.), *The Psychopath: A Comprehensive Study of Antisocial Disorders and Behaviours*, New York: Brunner & Mazel, pp.161-89.

Eysenck, H.J. (1967), *The Biological Basis of Personality*, Springfield, Ill: Charles C. Thomas, pp.36-7.

Falconer, M.A. & E.A. Serafentinides (1963), 'A Follow-up Study of Surgery in Temporal Lobe Epilepsy'. J. Neurol. Neurosurg. *Psychiatry*, Vol.26, p.154.

Fenwick, P., R. Howard, & G.F. Fenton (1983), 'Review of Cortical Excitability, Neurohumeral Transmission and the Dyscontrol Syndrome', (M.Parsonage et al, Eds.), *Advances in Epileptology: 14th Epilepsy International Symposium*, New York: Raven Press, pp.181-91.

Forssman, H. & G. Hambert (1967), 'Chromosomes and Antisocial Behaviour'. *Excerpta Criminologica*, Vol.7, pp.113-7.

Frank, A.E. (1992), 'Violence. The Neurologic Contribution: An Overview', *Arch. Neurol*, Vol.49, pp.595-603.

Gibbs, F.A., B.K. Bagchi & W. Bloomberg (1945), 'Electroencephalographic Study of Criminals'. *Am. J. Psychiat*, Vol.102, pp.294-8.

Goldzieher, J.W., T.S. Dozier, K.D. Smith & E. Steinberger (1976), 'Improving the Diagnostic Reliability of Rapidly Fluctuating Plasma Hormone Levels by Optimized Multiple Sampling Techniques', *J. Clin. Endocrinol. Metab*, Vol.43, pp.824-30.

Gove, R.W. & R.H. Crutchfield (1982), 'The Family and Juvenile Delinquency'.*The Sociological Quarterly*, Vol.23, pp.301-19.

Gunn, J.C. (1969), 'The Prevalence of Epilepsy Among Prisoners', *Proc. Ro.Soc. Med*, Vol.62, pp.60-3.

Heath, R.G. (1963), 'Electrical Self-stimulation of the Brain of Man', *American Journal of Psychiatry*, Vol.120, pp. 571-7.

Heath, R.G. & W.A. Michael (1960), 'Evaluation of Seven Years Experience with Depth Electrode Studies in Human Patients', E.R. Ramey & D. O'Doherty (Eds.), *Electrical Studies of the Unanesthetized Brain*, New York: Paul B.Hoeber, pp.214-24.

Hermann, W.M. & R.C. Beach (1976), 'Psychotropic Effects of Androgens: A Review of Clinical Observations and New Human Experimental Findings', *Pharmakopsych*, Vol.9, pp.205-11.

Hill, D. (1944), 'Cerebral Dysthemia: Its Significance in Aggressive Behaviour', *Proc. Roy. Soc. Med*, Vol.37, pp.317-28.

Hill, D. (1950), 'Encephalography as an Instrument in Research in Psychiatry', D. Lewis (ed.), *Perspectives in Neuropsychiatry*, London: Lewis, pp.47-59.

Hill, D. (1952), 'E.E.G. in Epistopic Psychiatric and Psychopathic Behaviour Electroenceph', *Clin. Neurophysiol*, Vol.4, p.419.

Hirschi, T. (1969), *Causes of Delinquency*, Berkeley: University of California Press, pp.16-26.

Irwin, J. & D. Cressey (1962), 'Thieves, Convicts and the Inmate Culture', *Social Problems*, Vol.10: pp.142-55.

Jacobs, P.A., M. Branton & M. Melville (1965). 'Aggressive Behaviour, Mental Subnormality and XXY Male', *Nature*, Vol.208, pp.1351-2.

Kennard, M.A. (1965), 'Effects of Bilateral Ablation of Cingulate Area on Behaviour of Cats', *Journal of Neurophysiology*, Vol.18,pp.159-69.

Kim, Y.& W. Umbach (1973), 'Combined Stereotactic Lesions for Treatment of Behavioural Disorders and Severe Pain', L. Laitinein & K. Livingstone (Eds.), *Surgical Approaches to Psychiatry*, Baltimore, MD: Baltimore University Park, pp.195-202.

Klein, S.G. & H.J. Schlesinger (1950), 'Perceptual Attitudes of Form-Boundlessness and Form-Liability Rorschach Responses', *Abstract Am.Psychol*, Vol.5, p.321.

Kling, A. (1975), 'Testosterone and Aggressive Behavior in Man and Non-Human Primates', Eleftheriou and R.L. Sprott (Eds.), *Hormonal Correlates of Behaviour*, Vol.1: *A Lifespan View*, B.E. New York: Plenum, pp.304-23.

Kornhauser, R. (1978), *Social Sources of Delinquency: An appraisal of analytic models*, Chicago: University of Chicago, p.85.

Kruez, L.E. & R.M. Rose (1972), 'Assessment of Aggressive Behaviour and Plasma Testosterone in a Young Criminal Population', *Psychosom. Med*, Vol.36, pp.321-2.

Lairy, G.C. (1964), 'Quelques Remarques sur le Probleme EEG, Psychologie du Comportement E.E.G.', *Clin. Neurophysiol*, Vol.16, pp.130-35.

Lane, P.J. (1978), 'Annotated Bibliography of the Overcontrolled-Undercontrolled Assaultive Personality Literature and the Overcontrolled-Undercontrolled-Hostility (0-4) Scale of the MMPI', *JSAS Catalog of Selected Documents in Pyschology* (JSAS ms. No. 1790).

Levy, S. (1952), 'A Study of the Electroencephalogram as Related to Personality Structure in a Group of Inmates of a State Penitentiary', *Clin. Neurophysiol*, Vol.4, p.113.

Levy, S. & M.A. Kennard (1953), 'A Study of the Electroencephalograph as Related to a Group of Inmates of a State Penitentiary', *American J. of Psychiatry*, Vol. 109, pp.832-9.

Lorne, T. Yeudall, Delee Fromm-Auch & Priscilla Davies (1970), 'Neuropsychological Impairment of Persistent Deliquency', *Neuroscience & Behav. Rev*, Vol.7, pp.394-407.

Linnoila, A.M., M. Virkunen, M. Scheinin, A. Nuntile, A. Rimon & F. Goodwin (1983), 'Low Cerebrospinal Fluid 5-Hydroxindol Acetic Acid Concentration Differentiates Impulsive from Non-Impulsive Violent Behaviour', *Life Sci*, Vol.33, pp.2609-14.

Maclean, P.D. & J. Delgado (1953), 'Electrical and Chemical Stimulation of Fronto-Temporal Portion of Limbic System in Waking Animal', *Electroencephalography and Clinical Neurophysiology*, Vol.5, pp.91-100.

Mark, V.H. & F. Ervin (1970), *Violence and the Brain*, New York: Harper and Row.

Mednick, S. & K.O. Christiansen (1970), *Biosocial Basis of Criminal Behaviour*, New York: Gardner Press.

Megargee, E.I. (1966), 'Undercontrolled and Overcontrolled Personality Types in Extreme Antisocial Aggression', *Psychological Monographs*, Vol.3, Whole No. 611.

Megargee, I.E. (1976), 'Population Density and Disruptive Behaviour in Prison Setting', pp.135-44.

Meyer-Bahilburg, H.F.L., B.A. Boon, M. Sharma & J.A. Edwards (1974), 'Aggressiveness and Testosterone Measures in Man, *Psychosom. Med*, Vol.36, pp.269-74.

Monroe, E. (1970), *Episodic Behavioural Disorders: A Psycodynamic and Neurophysiological Analysis*, Cambridge, Mass: Harvard University Press.

Monti, P.M., W.A. Brown & D.P. Corriveau (1977), 'Testosterone and Components of Aggressive and Sexual Behaviour in Man'. *Amer. J. Psychiat*, Vol.134, pp.692-4.

Narabayashai, H., T. Nagao, Y. Saito, M. Yeshuda & M. Nagohatta (1963), 'Sterotaxic Amygdaloctomy for Behaviour Disorders', *Archives of Neurology*, Vol.9, pp.643-59.

Parsons, T. (1947), 'Certain Primal Sources and Patterns of Aggression in the Social Structure of the Western World', *Psychiatry*, Vol.2, pp.167-81.

Perks, H., K.D. Smith, & G.K. Basu (1971), 'Relation of Psychologic Measures of Aggression and Hostility to Testosterone Production in Man', *Psychosom. Med*, Vol.2, pp.265-77.

Persky, H., C.P. O'Brian, E. Fine, W.J. Howard, M.A. Khan & R.W. Beck. (1977), 'The Effect of Alcohol and Smoking on Testosterone Function and Aggression in Chronic Alcoholics', *Amer. J. Psychiat*, Vol.134, pp.621-5.

Petrie, A. (1980), 'The Tolerance of Pain and Sensory Deprivation', *A.J. Psych*, Vol.1-3, No.1, pp.80-90.

Pincus, J.H. (1980), 'Can Violence be a Manifestation of Epilepsy?', *Neurology*, Vol.30, pp.304-7.

Poeck, K. (1969), 'Pathophysiology of Emotional Disorders Associated with Brain Damage', Du Vinken, P.J. Bruyen Gwelds, (Eds.), *Handbook of Clinical Neurology, Vol.3: Disorders of higher nervous activity*, Amsterdam,Holland: Elsevier Science Publisher, pp.343-67.

Quay, H.C. (1965), 'Psychopathic Personality as Pathological Stimulation Seeking', *American Journal of Psychiatry*, Vol.122, pp.180-3.

Rada, R.T., D.R. Laws & R. Kellner (1976), 'Plasma Testosterone Levels in the Rapist', *Psychosom. Med*, Vol.38, pp.257-68.

Rahav, G. (1983), 'Models of Delinquency', *International Journal of Group Tensions*, Vol.10, pp.61-72.

Reeves, A.G. & I. Plum (1969), 'Hyperphagia, Rage and Dementia Accompanying a Ventro-Medial Hypothalamic Neoplasm', *Arch. Neurol*, Vol.20, pp.616-24.

Romamuk, A. (1965), 'Representation of Aggression and Flight Reactions in the Hypothalamus of the Cat', *Acta Biologicae Experimentalis Sinica*, Warsaw, Poland, Vol.25, pp.177-86.

Rosenzweig, S. (1965), Notes of Correction of Schwartz, Cohen and Pavlik's 'The Effects of Subject and Experimenter Induced Defensive Responsive Sets on Picture Frustration Tests Reactions', *J. Proj. Tech. & Pers. Assess*, Vol.29, pp.352-3.

Sano, K., Y. Mayaanagi, H.E. Agashiwa & B. Ishyima (1970), 'Results of Stimulation and Destruction of the Posterior Hypothalamus in Man', *Journal of Neurosurgery*, Vol.33, pp.689-707.

Schreiner, L., & A. Kling (1953), 'Behavioural Change Following Encephalic Injury in Cats', *Journal of Neuropsychology*, Vol.16, pp.643-59.

Schulsinger, F. (1964), *The Premenstrual Syndrome*, Springfield, Ill: Charles C. Thomas Publishers.

Shah, S.A. & L.H. Roth (1974), 'Biological and Psychophysiological Factors in Criminality', D. Glaser (Ed.), *Handbook of Criminology*, New York: Rand McNally, pp.101-73.

Shealy, C. & T. Peele (1957), 'Studies on Amygdaloid Nucleus of Cats', *Journal of Neurophysiology*, Vol. 20, pp.125-39.

Shoham, S.G., G. Nehemia, R. Markowski & N. Kaplinsky (1976), 'Internationalism of Norms, Risk-Perceptions and Anxiety as Related to Driving Offences', *British Journal of Criminology.*

Shoham, S.G. (1979), *The Myth of Tantalus,* St. Lucia: University of Queensland Press.

Shoham, S.G.(1968), 'Points of No Return: Some Situational Aspects of Violence', *The Prison Journal,* Vol.48, p.2.

Shoham, S.G., G.Rahav, R. Markowsky, & F. Chard (1986), 'Reckless and Anxious Drivers,' *International Conference on Changes and Innovations in Road Safety,* Tel Aviv University.

Siegel, A. & H.M. Edinger (1983), 'Role of the Limbic System in Hypothalamically Elicited Attack Behaviour', *Neuroscience & Behav. rev,* Vol.7, pp.395-407.

Singer, J.L. (1971), *The Psychological Study of Aggression: The Control of Aggression and Violence,* New York & London: Academic Press.

Stafford, Clark D. (1959), 'The Foundations of Research in Psychiatry', *Brit.Med. J,* Vol.2, p.1100.

Stafford,Clark D., D. Pond, & J.W.L. Doust (1951), 'The Psycopath in Prison. A Preliminary Report of a Cooperative Research', *Br. J. Delinquency,* Vol.2, pp.117-29.

Stacey, W. & A. Shupe (1983), *The Family Secret: Domestic Violence in America,* Boston,Mass: Beacon Press.

Stevens, J.R. & B. Hermann (1981), 'Temporal Lobe Epilepsy, Psychopathology and Violence: The State of Evidence', *Neurology,* New York, Vol.31, pp.1127-32.

Stumpf, W.E. & M. Sar (1976), 'Steroid Hormone Target Sites in the Brain: The Differential Distribution of Estrogen, Progestin, Androgen and Glucocortiscosteroid', *J. Steroid Biochem,* Vol.7, pp.1163-70.

Sweet, W.H., F.R. Ervin, & V.R. Mark (1975), 'The Relationship of Violent Behaviour to Focal Cerebral Disease'. S.Garatini & E.B. Sigg, (Eds.), *Aggressive Behaviour,* Amsterdam Exerpta Medica Foundation, pp.336-52.

Tellegen, A., D.T. Lykken, T.J. Bouchard, K.J. Wilcox, N.L. Segal, S. Rich (1988), 'Personality Similarity in Twins Reared Apart and Together'. *J. Pers. Soc. Psychol,* Vol.54, pp.1031-9.

Thibaut, J.W. & H.H. Kelly (1959), *The Social Psychology of Groups,* New York: J.Wiley and Sons Inc., p.239.

Trimble, M.R. (1988), *Biological Psychiatry,* New York: John Wiley & Sons Inc.

Wasman, M. & J.P. Flynn (1962), 'Directed Attack Elicited from Hypothalamus', *Arch. Neurol,* Vol. 6, pp.220-7.

Watson, R.E., H.M. Edinger, & A. Siegel (1983), 'An Analysis of the Mechanism for Underlying Hippocampal Control of Hypothalamically-Elicited Aggression in the Cat'. *Brain Res,* Vol.269, pp.327-45.

Wieser, H.G. (1983), 'Depth Recorded Limbic Seizures and Psychopathology'. *Neuroscience Journal Reviews* 7.

Wilkinson, K.(1974), 'The Broken Family and Juvenile Delinquency: Scientific Explanation or Ideology?', *Social Problems,* Vol.21(June), pp.726-39.

Witkin, H.A., H.F. Paterson, D.R. Dyk, D.R. Goodenough, & S.A. Karp (1962), *Psychological Differentiation,* New York: John Wiley & Sons Inc.

Williams, D.P. (1941), 'The Significance of an Abnormal Electro-Encephalogram', *J. Neurol. Psychiat,* Vol.4, pp.257-68.

Williams, D. (1969), Neural Factors Related to Habitual Aggression', *Brain,* Vol.92, pp.503-20.

Yasukochi, G. (1960), Emotional Responses Elicited by Electrical Stimulation of the Hypothalamus in Cats, *Folio. Psychiatr. Neurol.,* Japan, Vol.14, pp.260-7.

Yarzura-Tobias J.A. & F.A. Neziroglu (1975), 'Violent Behaviour, Brain Dystrophy, Trauma and Glucose Dysfunction: A New Syndrome', *J. Onthromol. Psychiatry,* Vol.4, pp.182-8.

Zaman, W. & F.A. King (1958), 'Tumour of the Septum Pellicidum and Adjacent Structure with Abnormal Affective Behaviour. An Anterior or Midline Structure Syndrome', *J. Nerv. Ment. Dis,* pp.127-490.

Zimmerman, I.D. & K. Isaacs (1975), 'A Possible Effect of Testosterone on the Adenosine 3-5 Cyclic Monophosphate Levels in Rat Cerebral Cortex. A brief note', *Mechanisms of Aging and Development* , Vol.4, pp.215-9.

Zuckerman, M., E.A. Kolin & I. Koob (1964), 'Development of Sensation Seeking Scale', *Journal of Consulting Psychology,* Vol.28, 61, pp.477-82.

2   Biological Predispositions

When Man incites himself and goes to fornicate all his limbs obey him. When he goes to perform a righteous deed all his limbs become lazy; since the evil inclination on his guts reigns on the two hundred forty eight limbs of Man; whereas the righteous impulse may be likened to an incarcerated prisoner.

Rabbi Natan, *Ethics of the Fathers*

SUBJECTS

Prisoners were selected from the Jewish prison population and classified as violent or non-violent on the basis of court records. Sixty-five violent subjects and 35 non-violent subjects were selected. Subjects were also self-selected by volunteering to participate in this study. As the study was expected to take several months, only prisoners who were not due to be released within six months participated; thus, the sample is not probabilistic and may not be representative. In the early stages of the study, there was a large response from volunteers, but as time passed, subjects dropped out at a rate which increased when they were asked to undergo physiological examinations. Two of the measures (impulsiveness and plannedness), were taken only for the 65 subjects with violent offences.

The subjects of the electrophysiological part of our study were those to whom the psychological tests were administered. However, 35 of the prisoners chose not to volunteer for the neurophysiological study, leaving 65 out of the original 100 subjects.

METHODOLOGY

Variables

The dependent variables were the number of offences in a subject's criminal record, the number of violent offences (murder, manslaughter, attempted murder, assault, armed robbery, rape, quarrels and causing physical injury), compiled as detailed below, from the type of violent offence and the circumstances under which a crime was perpetrated. This information was extracted from court files. The subject's criminal records were examined, including the type of crime, age at perpetration, method of choosing the victim, relationship with the victim, whether the subject was provoked, whether a quarrel preceded the crime, whether drugs or alcohol were taken during the crime, pleas of insanity, and the underlying motivation. One hundred and twenty-seven crimes (all the crimes our violent offenders had been charged with), were scored on these variables. The scores were factor-analysed using SPSS. After orthogonal rotation, eight factors remained, of which only four had an eigenvalue of greater than 1.00. Of these, the first factor was responsible for 30 per cent of the variance and the second for a further 23 per cent. The remaining factors explained a considerably lower percentage of the common variance and were therefore excluded from further analysis. On each of the two major factors, variables whose factor weights were greater than 0.3 were marked, resulting in the following two factors:

Factor 1: Planned Violence

On this factor, the following variables had high factor weights: profit motivation, previous planning, professional performance, calm behaviour by the offender, group crime, damage to property and the use of weapons.

Factor 2: Impulsive Violence

This factor was strongly correlated with close relationships between victim and offender, choice of the victim by the offender, degree of physical harm, quarrel preceding the crime, slight damage to property and non-material motivation. One must note that the impulsiveness discussed here is not of the type which characterises the syndrome of periodic dyscontrol (Hare and Schalling, 1978), but; rather, is more likely to be triggered by situational factors. To ensure the validity of the results, a second analysis using oblique rotation was undertaken. The first factor showed no difference, while the second factor appeared to be less evident. The major variables in the latter were: offender's age (older), fewer offences, and female victims. The correlation between the two factors was R=0.24. We shall not reconsider the controversy over the validity of the criminal record again (Sellin and Wolfgang, 1964), but accept it as representing the tendency of a person to come into confrontation with the formal system of law enforcement (Black and Reiss, 1970).

ELECTROPHYSIOLOGIC TECHNIQUES

As shown in the review of electrophysiological correlates of violence, the limbic system is the most relevant. The sectoral temporal scalp electroencephalography, which focused on right and left temporal lobes, was designated to record the limbic electrical output. A monopolar six channel recording, using the 10/20 international system, was displayed in two montages by means of an Alvar Reega Minuit electroencephalograph instrument. The first recording montage included three monopolar channels monitoring the anterior, medial and posterior temporal right and left lobes. The second montage included three monopolar channels monitoring the right and left medial temporal, central and parietal lobes (see figure 1).

Figure 1. *Placement of channels of the Parietal Lobes*

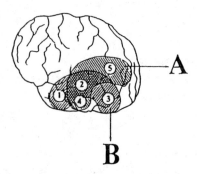

The subjects were asked to relax, while the EEG was recorded with open eyes for two minutes and with closed eyes for two minutes. Following this basic relaxed sectoral EEG recording, a dynamic electrography was performed, as a reaction to light flashes generated by an Alvar Soneclaf TR stimulator equivalent source about 6000 K, duration 200 micro sec, energy of 0.3 joule per flash and light intensity 24.600 Lux at subject's eye. The flash was given at a distance of 13 cm from the subject's eye. The alpha frequency was determined for each subject during the basic relaxed electroencephalography. The flash stimulator was fed with the individual alpha and

26

triggered to display six frequencies on the basis of the following paradigm: alpha/2-1; alpha/2; alpha/2+1; alpha-1; alpha; alpha+3. The flash light stimulator was controlled and operated by the display controller, which received its input from a stereocassette obeying a pseudo-random time sequence according to the following formula: T=1+n to (sec). To = 0.11 sec. 'n' was chosen from a random numbers table. Thus, the interflash interchange was between 1 sec. and 1.77 sec. The prerecorded signals which served as an input to the display controller were coded to 2.5 KHZ and 50 msc. duration. The above paradigm was given with closed and open eyes 10 times each, for a total of 120 flashes.

The sectorial electroencephalograms were visually scored by two scorers and the results confronted. The scoring comprised measurements of the frequency, amplitude, wave forms, stability, periodicity and reaction with open eyes. The responses to photic stimulation were recorded on cassettes. A computer program performed the spectrum analysis and displayed the resultant diagrams on six channels for each one of the two patterns for each subject. On each diagram, the Y axis displayed the brain wave amplitude, and the X axis displayed the frequency in the range of delta, theta, alpha and beta. The maximal and minimal energy of response related to the frequency and the maximal and minimal standard deviation of the energy for each frequency were calculated.

ENDOCRINOLOGICAL TECHNIQUES

Three blood samples were taken through a needle placed in an arm vein, at 20 minute intervals, after an hour's rest period following the insertion of the needle. Each blood sample was about 10 ml, so that in total 30 mls of blood were taken from each subject. The blood samples were taken from each prisoner at the same time of day, to eliminate circadian variations. Blood samples were centrifuged immediately and the serum taken off, frozen and transported to Dr R.T. Rubin's laboratory at Harbor General Hospital in Los Angeles. Four hormones, testosterone, luteinising hormone, prolactin and cortisol were analysed on each sample, a total of almost 1,800 separate hormone determinations.

RESULTS: ELECTROPHYSIOLOGICAL CORRELATES OF VIOLENT PRISONERS

Visual scoring and the computerised analysis of the electroencephalograms performed on the temporal brain regions showed significant correlations. The four types of brain

27

waves in decreasing order of frequency, were beta (-13c/s), alpha (8-12c/s), theta (4-7c/s) and delta (-3c/s). Only theta waves in the central area showed a significant correlation with the average of yearly accumulated prison terms in the violent group of criminals, $(R = 0.25; p < .038)$.

Table 1. *Correlation between theta waves in central area and dependent variables*

	R	P<
1. Average of yearly accumulated prison term with average theta waves in central area	0.25	0.038
2. Total number of offences committed by 1978 with average theta waves in central area.	0.41	0.001

It was found that with violent criminals, there was a significant correlation beween the total number of offences committed between 1968 and 1978 and theta waves in central area $(R = 0.41; P < .001)$ (see table 1).

The analysis of a more precise location of the theta activity of the sectoral electroencephalograms showed a preferential appearance in middle temporal and central areas of the left hemisphere. This location suggests a limbic origin and points out the dominant hemisphere.

With six offenders, theta activity occurred in bursts of 14 cycles per second. The form of theta waves was sharp, biphasic and triphasic. The 14 cycles per second consisted of positive spikes.

When analysing the response of offenders to photic drives, significant correlations were found: first, between the score on the impulsiveness scale, and the amplitude of alpha and beta waves in response to light flashes, when eyes were either open or closed (see table 2); and second, between the highest variability of the amplitude of driven waves and the score on the impulsiveness scale (see table 3).

In other words, the energy of the driven waves, as a response to the randomised flashes, varies significantly in the most impulsive violent offenders. The energetic instability in driven responses, characterises impulsive violence (see table 3).

Table 2. *Significant Pearson correlations between score on impulsiveness scale and amplitude of EEG in response to light flashes with open and closed eyes*

Variable	R	P<
Amplitude of alpha waves with closed eyes	0.30	0.02
Amplitude of beta waves with closed eyes	0.29	0.02
Amplitude of gama waves with open eyes	0.25	0.05

Table 3. *Significant Pearson correlations between impulsiveness and mean standard deviation of the amplitudes of various frequencies in examined cerebral areas*

Mean Standard Deviation	R	P<
Alpha	0.29	0.02
Theta	0.30	0.02
Beta	0.33	0.01
	R	P<
All Frequencies	0.32	0.012

HORMONAL CORRELATES OF VIOLENT PRISONERS

The violent group tended to have a high level of prolactin and testosterone compared to a low level of the same hormones among non-violent offenders (see table 4), but this result was not found to be significant.

Table 4. *Discriminant function analysis of hormonal variables between violent and non-violent prisoners (n=47).*

	Standardised Coeffecients:
Testosterone	0.86
Prolactin	0.72
Wilk's Lambda	0.93
Canonical Correlation	0.26
P<	0.21
	Group Centroids:
Violent	0.23
Non-Violent	0.29

DISCUSSION

The present study shows a significant correlation between theta rhythm and violent crime. It shows that more violent offenders, as expressed by yearly accumulated prison terms and total number of offences, displayed more theta rhythm. These two factors were shown, in a previously unpublished study, to be significantly related to violence. This result did not shed light on whether the conditions of imprisonment of the violent offenders determined the significant correlation. These findings confirm a number of previous studies dedicated to the usefulness of electroencephalography in detecting violent behaviour (Saul et al., 1949; Hill, 1950; Verdeaux, 1970; Gibbs et al, 1945; Ellingson, 1954; Williams, 1941; Williams, 1969; Lairy, 1964; Kim and Umbach, 1973; Grossman, 1954).

The interesting finding which points toward a predominance of theta activity in the middle temporal and central areas of the left hemisphere suggests a relationship with the dominant limbic structures. Stereotaxic electroencephalographic observations and neurosurgical extractions of par structures showed this relationship (Siegel and Edinger, 1983; Wieser, 1983).

The presence of bursts of sharp bi-and triphasic theta, with bursts of 14 cycles per second positive spikes in six violent offenders, suggests episodic behavioural dyscontrol syndrome.

The above electroencephalographic picture has been related to a propensity to violence by Monroe 1970; Mark and Ervin 1970, Bach-Rita et al. 1971, Maletzky 1973, Mednink and Volovka 1980, Pincus 1980, Thompson 1981, Delgado et al.

1981. The electroencephalographic picture, when associated with violence, was termed 'episodic behavioural dyscontrol'.

Another feature of the present study has been a dynamic approach intended to test the sensitivity of offenders to photic drives. Photic drives showed that amplitude variability to flashes was significantly increased with impulsive violent prisoners. The randomised flashes reached the perceptive occipital areas with a certain energy expressed by the amplitude of the waves. From the occipital areas, the energy passed towards the associative parietal, central and temporal areas displaying significant changes in the violent brain when compared to a non-violent one. This result emphasises the characteristic energetic instability of the temporal lobe and limbic structures of the impulsive violent offender.

Finally we have to comment on the increased rate of prolactin in violent prisoners. In the absence of drugs such as phenothiasines, alphamethyldopa or reserpine, which induce excessive prolactin secretion, it may be suggested that the control mechanism for prolactin was impaired. Hypothyroidism, through a mechanism not entirely understood, increases prolactin, but this may be due to altered sensitivity of the pituitary on the prolactin, releasing effects of TRH or PIF secretion. The inhibition of sexual life in prison may be the reason for high prolactin level amongst the research population. The violent group displayed significantly higher prolactin when compared with the non-violent group. It may be suggested that the correctional system produces abnormal hormones in the violent group. This observation suggests that imprisonment may affect the hormonal state of violent offenders adversely. This matter deserves further investigation.

References

Adams, R.D. (1982), 'The Limbic Lobes and the Neurology of Emotion', *Test book of Neurology*, pp.381-92.

Allsop, J.F. (1965), In H.J. Eysenck (1967), *The Biological Basis of Personality*, Springfield Ill: Charles C. Thomas, pp.36-7.

Alpers, R.J. (1937), 'Relation of the Hypothalamus to Disorders of Personality', *Arch. Neurol*, Vol.38, pp.291-303.

Andy, O.J. (1970), 'Thalamotomy in Hyperactive and Aggressive Behaviour', *Conference Neurol*, Vol.32, pp. 322-5.

Arthur, R.G.S. & E.B. Cahoon (1964), 'A Clinical and Electroencephalographic Survey of Psychopathic Personality', *Am. J. of Psychiatry*, Vol.120, pp.875-82.

Askenasy, J.J., P. Hackett, S. Ron & D. Hary (1983), 'Violence and Episodic Behavioural Dyscontrol', *Biological Psychiatry*, Vol.18, pp.604-7.

Bach, Rita G., J.R. Lion, C.E. Clement & F.R. Ervin (1971), 'Episodic Dyscontrol: Study of 130 Violent Patients', *Am. J. of Psychiatry*, Vol.127, pp.1473-8.

Bandler, R.J., C.C. Chi & J.P. Flynn (1972), 'Biting Attack Elicited by Stimulation of the Ventral Middlerain Tegmentum of Cats', *Science* , Vol.177, pp.364-6.

Berntson, G.G.(1973), 'Attack, Grooming and Threat Elicited by Stimulation of the Pontine Tegmentum in Cats', *Physiol Behav*, Vol.1, pp.81-7.

Bingley, T. (1958), 'Mental Symptoms in Temporal Lobe Epilepsy and Temporal Lobe Gliomas', *Acta Phychiatr. Scand,* Vol.33 (suppl. 120).

Bonnet, H. (1957), 'La Response Myoclonique a la SLI, en Psychiatrie', *Ann. Med. Psychol,* Vol.1, pp.865-92.

Burr, E. (1983), 'The Limbic System and Aggression in Humans', *Neuroscience J. Behavioural Reviews,* Vol.7, pp.391-4.

Casey, M.D., J.C.E. Blank & D. Street (1966), 'YY Chromosomes and Antisocial Behaviour', *Lancet,* Vol.2, pp.859-60.

Cleaver, P.T., A.D. Mylonas & W.C. Reckless (1968), 'Gradients in Attitudes Towards Law, Courts and Police', *Social Focus,* Vol.2, pp.29-48.

Cohn R. & J.E.Nardini (1958-9), 'The Correlation of Bilateral Occipital Slow Activity in the Human EEG with Certain Disorders of Behaviour', *Amer. J. Psychiat,* Vol.44, p.115.

Currie, S.K., W.G. Heathfield, R.A. Hearson & D.F. Scott (1971), 'Clinical Course and Prognosis of Temporal Lobe Epilepsy', *Brain,* Vol.94, pp.173-90.

Doering, C.H., H.K.H. Brodie, H.C. Dramer, R.H. Moos, H.B. Becker & D.A.Hamburg (1975), 'Negative Affect and Plasma Testosterone: A Longitudinal Human Study', *Psychosom Med,* Vol.37, pp.484-91.

Ehrenkranz, J., E. Bliss & M.H. Sheard (1974), 'Plasma Testosterone: Correlation with Aggressive Behaviour and Social Dominance in Man', *Psychosom. Med.* Vol.36, pp.469-75.

Eichelman, B., G.R. Elliot & J.D. Barchas (1981), 'Biochemical, Pharmacological and Genetic Aspects of Aggression', D.A. Hamburg & M.B. Touderau (Eds.), *Biobehavioural Aspects of Aggression,* New York.

Ellingson, R.Y. (1954-55), 'The Incidence of EEG Abnormality Among Patients with Mental Disorders of Apparently Non-Organic Origin: A Critical Review', *Amer. J. Psychiatr,* Vol.111, p.263.

Eysenck. H.J. (1967), *The Biological Basis of Personality,* Springfield, Ill: Charles C. Thomas, pp.36-7.

Falconer, M.A. & E.A. Serafentinides (1963), 'A Follow-up Study of Surgery in Temporal Lobe Epilepsy', *J. Neurol Neurosurg. Psychiatry,* Vol.26, p.154.

Forssman, H. & G. Hambert (1967), 'Chromosomes and Antisocial Behaviour'. *Excerpta Criminologica,* Vol.7, pp.113-7.

Gibbs, F.A., B.K. Bagchi & W. Bloomberg (1945), 'Electroencephalographic Study of Criminals', *A. J. Psychiat,* Vol.102, pp.294-8.

Goldzieher, J.W., T.S. Dozier, K.D. Smith, & E. Steinberger (1976), 'Improving the Diagnostic Reliability of Rapidly Fluctuating Plasma Hormone Levels by Optimized Multiple-sampling Techniques', *J. Clin Endocrinol. Metab,* Vol.43, pp.824-30.

Goodman, R.M., W.S. Smith & C.J. Migeon (1967), 'Sex Chromosome Abnormalities', *Nature,* Vol.216, pp.942-3.

Gove. J.R.W. & R.H. Crutchield (1982), 'The Family and Juvenile Delinquency', *The Sociological Quarterly,* Vol.23, pp.301-19.

Grossman, C. (1954), 'Laminar Cortical Blocking and its Relation to Episodic Aggressive Outbursts', *Arch Neurol. Psychiatr,* Vol.71, p.576.

Gunn, J.C. (1969), 'The Prevalence of Epilepsy Among Prisoners'. *Proc. Ro. Soc. Med,* Vol.62, pp.60-3.

Heath, R.G. & W.A. Mickle (1960), 'Evaluation of Seven Years' Experience with Depth Electrode Studies in Human Patients', E.R. Ramey and D. O'Doherty, (Eds.), *Electrical Studies of the Unanesthetized Brain,* New York: Paul. B. Hoeber, pp. 214-24.

Henderson, D.K. (1939), *Psychopathic States,* New York: Morton Publishers Inc.

Herrmann, W.M. & R.C. Beach (1976), 'Psychotropic Effects of Androgens: A Review of Clinical Observations and New Human Experimental Findings', *Pharmakopsych,* Vol.9, pp.205-19.

Hill, D. & W.W. Sargent (1943), 'A Case of Matricide'. *Lancet,* Vol.1, pp.526-7.

Hill, D. (1944), 'Cerebral Dysthymia: its Significance in Aggressive Behaviour, *Proc. Roy. Soc. Med,* Vol. 37, pp.317-8.

Hill, D. (1950), 'Encephalography as an Instrument in Research in Psychiatry', D. Lewis (Ed.), *Perspectives in Neuropsychiatry*, London: Lewis, pp.47-59.

Hill, D. (1952), 'EEG in Epistopic Psychiatric and Psychopathic Behaviour', *Electroenceph. Clin. Neurophysiol*, Vol.4, p.419.

Hirschi, T. (1969), *Causes of Delinquency*, Berkeley: University of California Press, pp.16-26.

Hitchcock, E. & V. Cainus (1973), 'Amygdalotomy', *Postgrad. Med. J*, Vol.49, pp.894-904.

Irwin, J. & D. Cressey (1962), 'Convicts and the Inmate Culture', *Social Problems*, Fall.

Irwin, J. (1970), *The Felon*. Englewood Cliffs, NJ: Prentice-Hall.

Jacobs, P.A., M. Branton, M. Melville (1965), 'Aggressive Behaviour, Mental Subnormality and XYY Male', *Nature*, Vol. 208, pp.1351-52.

Keating, L.F. (1961), 'Epilepsy and Behaviour Disorders in School Children'. *J. Ment. Sci*, Vol.107, pp.161-80.

Kelly, S., R. Almy & M. Barnard (1967), 'Another XYY Phenotype', *Nature*, Vol.215, p.405.

Kim, Y.K. & W. Umbach (1973), 'Combined Stereotaxic Lesions for Treatment of Behavioural Disorders and Severe Pain'. L. Laitman and K.E. Livingstone, Eds.), *Surgical Approaches in Psychiatry*, Baltimore University Park Press, pp. 182-8.

Klein, S.G. & H.J. Schlesinger (1950), 'Perceptual Attitudes of Form-Boundedness and Form-Liability', *Rorschach Responses, Abstract, Am. Psychol*. Vol. 5, p.321.

Kling, A. (1975), 'Testosterone and Aggressive Behaviour in Man and Non-Human Primates' B.E. Eleftheriou and R.L. Sprott (Eds.), *Hormonal Correlates of Behaviour, A Lifespan View*, New York: Plenum Press, Vol. 1, pp. 305-23.

Kluver, H., & P.C. Bucy (1938), 'An Analysis of Certain Effects of Bilateral Temporal Lobotomy in the Rhesus Monkey with Special Reference to Psychic Blindness', *J. Psychol*, Vol.5, p.33.

Kornhauser, R. (1978), *Social Sources of Delinquency: Appraisal of Analytic Models*, Chicago University Press, p.85.

Kreuz, L.E. & R.M. Rose (1972), 'Assessment of Aggressive Behaviour and Plasma Testosterone in a Young Criminal Population', *Psychosom. Med*, Vol.34, pp.321-2.

Lane, P.J. (1978), 'Annotated Bibliography of the Overcontrolled-Undercontrolled Assaultive Personality Literature and the Overcontrolled-Hostility (0-4) Scale of the MMPI.' *JSAS Catalog of Selected Documents in Psychology* (JSAS ms. No. 1790).

Leslie, W. (1940), 'Cyst of the Cavum Vergae', *Can. Med. Assoc. J*, Vol. 43, pp.433-5.

Levy, S. (1952), 'A Study of the Electrocephalogram as Related to Personality Structure in a Group of Inmates of a state penitentiary', *Electro-Enceph. Clin. Neurophysiol*, Vol.4, p.113.

Levy, S. & M.A. Kennard (1953), 'A Study of the Electro-Encephalograph as Related to a Group of Inmates of a State Penitentiary', *American Journal of Psychiatry*, Vol.109, pp.832-9.

Lorne, T. Yeudall, Ph.D., Dealee Fromm-Auch, M.A., & Priscilla Davies B.A. (1973), *Neuroscience and Behavioural Reviews*, Vol.7, pp. 394-407.

Lairy, G.C. (1964), 'Quelques Remarques sur le Probleme EEG', Psychologie du comportement, *EEG Clin Neurophysiol*, Vol.16, pp.130-5.

Malamud, N. (1967), 'Psychiatric Disorder with Intracranial Tumors of Limbic Systems', *Arch Neurol*, Vol.17, pp.113-23.

Maletzky, B.M. (1973), 'The Episodic Dyscontrol Syndrome', *Dis. Nerv. Syst*. Vol.34, pp.178-85.

Mark, V.H. & F.R. Ervin (1970), *Violence and the Brain*, New York: Harper & Row.

33

Marabayashi, H.T, Y. Nagao, M. Saito, Yoshuda & M. Nagohatta (1963), 'Stereotaxic Amygdalobotomy for Behaviour Disorders', *Arch. Neurol J*, pp.9-16.

Mark, V.H, W. Sweet & F.R. Ervin (1975), 'Deep Temporal Lobe Stimulation and Destructive lesions in Episodically Violent Temporal Lobe Epileptics'. W.S. Fields & W.H. Sweet, (Eds.), *Neural Basis of Violence and Aggression*, St. Somis: Warren H. Green, pp.379-91.

Marlowe,W.B., E.J. Mancall & J.J. Thomas (1975), 'Complete Kluver Bucy Syndrome in Man', *Cortex*, Vol.11, p.53.

McTwin, R.C. & F. Helmer (1965), 'The Symptoms of Temporal Lobe Contusion'. *J. Neurology* , Vol.23, pp.296-304.

Mednick, S. & K.O. Christiansen (1977), *Biosocial Basis of Criminal Behaviour*, New York: Gardner Press.

Megargee, E.I. (1966), 'Undercontrolled and Overcontrolled Personality Types in Extreme Antisocial Aggression', *Psychological Monographs*, (3,Whole No. 611).

Megargee, E.I. (1976), 'Population Density and Disruptive Behaviour in Prison Settings,' M.E. Wolfgang & N.A. Weiner (Eds.), *Criminal Violence*, Beverly Hills: Sage Publication, pp.135-44.

Megargee, E.I. (1982), 'Psychological Determinants and Correlates of Criminal Violence', M.E.Wolfgang, and N.A.Weiner, (Eds.), *Criminal Violence*, Beverly Hills/London/New Delhi: Sage Publications. pp.81-160.

Memple, E. (1971), 'Influence of Partial Amygdalectomy on Emotional Disorders and Epileptic Seizures', *Neurochir Pol*, Vol.21, pp.81-6.

Meyer-Bahlburg, H.F., B.A. Boon, M. Sharma & J.A. Edwards (1974), 'Aggressiveness and Testosterone Measures in Man', *Psychosom. Med*, Vol.36, pp.269-74.

Monroe, R. (1970), *Episodic Behavioural Disorders: A Psychodynamic and Neurophysiologic Analysis*, Cambridge: Harvard University Press.

Monti, P.M, W.A. Brown & J.D.P. Corriveau (1977), 'Testosterone and Components of Aggressive and Sexual Behaviour in Men', *Amer. J. Psychiat.*, Vol.134, pp.692-4.

Nuffield, E.J. (1969), 'Neurophysiology and Behaviour Disorders in Epileptic Children', *J. Ment. Sci*, Vol.107, pp.438-58.

Ounsted, C. (1969), 'Aggression and Epilepsy: Rage in Children with Temporal Lobe Epilepsy'. *J. Psychosom. Res*, Vol.13, pp.237-42.

Parsons, T. (1947), Certain Primary Sources of Patterns and Aggression in the Social Structure of the Western World', *Psychiatry*, Vol.2, pp.167-81.

Persky, H., K.D. Smith & J.G.K. Basu (1971), 'Relation of Psychologic Measures of Aggression and Hostility to Testosterone Production in Man', *Psychosom. Med*, Vol.32, pp.265-77.

Persky, H, C.P. O'Brien, E. Fine, W.J. Howard, M.A. Khan, & R.W. Beck (1977), 'The Effect of Alcohol and Smoking on Testosterone Function and Aggression in Chronic Alcoholics', *Amer. J. Psychiat*, Vol.134, pp.621-5.

Person, T. (1967), 'An XYY Man and his Relatives', *Journal of Mental Deficiency Research*, Vol.11, pp.239-45.

Petrie, A. (1980), 'The Tolerance of Pain and Sensory Deprivation', *A.J. Psych*, Vol. 1-3, No. 1, pp.80-90.

Pillien, G. (1967), 'The Kluver-Bucy Syndrome in Man', *Psychitar. Neurol*, Vol.152, p.65.

Poeck, K. (1969), 'Pathophysiology of Emotional Disorders Associated with Brain Damage', Du Vinken PJ, Bruyen Gwleds *Handbook of Clinical Neurology*, Vol. 3: Disorders of Higher Nervous Activity Amsterdam, North Holland, Chap. 20, pp. 343-67.

Quay, H.C. (1965), 'Psychopathic Personality as Stimulation Seeking', *American Journal of Psychiatry*, Vol.122, pp.180-3.

Rada, R.T., D.R. Laws & R. Kellner (1976), 'Plasma Testosterone Levels in the Rapist', *Psychosom. Med*, Vol.38, pp.257-68.

Rahav, G. (1983), 'Models of Delinquency', *International Journal of Group Tensions*, Vol.10, pp. 61-72.

Reeves, A.G. & F. Plum (1969), 'Hyperphagia, Rage and Dementia Accompanying a Ventro Medial Hypothalamic Neoplasm', *Arch. Neurol*, Vol.20, pp.616-24.

Rose, R.M., T.P. Gordon, & I.S. Bernstein (1972), 'Plasma Testosterone Levels in the Male Rhesus: Influences of Sexual and Social Stimuli', *Science*, Vol.178, pp.643-5.

Rose, R.M. (1975), 'Testosterone, Aggression, and Homosexuality: A Review of the Literature and Implications for Future Research', E.J. Sachar (Ed.),*Topics in Psychoendocrinology*, New York: Grune and Stratton, pp. 83-103.

Rosen, L. (1970), 'The Broken Home and Male Delinquency', Wolfang M.E., Savitz E. & N. Johnson (Eds.), *The Sociology of Crime and Delinquency*, New York: John Wiley & Sons Inc.

Rosenzweig, S. (1965), Note of Correction for Schwartz, Cohen and Pavlik's 'The Effects of Subject and Experimenter Induced Defensive Response Sets on Picture-Frustration Test Reactions', *J. Proj. Tech. & Pers. Assess*, Vol.29, pp. 352-3.

Rotter, J.B, M. Seeman & S. Liverant (1962), 'Internal V. External Controls of Reinforcements, A Major Variable in Behavior Theory', N.F. Washburne (Ed.), *Decisions, Values and Groups*, London: Pergamon Press, Vol. 2, pp. 473-959.

Saul, L., J.H. Dans & P.A. David (1949), 'Psychologic Corrections with the Electroencephalogram', *Psychsom Med*, p.361.

Shah, S.A. & L.H. Roth (1974), 'Biological and Psychophysiological Factors in Criminality', D. Glaser (Ed.), *Handbook of Criminology*, New York: Rand McNally, pp.101-73.

Shoham, S.G. (1964), 'Conflict Situations and Delinquent Solutions', *Journal of Social Psychology*, The Journal Press Vol. 64, pp. 185-215.

Shoham, S.G. (1968), 'Points of No Return: Some Situational Aspects of Violence', *The Prison Journal*, Vol.48, p.2.

Shoham, S.G, G.Nehemia, R.Markowski & N. Kaplinsky (1976), 'Internalisation of Norms, Risk-Perceptions and Anxiety as Related to Driving Offences', *British J. of Criminology* Vol.16, p.2.

Shoham, S.G. (1979), *The Myth of Tantalus*, St. Lucia: University of Queensland Press.

Shoham, S.G, G. Rahav, R. Markowsky & F. Chard (1986), 'Reckless and Anxious Drivers,' *International Conference on Changes and Innovations in Road Safety*, Tel Aviv University.

Shoham, S.G, Z. Schwartzman, G. Rahav, R. Markowski, F. Chard, & A. Adelstein (1987), 'An Instrument to Diagnose Personality Types According to the Personality Theory of Shoham', *Medicine and Law*, p.6.

Siegel, A. & H.M. Edinger (1983), 'Role of the Limbic System in Hypothalamically Elicited Attack Behaviour', *Nervose. & Behav. Rev*, Vol.7, pp.395-407.

Singer, J.L. (1971), 'The Psychological Study of Aggression', *The Control of Aggression and Violence*, New York & London: Academic Press.

Stafford, D. Clark, D. Pond & J.W.L. Doust (1951), 'The Psychopath in Prison. A Preliminary Report of a Cooperative Research', *Br. J. Delinq.* Vol. 2, pp.117-29.

Stafford, D. Clark (1959), 'The Foundations of Research in Psychiatry', *Brit. Med. J*, Vol.2, p.1100.

Stumpf , W.E. & M. Sar (1976), 'Steroid Hormone Target Sites in the Brain: The Differential Distribution of Estrogen, Progestin, Androgen and Glucocorti-costeroid', *J. Steroid Biochem*, Vol.7, pp.1163-70.

Sutherland, E.H. & D.R.Cressey (1960), *Criminology*, Philadelphia: Lippincott.

Sweet, W.H., F.R. Ervin & V.H. Mark (1969), 'The Relationship of Violent Behaviour to Focal Cerebral Disease', S. Garattini and E.B. Sigg, (Eds.), *Aggressive Behaviour*, Amsterdam Exerpta Medica Foundation, pp. 336-52.

Verdeaux, G. (1970), 'Encephalography in Criminology', *Medicine legale et Dommage Corporel*, Vol.6, pp.39-46.

Viets, H.R. (1926), 'A Case of Hydrophobia with Negri Bodies in the Brian', *Arch. Neurol. Psychiatry* , Vol.15, pp.735-7.

35

Wasman, M. & J.P. Flynn (1962), 'Directed Attack Elicited from Hypothalamus', *Arch. Neurol* , Vol.6, pp.220-7.

Watson, R.E, H.M. Edinger & A. Siegel (1983), 'An Analysis of the Mechanism for Underlying Hippocampal Control of Hypothalamically-Elicited Aggression in the Cat', *Brain Res.* Vol.269, pp.327-45.

Wieser, H.G. (1983), 'Depth Recorded Limbic Seizures and Psychopathology', *Neuroscience S.Reviews* , Vol.7, pp.427-40.

Williams, D.P. (1941), 'The Significance of an Abnormal Electroencephalogram', *J. Neurol. Psychiat,* Vol.4, pp.257-68.

Williams, D. (1972), 'Neural Factors Related to Habitual Aggression'. *Brain,* Vol. 92, pp.503-20.

Wilkinson, K. (1974), 'The Broken Family and Juvenile Delinquency: Scientific Explanation or Ideology?', *Social Problems,* 21 (June), pp.726-39.

Witkin, H.A., H.F. Faterson, D.R. Dyk, D.R. Goodenough & S.A. Karp (1962), *Psychological Differentiation,* New York: Wiley.

Yarzura-Tobias, J.A. & F.A. Neziroglu (1975), 'Violent Behaviour, Brain Dystropohy, Trauma and Glucose Dysfunction: A New Syndrome', *J. Onthromol. Psychiatry,* Vol.4, pp.182-8.

Zeman, W., F.A. King (1958), 'Tumours of the Septum Pellucidum and Adjacent Structures with Abnormal Affective Behaviour: An Anterior or Midline Structure Syndrome', *J. Nerv. Ment. Dis,* Vol.1227, p.490.

Zimmerman, I.D. & K. Isaacs (1975), A Possible Effect of Testosterone on the Adenosine 3-5 Cyclic Monophosphate Levels in Rat Cerebral Cortex: A Brief Note'. *Mechanisms of Aging and Development* , Vol.4, pp.215-9.

Zuckerman, M., E.A. Kolin, & I. Zoob (1964), 'Development of Sensation Seeking Scale', *Journal of Consulting Psychology,* Vol. 28, No, 61, pp.477-82.

3 Personality and Social Attitudes of Violent Prisoners

It was very good. (Gen 1, 31) Rabbi Nahman Ben Shmuel said: That is the evil inclination. But is the evil inclination very good? Yes, for if it were not for the evil inclination man would not build a house or take a wife or beget a child, or engage in business.

Genesis Raba, IX 7

METHODOLOGY

Independent Variables

These variables on the personality level, as related to the violence of the research population, were measured by the following instruments:

1. The Cattell (1970) Personality Factor Questionnaire (C.A.Q.), both forms A and B;

2. H. Levenson's Scale (1973) for measuring locus of control;

3. Christie's Machiavellianism Test (1970);

4. Budner's Test of Intolerance of Ambiguity (1962);

5. Shoham's Risk Taking Test;

6. The Raven Intelligence Test;

7. Witkin's Rod and Frame Test (1954);

8. Zuckerman's Sensation Seeking Scale (1964);

9. Gibson's Spiral Maze Test (1961);

10. Kagan's Matching Familiar Figures Test (1974); and

11. The Thematic Apperception Test. Murray (1938).

The social and attitudinal parameters of the prisoners, as related to violence, were measured by their attitudes toward the prison authorities, their relationships with other prisoners, their self-concepts as prisoners and their attitudes towards the police, the prosecutors and the judge.

FINDINGS

The analysis of the psychological correlates of the research population revealed that a majority of the personality tests we used did not differentiate between the violent and non-violent prisoners, nor between the various groups of violent prisoners (see table 1).

Table 1. *Level of significance in one-dimensional analysis of variances on various personality indices*

The Contrast

Dependent Variables	Violent/ non-violent	Impulsive/ non-impulsive	Premeditated/ not premeditated
CAQ sub scales:			
A. Affectothymia (warmhearted)	0.51	0.10	0.72
C. Emotionally stable	0.06	0.65	0.49
E. Assertive, aggressive	0.28	0.44	0.56
F. Impulsively lively	0.01	0.20	0.29
G. Conscientious	0.65	0.80	0.38
H. Venturesome	0.06	0.57	0.44
I. Tender	0.62	0.78	0.82
L. Suspicious	0.88	0.53	0.58
M. Imaginative	0.02	0.21	0.77
N. Shrewd	0.17	0.02	0.44
O. Apprehensive	0.10	0.75	0.22
Q1. Radicalism	0.63	0.57	0.67
Q2. Self-Sufficiency	0.83	0.26	0.22

Table 1 (continued)

Dependent Variables	Violent/ non-violent	Impulsive/ non-impulsive	Premeditated/ not premeditated
Q3. Controlled	0.35	0.14	0.85
Q4. Tense	0.64	0.37	0.35
D1. Hypochondria	0.001	0.52	0.80
D2. Suicidal depression	0.02	0.52	0.90
D3. Excitement-seeking	0.40	0.62	0.19
D4. Depression, anxiety	0.07	0.30	0.12
D5. Low energy depression	0.04	0.55	0.80
D6. Guilt and revulsion	0.48	0.31	0.97
D7. Boredom and disconnection	0.08	0.04	0.59
PA. Paranoia	0.01	0.99	0.38
PP. Psychopathy	0.09	0.40	0.82
SC. Schizophrenia	0.10	0.41	0.50
AS. Psychosthenia	0.18	0.67	0.88
PS. Inferiority; general psychosis	0.40	0.10	0.17
Raven (Intelligence)	0.31	0.30	0.69
TAT Themes:			
Post Positive theme	0.16	0.35	0.23
LOSSL Loss of life theme	0.09	0.38	0.26
PHAGG Physical aggression	0.82	0.001	0.02
AGG Other forms of aggression	0.13	0.09	0.31
IT Internal Tension	0.73	0.30	0.37
MS Success-major	0.89	0.78	0.25
SS Success-secondary	0.24	0.09	0.20
MF Failure-major	0.97	0.96	0.63
Risk taking	0.56	0.19	0.10
Machiavellianism	0.10	0.80	0.56

Table 1 (continued)

Dependent Variables	Violent/ non-violent	Impulsive/ non-impulsive	Pre-meditated/ not premeditated
Locus of Control:			
LOC IC Internal	0.07	0.78	0.84
LOC CH Luck	0.31	0.12	0.49
LOC PO Powerful Others	0.72	0.51	0.39
SSS Sensation Seeking Scale	0.87	0.10	0.51

Therefore, we decided to concentrate on those findings which were brought out by the CAQ analysis. Certain sub-scales of this test indicated significant differences between groups and were found to be significantly connected with the dependent variable.

Comparison of the violent and non-violent prisoners, with respect to their personality data and some demographic data.

The violent prisoners were found to be younger, to have spent a longer period in jail, to score higher on Zuckerman's Sensation Seeking Scale (SSS) (Zuckerman, 1964) and, according to Chana Levenson's Locus of Control Test, (Levenson, 1973) to have a marked tendency to locate control in powerful others. That is, the violent prisoners tend to view the world as managed by strong, all-engulfing others. Since it is possible that these variables are interconnected, we undertook a multi-variate analysis. Table 2 (Discriminant Analysis) presents the means of the distinguishing scores between the two principal groups under analysis--violent as opposed to non-violent prisoners. This analysis included only the various scales of the CAQ test, the age and length of imprisonment.

40

Table 2. *Results of discriminant analysis, distinguishing between violent and non - violent prisoners (normalised parameters)*

The Variable	R	Average Violent Group	Average Non- Violent Group	Standard Deviation
Age	0.64	27.2	32.3	10.7
Apprehension (o)	0.46	7.0	6.1	2.6
Tense (Q4)	0.35	8.0	7.9	3.4
Warmhearted (A)	0.36	8.0	8.6	2.6
Assertive (E)	0.23	8.5	8.8	2.5
Suspicious (L)	0.17	9.5	9.5	2.5
Imaginative	0.30	9.2	8.2	2.5
Hypochondria (D1)	0.48	8.6	6.6	4.7
Suicidal Depression (D2)	0.12	7.6	6.0	4.9
Paranoia (PA)	0.19	12.7	11.5	3.6
Length of Imprisonment	0.20	9.7	5.1	19.5
Canonical Correlation	0.44			

From the analysis, it appears that those scales which show the clearest distinction between violent and non-violent prisoners are: CAQ Sub-Scales hypochondria (D1), apprehension (O), warmhearted (A), tension (Q4) and imaginative (M). Furthermore, the age of the criminal carries considerable weight, over and above the various psychological variables. It was found that the violent criminals are more insecure (O), tend to reject criticism, are accident-prone and more given to depression (D2) and hypochondria (D1). The violent prisoners were also found to be more tense and frustrated (Q4) and lacking in warmheartedness (A).

The following conclusions can be drawn from these comparisons: the younger age of the violent prisoners is seemingly connected to the fact attested by prison service personnel that the criminals sent to jail are more and more violent with each passing year. Thus, the younger prisoners were also found to be the most violent ones. Another possibility is connected to the fact that many investigations have indicated an increase in aggressive and violent behaviour towards the end of youth and the beginning of adulthood. These findings are connected to the socio-biological theories of Wilson, Tiger and Trievers (Campbell, 1972). According to these theories, juvenile violence arises, amongst other things, from a need to display sexuality in choosing a partner. Youth, therefore, lends itself to a greater tendency to violence, provided that circumstantial factors allow it. These factors include: lack of normative barriers against

41

violent behaviour, and pre-dispositional characteristics towards violence, with which we are concerned in the report context.

PROFILE OF THE IMPULSIVE VIOLENT AND THE PREMEDITATIVE VIOLENT CRIMINAL

From the findings of CAQ sub-scales, it appears that impulsive, violent prisoners are cut off from their human environment. This alienation is also apparent in the fact that they were found to be more recessive (D7), to have a tendency towards boredom (D7) and to have fewer guilt feelings (D6). They were found to possess a higher level of cunning, to have a tendency towards indirect reactions (N), and to be dominated by emotion rather than reason (L). They were more daring and hedonistic, that is, more pleasure-seeking, and were impulsive decision makers. However, precisely because their decisions were impulsive, they were often not correct. In this context, we may say that their cunning is not connected to reality, since the hastiness and irrationality of their behaviour renders it non-functional.

We found (Shoham et al, 1987) that violent behaviour is more closely connected to deviant personality data, whereas non-violent crime is connected to processes of learning and socialisation. That is, the behaviour of criminals whose violence is pre-meditated is controlled by logical and functional considerations, and their violence is part of their criminal behaviour, which they learnt during their socialisation process. Their violence is less 'abnormal' from a personality standpoint; it stems from their criminal sub-culture, and is less connected to personality defects. We observed that even in those cases where the family legitimised criminal values, the violent and impulsive criminal felt rejected by his family. This report deals with the deviant personality data which characterise the violent and impulsive criminal. In this framework, it was found that the premeditative violent criminal does not necessarily have a more defective personality structure and is not necessarily more deviant in his personality parameters than the non-violent one.

PREMEDITATIVE VIOLENT CRIMINALS AND SITUATIONALLY VIOLENT (IMPULSIVE) ONES IN COMPARISON TO NON-VIOLENT CRIMINALS ACCORDING TO THE CAQ ANALYSIS

The following analysis compares five groups of prisoners:

1. Violent prisoners high in both situational-impulsive and premeditated violence;

42

2. Violent prisoners high in premeditated and low in situational-impulsive violence;

3. Violent prisoners high in situational-impulsive and low in pre-meditated violence;

4. Violent prisoners low in both situational-impulsive and pre-meditated violence;

5. Prisoners who had not committed violent offences.

Group 1

This group is characterised by high rates of both premeditated, and situational-impulsive, violence. Another characteristic of the group is an especially high level of anxiety, as measured by the CAQ high-level anxiety scale (Q4). Anxiety is connected to Shoham's theory (1977), according to which, if the opposing core personality vectors are not in balance, there is a general defect in functioning. This dynamic is expressed, amongst other things, in panic. The profile of this group expresses especially extreme parameters which are essentially in conflict and show a lack of balance, leading to anxiety. The significance of this finding, in our context, is that although the violent criminals in this group are supposed to be premeditative, in the course of the perpetration of violence, impulsive elements enter into their behaviour. Thus, they may direct their violence towards objects around them. That is, they have a tendency to react if unexpected changes occur in their environment, and their impulsive violent reaction will be directed at the originators of these changes. Impulsive violence represents a loss of control over professional objectives, and thus anxiety acts as a positive feedback, so that this group has an extreme profile in this parameter.

Another explanation of this finding is connected to additional data, characteristic of this group: lack of emotional stability (C), inability to cope with reality (Sc) accompanied by low inner control (Q3), and by defective interpersonal communication (H). These findings also agree with the profile of the violent criminal who aims to plan his violence, but finds himself carrying out impulsive acts of violence. As a result, the feeling of frustration with his self image as a premeditative violent criminal, whose professional reputation is built on his ability to execute his tasks quietly and efficiently, grows. This image is injured because of lack of stability, lack of self-discipline and inability to cope with changing reality. This endangers his relations with the criminal sub-culture, since this group, not unlike a legitimate group, approves the efficient execution of tasks and fulfilment of its aims. The unavoidable consequence is friction between the members of the group, and bad interpersonal relationships. The criminals who belong to this group possess few feelings of guilt, (D6) an indication of the psychopathic tendencies in their characters which cause a lack of moral orientation towards their actions (see figure 1).

Figure 1. *CAQ Profile of the group of prisoners, whose violence is high both in pre-plannedness and in impulsiveness*

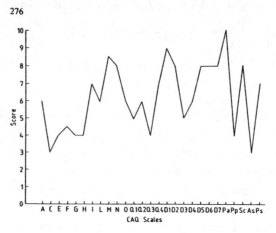

276

Group 2

This group is supposed to include the controlled, cool-tempered criminals, those who carry out their violent crimes after planning, without situational-impulsiveness on the CAQ sub-scales. This group is indeed characterised by a high level of pre-planning and a low level of impulsiveness. The subjects investigated were marked by a higher than normal level of anxiety, which was, however, lower than the level displayed by the members of the first group. In addition to this, their personal characteristics were as follows: higher emotional stability (C), greater ego powers, less introverted, less shy (A,F,M) and less self-disciplined (Q3). Their most characteristic trait is extraversion. They are happier and more vital. Compared to Group 1, their super-ego is weaker, they display lower feelings of social responsibility, they are more callous and less sensitive (I,M,A), they show more independence (E) and less sophistication (N). One can describe them as less conformist, possessing fewer emotional problems, tending more to crime and showing more psychopathic tendencies. All these characteristics conform, with a few exceptions, to the expected profile of the violent prisoner, to which we will devote a separate discussion. Emotional stability, stronger ego and less shyness all characterise the premeditative violent criminal and the expected profile of the professional underworld thug.

44

However, low self-discipline was discovered in the profile of the subjects investigated, whereas we expected that the premeditative violent criminal would have high self-discipline, in order to be able to carry out his tasks efficiently. This low self-discipline may be the reason for higher than normal anxiety in this group. The pre-meditative violent criminal is conscious of this defect, which prevents 'clear' execution of his tasks, and therefore displays greater anxiety. The other parameters that characterise the violent and classic callous prisoner are cruelty, lack of emotion and execution of his violent tasks in a cool and professional manner (see figure 2).

Figure 2. *The CAQ profile of the premeditated low-impulsive violent prisoner*

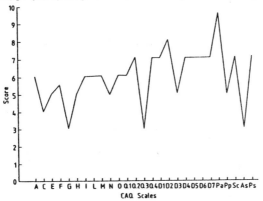

Group 3
This group is supposed to be the archetype of the impulsive violent criminal. Their crimes are carried out in the context of situational provocation and are not pre-planned. According to the CAQ, this group displays high inner feelings of guilt (O), weak ego forces, high personal tension (C,H) close to the average level of the extrovert (F,H,Q2), a greater tendency towards conformity (Q1,G) than the previous groups, but still less than the norm. These criminals are less callous (I,M,A), possess low emotional stability (C), a high level of imagination and a poor grip on reality (M) (see figure 3).

Figure 3. *A CAQ profile of the impulsive violent prisoners*

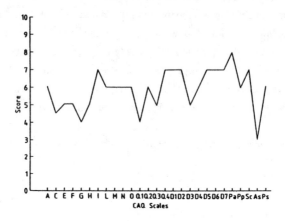

Group 4

This group is low in both premeditated and situational-impulsive violence. The most important result in relation to this group is that it was found to be the highest on the schizophrenia index (Sc) and to display a very high level of anxiety. According to the CAQ second order scales, this group has an especially weak ego (H), low self-esteem, lacks security, experiences feelings of guilt (O), has weak self-discipline (Q3), a high level of imagination, is disconnected from reality and is very easily emotionally hurt (I,M,A). Members of this group are characterised by a deficiency in their personality structure. Their violence is sudden and undirected and cannot be explained by pre-meditation or as an impulsive reaction to provocation. Rather, it is an expression of defects in their personality structure. In this it is apparently similar to what is known in the literature as the temporary loss of control syndrome (episodic dyscontrol). Here also, as in Group 1, there is a high level of anxiety. A possible explanation, according to Shoham's personality theory ('The Myth of Tantalus' 1979), is that once there is an imbalance between the personality core vectors, a high level of anxiety results, since the opposing tendencies in the core personality cause extreme manifestations of conflicting behaviour patterns (see figure 4).

Figure 4. *CAQ profile of the non-premeditative and non-impulsive violent prisoners*

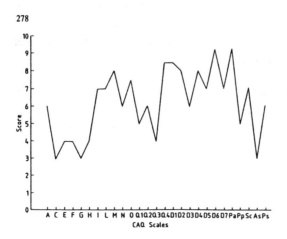

278

We have not deliberated on Group 5, (non-violent prisoners) because naturally, they had no violent parameters comparable to the other four groups.

The findings relating to the socio-psychological and social parameters of our research prisoners were as follows:

THE SOCIAL ATTITUDES OF VIOLENT PRISONERS

Self-Concept

The results (see table 3) show that prisoners who admit that they sometimes act against the prison regulations, in that they 'do what they want' (item 87), have committed a larger number of violent offences. Those prisoners who openly defy prison regulations are also the violent offenders. This finding sheds light on predictions about the prisoners' behaviour after their release and likewise on the behaviour of violent prisoners whilst still in prison. Assuming that this self-report is indicative of future

47

behaviour, it could be useful in the selection of prisoners suitable for open-prison frameworks.

Prisoners who claim that they prefer to abide by prison regulations, in spite of the fact that their fellow prisoners do not do so (question 85), thereby showing a certain conformity to society's normative system, were shown to have performed fewer violent offences (non-significant tendency). This finding could also be important as an initial predictor of a low risk tendency amongst prisoners being considered for an open framework.

Table 3. *Significant differences (P<) of dependent variable for different categories of independent variables (one-way analysis of variance).*

Item	No. of Offences	No. of violent offences	Planned violence	Impulsive violence
50. Did you know any of the prisoners before you entered prison?		0.09		0.02
51. How are relations between you and previous acquaintances serving terms with you today?		0.10		
53. Have you made new friends in prison?	0.03			
68. I will never have a fist fight when there is a prison guard nearby.	0.09		0.07	
69. Guards should speak politely to prisoners, and if they swear should be taught a lesson.		0.01		
73. A prisoner can gain respect without resorting to physical violence.		0.007		

Table 3
(continued)

Item	No. of Offences	No. of Violent offences	Planned Violence	Impulsive Violence
76. Violence does not help to educate 'rats'.			0.007	
77. Even if someone is strong and powerful...one should avoid the use of fists.		0.07		
87. I do what I want, even if it is against the law.		0.005		0.08
90. When everyone attacks a prisoner, it is advisable to stand clear and not interfere.				
103. In prison, one can learn a profession that will be useful later on.		0.005	0.10	0.08
107.Prosecutors try not to bring a case unless they are certain of the guilt of the accused.	0.04			
108.Prosecutors are not concerned with justice at all.	0.005			

Table 3
(continued)

Item	No. of Offences	No. of Violent Offences	Planned Violence	Impulsive Violence
114. Many fights occur in prison between guards and prisoners, because the guards are callous and do not understand the prisoners.	0.04			
116. Many highly-strung prisoners, who, if they receive additional punishment, run wild for a week.	0.07		0.1	
120. When many people are cooped up in one room...fights are inevitable.		0.03		
122. A prisoner who does not receive the things he needs becomes enraged and picks on others.	0.02			
124. Are your conditions in prison overcrowded? Absolutely not.	0.10			
125. How many people do you share a cell with?	0.001	0.03		
No. of significant items (p< 0.10)	9	10	3	4
No. of non-significant items (P<0.10)	12	11	18	17

The Sub-culture of Prisoners

The prisoners' negative attitude to violence is expressed, amongst other things, in the belief that a prisoner can command 'respect' without having to resort to violence (item

73). This means that the professional criminal, who is a member of a criminal sub-culture, views violence as an annoyance. This result accords with the finding reported earlier, which showed that those prisoners whose families legitimise violence, perform violent actions which interfere with the smooth running of life, both within the family and within the criminal sub-culture. This finding is strengthened by the prisoners' claim that they would 'never have a fist fight with a warden nearby' (item 68).

A sanction-orientated attitude towards life, and the avoidance of crime for fear of punishment, characterise the professional criminal. It is not that he grants legitimacy to norms that reject violence, rather he acts according to his own personal moral code. This attitude characterises the non-impulsive criminal, who weighs his actions, so that if he commits a violent crime, he will do so in a controlled manner.

The subject who agrees that 'if a warden does not speak politely one should teach him a lesson' (item 69), will tend to commit violent acts more spontaneously. This picture of prison life, in which the prisoners possess more power than the wardens, is unrealistic. A delusive view of reality is in accordance with the profile of the more impulsively violent group and matches the results obtained for the less planned violent group. The professional criminal appreciates the reality of the prisoners' situation and evaluates the balance of power correctly.

Item 70, in which it is claimed that if a prisoner owes cigarettes, there are ways other than physical violence to arrange the repayment of the debt, also indicates delusions of strength. Those who agreed with this statement were found to be comparatively high on situationally-impulsive violence. Here again, an unrealistic evaluation of their strength and of the division of power amongst the prisoners leads to frustration and thus, to situational violence.

Subjects who knew other prisoners serving a sentence with them during the research period (item 50), were lower on the situationally-impulsive violence factor. That is, the violence of those subjects who in all probability belong to the criminal sub-culture is not impulsive. Their behaviour is more rational and is executed with the goal of the criminal sub-culture in mind.

In cases where the subject replied that his relations with the 'veterans' serving with him in prison were very good (item 51), tended to have committed a great number of offences, that is, to belong to the criminal group.

The professional criminal is usually suspicious, a characteristic he develops within the criminal group as a valuable aid to survival. Further support for this finding is obtained from item 53, according to which those prisoners who responded negatively to the question of whether they had made new friends in prison, had committed more offences. The professional criminal 'knows the ropes', that is, he knows that the more emotional and 'professional' ties he has with other prisoners, the greater his chance of getting involved in conflicts which would unnecessarily extend his period of imprisonment. This is especially relevant because there is no opportunity to avoid meeting these prisoners-friends. Accordingly, the professional prisoner will detach himself from prison society as much as possible, and try to be a 'loner'.

Overcrowding in Prison

Those subjects who agreed that the overcrowding in prison led to more quarrels amongst the prisoners (item 120) had committed a larger number of violent offences. It is possible that these subjects had a lower tolerance threshold, and therefore tended to react violently to overcrowding. This finding is reinforced by item 124, according to which the more crowded the conditions in which the prisoner lives, the more offences he will tend to commit. This may be the result of certain imprisonment policies, whereby criminals with longer criminal records are concentrated together in more crowded cells. Those prisoners housed in cells with a small number of prisoners (less than 4), or those in crowded cells (more than 13), had committed a large number of violent offences (item 125). On the other hand, prisoners housed in cells of medium crowdedness had committed fewer violent offences. This finding might be connected to imprisonment policies, whereby hard-core, violent criminals are housed with other hard-core criminals. Other special cases of violent criminals were separated in small cells. This suggests two types of violent prisoners: professional criminals, whose violence is connected to their professional offences, such as 'settling of accounts', violent robbery and so on, and those offenders whose brush with the law is mainly connected to violent outbursts, which justify their being separated from the rest of the offenders in small cells. The hypothesis is that the violence of the first group is planned and that of the latter is impulsive.

The Outside World

Those prisoners who agree that violence in prison is connected to the denial of prisoners' rights, had committed a larger number of offences (item 122). This again provides evidence that the professional criminal guards his 'professional rights'. He also agrees with the claim that disputes in prison occur due to the strictness of prison guards (item 114). The professional criminal sees the guards as hostile representatives of the outside world; an enemy in a constant war in which he can never be vindicated. This result receives additional support from two items that deal with the general prisoner-guard relationship: the subjects who agreed that, in general, prison guards 'do not behave well' to prisoners (item 102) were found to be the hard-core criminals, (non-significant tendency), while subjects who claimed that generally the wardens are not fair (item 104) were found to be more violent (non-significant tendency). Here again we find evidence of the institutional barrier which the guards represent; a system of values and organisations that the prison population cannot, by definition, accept. The more a hard-core criminal is guarded, the more he will reject the system of values of the outside world, represented *inter alia* by the prison guards.

It should be stressed here that when items 85, 87, 102, 104, and 114, dealing with prisoner-guard relations, were combined to form one measure, (presented in table 4), they were found to be significantly connected to the dependent variable, that is, the number of violent offences (R=0.27, P<0.005).

Table 4. *List of items forming scale of prisoner-guard relations*

85. I prefer to stick to regulations although others do not always do so.

87. I do what I want, even if it is against the law.

102. The guards always behave badly towards the prisoners.

104. Most of the guards are honest.

114. Many fights occur in prison due to disagreements between the guards and prisoners, because the guards are callous and do not understand the prisoners.

This result supports our findings that the value content of the prisoner-guard relationship accurately describes the constant and uncompromising conflict between the prisoners' society, representing the criminal culture, and the prison guards, who represent the legitimate system of values and norms.

Subjects who agreed that if a guard 'swears he must be taught a lesson' (item 69) were found to be less planned in their violence. That is to say, these are the prisoners who do not fully appreciate the balance of power , who think in terms of principles and even expect 'honour' and 'justice' to be part of the prisoner-guard relationship. The professional and planned criminal knows that there is no point in having unrealistic expectations of the guards. The prisoners who stated that they would never have a fist fight with a guard nearby (item 68) were found to be lower on impulsive violence, that is, these are the prisoners who appreciate the balance of power within prison. They are

53

hard-core and professional criminals whose attitude towards the prison norm is sanction-orientated. They do not recognise the legitimacy of the prison norms; rather, they are afraid of the punishment they may receive if caught.

The subjects who agreed that the representatives of the law have absolutely no regard for justice (item 108), were found to be less violent. These subjects are more realistic and know that the connection between the law and justice is very feeble. They belong to the class of professional criminals who know that the prosecutor in a trial is usually looking for a conviction and that questions of guilt or justice are of secondary importance to him. Their lesser use of violence is related to the fact that the professional criminal is more pragmatic and generally avoids violence, since the result tends to be 'unecessary complications'. The prosecution will try not to bring a case unless it is certain of the guilt of the accused (item 107). Those who agreed with this statement had committed fewer violent offences. This result also points to the pragmatism of the professional criminal.

At this point, it is appropriate to present a scale (table 4) comprised of items 85, 87, 102, 104 and 114, which were found to be correlated with the number of violent offences committed. This scale also shows that the professional criminal, who is familiar with the norms and balance of power in prison, will have committed fewer violent offences. On the other hand, the prisoner who lacks a realistic appreciation of prisoner-guard relations, will have committed more violent offences.

MULTIVARIATE ANALYSIS

The multivariate analysis contains four multiple regression analyses of which only two were found to be significant (table 5).

Table 5. *Multivariate Regression*

A. Multiple regression of the amount of
situational impulsiveness present in the violence
of the research population for chosen variables

Variable	Beta
Age	0.18
Duration of Imprisonment	0.14
Item 70 'There are means other than physical violence...'	0.24*
Item 103 'One can learn a useful profession'	0.23*
Item 87 'I do what I want...'	0.21*
Item 68 'I will not have a fist fight...'	0.04

Table 5 (continued)

R^2	0.25
Variable	Beta
N	61
	*p.<0.10

B. Multiple regression of the measure of planned
violence for chosen variables

Variable	Beta
Age	0.08
Duration of imprisonment	0.11
Item 69: Guards need to talk politely...'	0.51

$$R^2 = 0.15$$
$$N = 47$$
$$P<0.10*$$

C. Multiple regression of the maximal measure
of plannedness in the violence for various
variables.

Variable	Beta
Age	0.03
Duration of imprisonment	0.35**
Item 125: 'Number of prisoners in cell.'	0.38**
Item 113: 'Each group wants to be strong...'	0.19*
Item 51: 'Relationship with friends serving sentences'	0.17*
Item 114: 'The wardens are strict and do not understand.'	0.17*
R^2	0.31
N	89
	P<0.10* P<0.01**

Variable	Beta
D. Multiple regression of number of violent offences for various variables	
Age	0.05
Duration of imprisonment	0.22*
Item 87: 'I do what I want'	0.30**
Item 108: 'The prosecutors are not concerned with justice.'	0.22**
Item 73: 'One can gain respect without fist fights.'	0.23**

55

Table 5 (continued)

Item 107: 'The prosecutors do not bring cases unless they are certain.'	0.17*

R^2	0.34
N	106
P<0.10*	P<0.001**

The first significant multiple regression analysis connected the number of violent offences, as the dependent variable, with the following variables:

Item 73:   'A prisoner can receive respect without resorting to fist fights.'

Item 87:   'I do what I want even if it is against prison regulations.'

Item 103: 'In prison one can learn a profession that can help later on in life.'

Item 107: 'Prosecutors try not to bring a case unless they are sure of the guilt of the accused.'

Item 108: 'The prosecution is not concerned with justice.'

These items, related to the duration of imprisonment, explain 34 per cent of the variance; that is, the attitude of the subject to the prosecution and to the prison systems and his outlook on violence, as an important means of adjustment to the system, are the best predictors of his violence.

The second significant multiple regression connected the following items to the total numbers of offences committed:

Item 51:   'How are the subject's relations with previous acquaintances serving with him today?'

Item 113: 'One of the main reasons for fights in prison is that each group wants to be strong and to have others listen to it.'

Item 114: 'Many fights occur in prison due to troubles between guards and prisoners, since the guards are strict and do not understand the prisoners.'

Item 125: 'Numbers of prisoners in cell'

(The above items explain 31 per cent of the variance in total number of offences).

It is important to stress that the number of prisoners in each cell (item 125) strongly influences the results. The greater the number of prisoners in the cell, the more offences the prisoner has. Similarly, the length of imprisonment also influences the results, a factor known in criminological literature to be clearly connected with hard-core, professional criminality. What emerges from this regression is the pragmatism of the professional criminal--he knows that he must take into account the conflictive relations between the criminal sub-culture and the prison authorities. Only an understanding of this system of relations will enable the prisoners to know how to serve his time without getting into unnecessary conflicts.

DISCUSSION

Our psychological analysis of violent prisoners revealed a profile of a powerful separant type, according to Shoham's theory. He tends to be outwardly-oriented and a sensation seeker, according to the Zuckerman's scale. The violent prisoner is also younger, as his violence is part of a socio-biological developmental dynamic.

The premeditated violent offender is a habitual professional criminal, whose violence was instrumental to his occupation. On the other hand, the impulsive violent prisoner was more unstable in his personality structure and alienated from both the normative and non-normative groups.

The typical professional criminal knows how to serve out a sentence, and holds no illusions as to the essence of the conflictual relations between prisoner and guards. He knows that the best way to sit out an imprisonment 'without problems' is to become acquainted with the relations within the prison society and with the internal dynamics of the law-enforcement authorities, and to reach a *modus vivendi* with them, irrespective of the external front these bodies represent. The prisoners who tend towards situationally-impulsive violence can be distinguished from these violent prisoners, in that they tend to have more illusions as to the nature of prisoners' groups and the intentions of the supervision agencies both in prison and without. Their conception of the dynamics between prisoners and the legal authorities is diffuse and unrealistic. It is possible that this is one reason why they find themselves in situations that lead to violence. The professional criminal rejects violence undirected toward profitable ends, since unplanned and impulsive violence presents a threat to him and to the successful performance of his crimes.

References

Allsop, J.F. In H.J. Eysenck (1967), *The Biological Basis of Personality,* Springfield, Mass: Charles C.Thomas.
Askenasy, J.J, P. Hacket, S. Ron & D. Mary (1983), 'Violence and Episodic Behavioural Dyscontrol', *Biological Psychiatry,* Vol.18, pp.604-7.

Black, D.J. & A.J. Reiss Jr. (1970), 'Police Control of Juveniles', *American Sociological Review,* Vol.35, pp.63-77.

Budner, Stanley (1962), 'Intolerance of Ambiguity as a Personality Variable', *Journal of Personality,* Vol.30, pp.29-50.

Cattell, R.B., M.W. Eber & M.M. Tatsuoka (1970), 'Handbook of the 16 Personality Factor Questionnaire', Champaign, Ill., (CAQ) *Institute for Personality and Ability Testing.*

Christie, R. & F.L.Geis (1970), *Machiavellianism,* New York: Academic Press.

Cleaver, P.T., A.D. Mylonas & W.C. Recless (1968), 'Gradients in Attitudes Towards Law, Courts and Police', *Social Focus,* 2 (winter), pp.29-48.

Eysenck, H.J. (1967),*The Biological Basis of Personality,* Springfield, Ill:Charles C.Thomas, pp. 36-7.

Gibson, H.B. (1961), *Manual of the Gibson Spiral Maize,* (2nd. ed.). Dundon Green: Kent, England: Hodder and Stoughton.

Irwin, J. & D. Cressey (1962), 'Thieves, Convicts and the Inmate Culture', *Social Problems.* (Fall).

Irwin, J. (1962), *The Felon,* Engelwood Cliffs, NJ: Prentice-Hall, pp. 142-55.

Kagan, J., B. Rosman, D. Day, J. Albert & W. Phillips (1974), 'Information Processing in the Child's Significance of Analytic and Reflective Attitudes', *Psychological Monographs,* Vol.78, p.578.

Klein, S.G. & H.J. Schlesinger (1950), 'Perceptual Attitudes of Form-Boundedness and Form-Liability in Rorschach Responses, Abstract *Am. Psychol,* Vol.5, p.321.

Lane, P.J. (1978), 'Annotated Bibliography of the Overcontrolled-Undercontrolled Assaultive Personality Literature and the Overcontrolled-Hostility (O-H) Scale of the MMPI', *JSAS Catalog of Selected Documents in Psychology,* (JSAS No.1760).

Levenson, H. (1973), 'Perceived Parental Antecedents of Internal Powerful Others and Chance Locus of Control Orientation', *Developmental Psychology,* Vol.9, pp.260-5.

Megargee, E.I. (1976), 'Population Density and Disruptive Behaviour in a Prison Setting,' M.E. Wolfgang & N.A. Weines (Eds.),*Criminal Violence,* Beverly Hills: Sage Publications, pp. 81-160.

Megargee, E.I. (1982), 'Psychological Determinants and Correlates of Criminal Violence'. M.E. Wolfgang & N.A.Weines (Eds.), *Criminal Violence,* Beverly Hills: Sage Publications, pp.81-160.

Megargee, E.I. (1966), 'Undercontrolled and Overcontrolled Personality Types in Extreme Antisocial Aggression', *Psychological Monographs,* Vol.80 (3, Whole No. 611).

Murray, M.A. (1938), *Explorations in Personality,* New York: Oxford University Press.

Petrie, A. (1960), 'The Tolerance of Pain and Sensory Deprivation', *A.J. Psychol.* Vol. 1-3, No.1 March, pp.80-90.

Quay, H.C. (1965), 'Psychopathic Personality as Pathological Stimulation-Seeking', *American Journal of Psychiatry,* Vol.122, pp.180-3.

Raven, S.C., *Standard Progressive Matrices. Sets, A,B,C,D,E.,* London; H.K. Lewis.

Rosenzweiz, S. (1965), Note of Correction for Schwartz, Cohen & Pavlik. 'The Effects of Subject and Experimenter Induced Defensive Response Sets on Picture-Frustration Test Reactions', *J. Proj. Tech. & Pers. Asses,* Vol.29, pp. 352-3, Sept. 1965.

Rotter, J.B. (1962), Seeman, M. & Liverant, S., 'Internal v. External Controls of Reinforcements, A Major Variable in Behaviour Theory', N.F.Washburne'. (Ed.), *Decisions, Values and Groups,* London; Pergamon Press, Vol. 2., pp. 473-959.

Schalling, D, & R.D. Hare (Eds.1978), *Psychopathic Behaviour: Approach to Research*, Chichester: John Wiley & Sons Inc.

Sellin, T. & W.E. Wolfgang (1964), *The Measurement of Delinquency*, New York: John Wiley & Sons Inc.

Shoham, S.G. (1964), 'Conflict Situations and Delinquent Solutions', *Journal of Social Psychology, The Journal Press*, Vol.64, pp. 185-215.

Shoham, S.G. (1968), 'Points of No Return: Some Situational Aspects of Violence', *The Prison Journal*, Vol. XLVIII, p.2.

Shoham, S, G. Nehemia, R. Markowski & N. Kaplinsky (1974), 'Internalisation of Norms, Risk-Perceptions and Anxiety as Related to Driving Offences', *British Journal of Criminology*, Vol. 16, No.2, April 1976, pp. 142-55.

Shoham, S.G. (1979), *The Myth of Tantalus*, St. Lucia; Univ. of Queensland Press.

Shoham, S.G., Z. Schwartzman, G. Rahav, R. Markowski, F. Chard & A. Adelstein (1967), 'An Instrument to Diagnose Personality Types According to the Personality Theory of Shoham', *Medicine and Law*, Vol.6, p. 164, (1987).

Singer, J.L. (1971), 'The Psychological Study of Aggression', *The Control of Aggression and Violence*, New York & London: Academic Press.

Sutherland, E.H. & D.R. Cressey (1970), *Criminology*, Philadelphia: Lippincott.

Thibaut, J.W. & H.H. Kelly (1959), *The Social Psychology of Groups*, New York: John Wiley and Sons Inc, pp. 239 *et seq.*

Trivers, R.L. (1972), *Parental Investment and Sexual Selection*, Chicago: Aldine, p. 164.

Wilson, E.O. (1976), *Sociobiology*, Cambridge,Mass: Harvard Univ. Press.

Witkin, H.A. H.F. Faterson, R.B. Dyk, D.R. Goodenough, & S.A. Karp (1962), *Psychological Differentiation*, New York: John Wiley & Sons Inc.

Zuckerman, M., & E.A. Kolin (1964), 'Development of Sensation Seeking Scale, *Journal of Consulting Psychology*, Vol. 28, No. 61, pp.477-82.

4 The Validation of Shoham's Personality Theory

Even Moses had roots in Cain.

The Lurianic Kabbala

INTRODUCTION

A study was conducted to construct an instrument suitable for measuring the direction and potency of the core personality vectors in accordance with Shoham's personality theory. As a result, the theory and instrument are now linked together and can thus be applied to empirical investigations. Adaptable to many languages, the questionnaire can be used to study cross-cultural differences and the universality of the theory.

The purpose of the study reported in this chapter was to construct an instrument with which to measure the direction and potency of the core personality vectors according to Shoham's personality theory (1977). The construction of an instrument measuring personality parameters links theory to empirical anchors.

The theoretical models formulated by Freud, Jung, Horney, Fromm and Sullivan enriched and stimulated thinking on personality structure, but were criticised by the behavioural scientists and empirical personologists as speculation without empirical bases. In the 1950s and 1960s, personality researchers sought quantitive behavioural parameters and personality inventories which could quantify human traits and situations. Examples of scales and personality inventories in current use include. the M.M.P.I. MPI, and CPI, and of Cattell's C.A.Q. All these instuments are based on self-reporting, and the total scores determine where the subject is positioned on the various personality scales.

60

According to Eysenck (1981), the human personality can be described by such traits as sociability, impulsiveness, activity etc. The traits, when correlated, form higher order patterns. Eysenck delineated his personality types following the work of Kant, Wundt, Gross and Hymans. The two main personality types described by Eysenck were the introvert and extravert.

These personality types were introduced by Jung, who recognised their value intuitively without providing them an empirical basis. Eysenck believed that these personality types were genetically formed, and postulated that there was a difference in cortical functioning between introverts and extraverts. This difference expressed itself in higher cortical arousal in introverts and more pronounced cortical inhibition in extraverts (Eysenck, 1969).

Eysenck described the 'pure' introvert and extravert, although he stressed that a pure type does not exist in reality. He also presented a continuum of traits, from a 'higher' pole to a 'lower' one, with the classification of each individual related to his position on the continuum. His theoretical structures were based on a dual continuum of introversion-extraversion and neuroticism-stability (Eysenck, 1964). Eysenck's theoretical premises concerning personality types and his attempts to give a theoretical explanation for their existence together with instruments for their measurement, were an initial step towards the concept of a comprehensive personality theory with an empirical basis. Some of the overt features of Eysenck's parameters are included in Shoham's personality theory (Shoham, 1977), which is also based on the assumption that these traits and types can be described and measured.

It should be stressed, however, that there is a crucial, conceptual and methodological difference between Jung's and Eysenck's theoretical analysis of the introversion-extraversion continuum and Shoham's theoretical analysis. Furthermore, Eysenck's theory of the core of the human personality is totally different from Shoham's model.

Shoham's theory follows the trend that started in the late 1970s, when personologists started to regard the fragmented and atomistic personality inventories more and more critically and to look for a holistic integration of these theories. Shoham tried to explain the complexity of the human personality in the holistic theoretical style of the 1940s and the 1950s, but also employed some innovative conceptual frameworks and empirical anchors. The detailed parameters offered by Shoham, together with some conceptual frameworks which had already been used in professional literature, enabled us, in the present study, to construct a measuring instrument similar in methodology to Eysenck's. The theory and the instrument together allow a new scientific approach to the nature and prediction of personality process.

SHOHAM'S PERSONALITY THEORY

The personality continuum, according to Shoham's theory, has two ontological systems, which are in conflict: in one, surroundings are perceived as space, time and causality, whereas the other is boundless, timeless and non-synchronic. The cognitive system of the first is based on logic, and discrete sequences, whereas the other can be perceived by intuition and through mystical experiences. These cognitive systems interact dialectically within the core personality of the individual.

These two conflicting entities are formed from the basic vectors of human existence; the powers of growth and development as opposed to the desire to revert back to the nothingness of pre-being. After neonates leave the womb, they experience the transition from pantheistic togetherness with their mothers and objective surroundings in early orality to existence as a separate entity. But the ego feels a constant longing to revert to the feeling of wholeness and completeness experienced in pre-being. The very nature of this desire means that it cannot be realised and that it will therefore continue to manifest itself in various ways and degrees of potency throughout life. This longing is in dialectical conflict with the powers of growth and development, which is the second basic vector of our core personality. This vector is that of separation through growth, initiated by fertilisation, birth, the crystallisation of separate cells and other developmental phases of the personality, which are registered by the organism as disasters. The other vector aims at 'participation,' which is structured around the quest of the individual's striving to revert to earlier developmental phases and to the completeness of non-being. The dialectical interaction between the two vectors form and structure the core personality and crystallises the ego boundaries.

Shoham sees the biophysiology of the organism as potential raw material for the personality structure, and the interrelationship of the organism with its surroundings as the crystallising dynamic of these structures. His model is thus an interdisciplinary and multidimensional one, which takes into account the biophysiological potential, the personality dimension and sociocultural imprints.

The Vectors of Participation and Separation

'Participation' means identification of the ego with people, life forms or objects which are outside the organism and its yearning to negate itself by merging with these life forms, objects and symbols. 'Separation' means the definition of the self as separate from people, life forms, objects and symbols which are outside the personality and its attempt to negate their separate existence by 'swallowing' them within itself. Both vectors are apparent in the three main phases of personality development, which are in

62

essence three separate foci: birth, the crystallisation of the 'ego boundary' and the formation of the 'ego identity'.

1. The process of birth: The sudden transition when the neonate, from being a part of the mother within the womb, becomes an independent biological and mental entity, constitutes a separation crisis which engenders a constant yearning for participation.

2. The crystallisation of the ego boundary: The traumas and suffering that the neonate encounters through periods of hunger, thirst, changing temperatures, clashes with hard surfaces and, of course, with the mother, who is often not 'good' and 'caring' but 'bad' and depriving. All these push the newborn child to crystallise a separate entity and to depart from pantheistic togetherness with his surroundings. There is also an especially painful separation from the mother or her surrogate.

3. The formation of an ego identity: the continuation of the separation process is effected mainly by subsequent socio-normative pressures exerted on the child by the various socialisation agencies, such as the family, schools and religious institutions, to 'grow up' and become a responsible and independent person in the framework of society.

Throughout the process of developmental separation the child struggles against the separant pressures and longs to revert to the togetherness of early orality and of life *in utero*. It seems, therefore, that the separant vector operates on the ego from without, whereas the urges towards participation are subjective and internal. Achievement of the longed for participation is attempted by negating one of the three main foci of separation. These attempts may be either deviant or institutionalised: mystics yearn to achieve perfect participation by the reversal of birth and the obliteration of self. Madness is one way of blotting out the ego boundary, and crime and social deviation can be ways of neutralising the social stage of normative separation. Institutionalised means of participation include creativity, revelation and love. Creativity may bridge the gap between subject and object; love may temporarily melt the ontological partition between human beings; and revelation may momentarily expose the individual to the wholeness of nothingness.

63

The Interrelationship Between the Vectors of Separation and Participation as Core Dynamics of Shoham's Personality Model

The theory is based on two cycles of conflict: an internal one, which includes the separant pressures on the individual stemming both from the biological basis and the object relationships, and the participation vector, which stems from the inner self. The inner conflictive cycle occurs within the ego itself. The outer cycle includes the conflictive interaction of the ego with its surroundings , which also involves separant and participant pressures. If, in the internal cycle, the ego aims to melt its ego boundaries and revert to pre-separation nothingness, in the outer cycle, the ego aims for ontological participation with the alter ego and for social solidarity. The opposition of the objective and human environment to this aim is introjected by the ego and becomes a separate component within the personality.

As the participant vector opposes the powers of growth, the libidinal forces and the object relationships, it is mainly responsible for the dualism of the personality core. The process of separation, which crystallises the separate cell and forms the ego boundaries, is inherent in the conflictive interaction with a painful, neglectful or rejecting object. The separate ego and the ego boundaries are formed through a dialectical interaction with a nipple, which many times does not secrete food and with a mother who does not always ease pain, tension and discomfort. Thus, unlike Freud and Erikson, Shoham claims that social separation is not achieved by psychosexual developmental phases, but by conflictive socialisation within the family. The separant powers always overcome the participant, except in the case of death, yet people are always moved by the quest for non-being, which stems from the participant vectors. The dialectics between the separant and participant vectors within the core personality constitute the Tantalus Ratio. The Tantalus Ratio depends mainly on the following factors:

1. The potency of the participant vectors, which are related to age, and the distance as measured by the time span, from the developmental events of birth, the crystallisation of ego, and the achievement of the 'ego identity'.

2. The fixation, in the Freudian sense, that has been suffered by the ego in its various developmental stages.

3. The type of culture in which the ego grew up.

The Tantalus Ratio is higher at the start of life and declines with each consecutive developmental phase. The potency of the separant force in childhood causes the participant vectors to generate countering pressures of corresponding potency. These are the constant dialectics of a system in balance. The developmental events after birth implant memories of the loss of participant grace and generate attempts to revert to pre-separation wholeness. The more traumatic the process of birth, the more intense the desire to return to the womb. This might explain the 'attachment instinct' of mammals to their mothers, as a function not only of the search for food and shelter, but also of the neonate's quest for participation.

The crystallisation of the ego boundary is the synthetic result of the conflict between the participant and the separant vectors. In his theory, Shoham relies on the oralist off-shoots of psychoanalysis stemming from the teachings of Melanie Klein, which stress the early developmental phases of the neonate, which are crystallised in the interaction of the oral 'mouth ego' with the object. In early orality, the neonate aims, by suckling, to empty the breast-object, which does not fulfil expectations. The emptying of the breast in early orality or its swallowing and destruction in later orality are expressions of the quest for participation, in opposition to the separant powers expressed in development and biological growth and against the frustrating interaction which pushes the nascent ego to crystallise as a separate ego.

The Tantalus Ratio is exceptionally potent at the stage of the crystallisation of the separate ego, because of the violent pressures which culminate in the 'expulsion' of the separate ego. The crystallisation of the ego identity is also a result of the struggle of the participant and separant vectors due to the encounter of the ego-centred child with parents and other socialising agencies which pressure him to be socialised, to adopt the viewpoint of others, and to internalise social norms. At a later stage, towards puberty, the separant forces continue to operate from without, through the normative pressures on the adolescent, who reacts in a participant manner by yearning for the grace of the mother and for the forgiveness and non-responsibility of the family unit. At this stage, the Tantalus Ratio is still very strong, but after middle age there is a gradual but constant decrease, due to the slow waning of the separant powers. The event of birth has long since receded into the background, and there is a marked decrease in the biological powers of growth and in libidinal energy and an ever-increasing alienation from the environment.

Fixation

The notion of fixation is taken from Freud. But according to Freud, fixation is generated both by deprivational interaction with one's surroundings and through parental over-protection, while Shoham sees fixation as generated only by a deprivational interaction. The participation vector generates a basic yearning to revert to earlier developmental phases, and this yearning does not receive any special reinforcement from the parents. Therefore, only deprivational interaction with the parents and with the surroundings, or severe trauma, can cause a fixation.

Formation of Personality Types According to the Period in Which Fixations Occurred

Shoham sees the ontological division between the object and subject as a basis for the personality dichotomy. This division is crucial in relation to two developmental periods: from birth up to the end of early orality, when an ego boundary is crystallised around a separate individual, and from later orality, up to the formation of an ego identity later on.

In the first stage, i.e., in early orality, every fixation is experienced not by a separate, individualised entity which is capable of distinguishing between itself and the trauma-generating objects, but by a pantheistic holistic essence for which the outside and inside are one. At the second stage, separation between the individual and the object has already taken place and the individual can attribute pain and deprivation to an external object. The difference in the way the traumatic fixation is internalised determines the personality type: if the traumatic fixation has occurred before the generation of a separate self, it results in a participant type, constantly longing to revert to early orality and to the suspended animation *in utero*. If the traumatic fixation occurs after crystallisation of the separate self, the result is a separant type, who struggles to cope with the surrounding objects and life forms.

Characteristics of the Separant and Participant Personality Types

Shoham's characterisation of the oral stage of development is, as we have already mentioned, based on the English oralists Klein, Fairbern, Winnocot and Guntrip. Fixation in the early oral phase takes place before differentiation beween the neonate and his surroundings starts. Hence, whatever hardship is experienced, e.g., an empty breast, a neglectful mother, or hard objects, inconvenience and suffering are perceived as happening within the pantheistic ego and therefore lead to an ego boundary characterised by a feeling of badness surrounded by an outer amorphic 'goodness'.

Fixation at a later stage in the oral phase, created by interaction with a 'bad' mother, is effected after the period of separation between the individual and the object. Hence, the ego boundary will regard itself in a positive manner and view the object as frightening, depriving and 'bad'. Because fixations are related to frustrations experienced during orality, Shoham adopts Rosensweig's typology of reactions to frustrations for the description of the two resultant types (Shoham, 1977). The extrapunitive reaction is characterised by aggression towards the outside and by a defence mechanism of projection, and the intropunitive reaction by inner aggression and by defence mechanisms of transference and regression.

The participant type is therefore characterised by a feeling of a 'bad me' and an anxious fixation of destroying the 'good object' (according to the oralists, anxiety of the possibility of destroying the object by swallowing it). Hence, the participant vector of the participant type will seek to annul the temporal self in order to achieve the longed-for participation. On the other hand, the characteristics of the separant type are the feeling of a 'good me' surrounded by a 'bad object' and a fixation on the quest to dominate the object. Hence, the participant vector of the separant type will seek to merge--realistically or symbolically --with the object within his personality.

Because the participant type seeks the negation of his separate existence, his reactions are passive and quietist, whereas the separant type, who seeks to dominate and swallow the 'object', tends to be activist in his reactions. The quietist characteristics of the participant type signify a lower Tantalus Ratio than is present in the separant type, whose wish to dominate and swallow the object meets a stronger reaction by the separant vectors and generates a stronger conflictive system within the core personality. The dichotomous characteristics of the quietist versus the activist, as a means of distinguishing between the separant and participant personality types, provide the first pair in a series of twenty-five dichotomies of personality characteristics that have been identified by Shoham to portray the two types. Fifteen of these characteristics were defined by Shoham in his development of the hypothesis of the crystallisation of personality types according to the period in which fixation occurred.

Personality Types

Participant	Separant
Passive	*Active*
Aversion to stimuli	Hungry for stimuli
Low vulnerability to sensory deprivation	High vulnerability to sensory deprivation
Low sensory threshold	High sensory threshold
Sensitivity to pain	Insensitivity to pain
Augmentor	Reducer
Solitary performers	Group performers
Field-independent	Field-dependent
Tolerance of objective ambiguity	Intolerance of objective ambiguity
Intolerance of ideational ambiguity	Tolerance of ideational ambiguity
Intropunitive	Extrapunitive
Moral orientation	Sanction orientation
Low risk takers	High risk takers
Inner orientation	Outer orientation
Non-conformity	Conformity

According to Eysenck, the extravert is hungry for stimuli, in contrast to the introvert, who is averse to stimuli. In a like manner, Shoham's separant seeks the object, while his participant longs for inaction. The introvert reacts favourably to sensory deprivation, whereas the extravert suffers under it. According to Shoham, the participant type is less vulnerable to sensory deprivation but is very sensitive to pain. We should recapitulate that in early orality the neonate feels pain within his pantheistic totality and fixation at this stage creates the participant type. The separant type needs activity and stimuli, while the participant suffers from stimuli, since it distances him from his goals of inactivity and passivity. Therefore, the participant type develops a defence shield against stimuli and activity. However, even a very few stimuli can 'engulf' this type, signifying a very low sensory threshold. Petri found that introverts tend subjectively to augment the pitch and volume of stimuli, whereas extraverts reduce them. Shoham tried to utilise these concepts and their empirical anchors to characterise the participant type as one who reacts to the strength of stimuli more intensively, whereas the separant type reacts less intensively. The following four pairs of characteristics: solitary performers versus group performers, field dependence versus field independence, tolerance versus intolerance of objective ambiguity and intolerance versus tolerance to ideational ambiguity are linked to the tendency of each type to relate to the object, i.e. the goal of the separant type to swallow the object and the wish of the participant type to merge within it. W.P. Colquhoun and D.W.J. Corcoran showed that introverts perform better when they are by themselves and extraverts perform better in a group. In like manner, Shoham claims that the higher motivation of the separant for interpersonal relationships and his more intense achievement motive are linked to his tendency to perform in groups, whereas the participant type prefers to work alone. Vitkin et al. related themselves to the objective context and to the ego's perception of the environment while performing a certain task, and coined the concepts of field dependence and field independence. The type who is field-dependent, who has a lower psychological differentiation because he depends on cues which are linked to the objective background, has the characteristics of the separant type. On the other hand, the participant type fits the field-independent type, who is characterised by a better psychological differentiation, because he anchors on his inner self and not on the outer structure of the objects which surround him.

Shoham (1977) added two more characteristics to the personality types in the context of object relationships, even though he did not find empirical anchors for them in the existing literature. Shoham hypothesised that the separant type is intolerant of objective ambiguity. He will perceive himself and others better in situations which are well defined by outer boundaries. Yet he is tolerant of ideational ambiguity, that is, he does not seek maximum clarity in abstract matters. The participant, on the other hand, seeks ideational clarity, whereas objective ambiguity serves his mystical tendencies.

Five pairs of characteristics concern the normative parameters, and are related to the interaction of ego with his surroundings. There are conceptual parallels in the literature, but no empirical anchors. Shoham hypothesised that the participant type will internalise moral standards in a deeper manner, and hence will be moral-orientated, whereas the separant type will tend to comply with social norms for fear of sanction for their infringement. The separant type will also tend to take risks, whereas the participant type will be more hesitant and cautious. The separant will have an external orientation, i.e., seek the approval of others for his or her actions (according to Riesman's conceptualisation). He will also tend to be conformist, because his membership group will be very important to him. The participant type will have an inner orientation and will tend to be non-conformist.

The type of culture is the third dimension that links the core vectors of the personality to the society in which the individual has been socialised. The socialising agencies which imprint social norms on the individual may also be classified and placed on the separant-participant continuum. Shoham assumed that cultures have composite patterns, which may be described as 'social characters', which could be related in turn to the character of a given individual. For these two assumptions we found ample support in the sociological and anthropological literature (Shoham, 1977), especially from the works of scholars with the cultural relativist approach, which characterises the social character of the culture as the composite portrait of a society and placed this social character between two poles of a continuum, although the position on this continuum is never static, but moves with every change in the social structure (Shoham, 1977).

The Continuum of Social Characters

The classification of social character according to the participant-separant continuum of cultures was constructed by Shoham with five dimensions:

Participant social character	Separant social character
Quietism	Activism
Individual	Pluralism
Stability	Relationship
Intuition	Logic
Anchoring on the self	Object manipulation

Quietism vs Activism

Separant cultures preach salvation through activism, which will unify the subject and the object by Hegelian dialectics or by Marxist *praxis* and historical materialism. Participant cultures, on the other hand, perceive reality as static. According to participant cultures such as Taoism and Hinayaic Buddhism, etc., it is necessary to release oneself from the illusion of a manifest world and reach the true stability beyond it.

Unity vs Plurality

Participant cultures preach release from the false perception of the senses and anchor on unity. Separant cultures see the world as a system within a plurality, which is organised by sequences in a dynamic harmony, as explained by Pythagoras and Heraclitus.

Stability vs Relationship

Participant cultures reject the possiblity of viable relationships between the ego and its surroundings and see them as the basis of evil and suffering. Separant cultures, on the other hand, perceive the relationship of individuals with space, time, and other human beings as very significant. They also stress the need for interpersonal adjustment and social solidarity.

Intuition vs Logic

Participant cultures reject the logic of separant cultures and anchor more on intuition in their relationship with the environment, and on revelation in their relationship with transcendence.

Anchoring on Self vs Object Manipulation

Participant cultures negate salvation through interaction with others and the objective surroundings. They stress personal freedom and release. Separant cultures anchor on the interaction of individuals with their objective and human surroundings.

The type of culture in which the individual is socialised constitutes the third layer of factors that form the personality of the individual. The social character is imprinted in the individual by socialising agencies. Hence, the five pairs of patterns of the individual and of his Tantalus Ratio.

Measurement of Personality Type and the Tantalus Ratio

The first factor which determines the Tantalus Ratio is, as we have specified, the potency of the core personality vectors, which are linked to age. Age is an external and constant factor influencing the potency of the Tantalus Ratio, but is not itself involved in the structuring of the separant or participant personality type. This is the reason for keeping age constant when personality types are diagnosed. The other two groups of factors, the personality parameters and the type of culture in which the individual was raised, were measured by ourselves as we have seen, with reference to 25 pairs of characteristics which lent themselves by nature to a description as continua.

The crystallisation of the core personality of the individual is dynamic and is related to the interaction with the mother in the oral phase of development, to the inter-relationships within the whole family and to interaction with the socialisation agencies. Hence, it is clear that those who grow up in a separant culture will not all necessarily be separant and those who are socialised in a participant culture will not necessarily be participant types.

Furthermore, those who are fixated in early orality and those fixated at later orality will be influenced differentially by the imprints of social norms stemming from a more separant or a more participant social milieu.

As a result, we have a personality type whose placement on a continuum between the separant and participant poles is determined by fixation in the oral phase of development and by internalisation of the culture in which the individual has been socialised. The overall position on the continuum is derived from the sum total of the placement on the continua of each of our 25 pairs of parameters. These personality parameters are manifestations of the dynamics of the core personality, which are always in conflict between participation and separation. The position of the individual on each scale of the parameter and the interrelationship between the scales will show us the system of vectors and dynamics which operate within a given personality core, and the internal consistency in balance between the vectors of participation and separation. When the polarity is greater, that is, when a person's position is skewed towards the pole of separation or participation on each parameter, the conflict in his core personality is more intense, constituting evidence of a higher Tantalus Ratio. Conversely, the more a person's personality parameters are symmetrically placed between the separant and participant poles of the continua, the more balanced is his core personality. To measure the placement of each individual on the separant-participant continuum, we have constructed a questionnaire to measure our 25 pairs of parameters.

We have adopted Block's (1977) assumption on the advantages of constructing a self-reporting questionnaire for personality type, so a questionnaire of this type was classified by Cattell (1977) as the collection of type-S information. Block claimed that self-reporting questionnaires for the collection of personality data had a long history and were in wide use. The prevailing personality inventories of this type are the MMPI, Cattell's 16PF, and Jackson's personality research form.

An important aspect of the construction of any questionnaire relates to its reliability and validation. We had therefore to ascertain whether the questionnaire did indeed succeed in differentiating between the separant and participant types. For this purpose, we had to choose a specific group of persons which was characterised as extremely separant, and another specific group of persons characterised as extremely participant. These two groups were selected with reference to the parameters of the separant and participant personality types and social characters. In addition to this, we adopted Shoham's (1977) recommendation that for an empirical verification of his theories, it is desirable to take a group of practising mystics as representative of the participating pole of his personality continuum, and a group of extremely ambitious people active in business or professional life, as representative of the separant pole.

METHOD

Procedure

a) *Construction of Initial Questionnaire.* Four researchers who were familiar with Shoham's theory of personality (Shoham, 1977) proposed statements representing each of Shoham's 25 personality characteristics (at least 5 statements for each characteristic). The statements were assumed to differentiate between separant and participant character types. A total of 151 sentences were collected and edited by two grammar experts. The sentences were arranged in a list according to a table of random numbers.

The questionnaire was then administered to five independent judges proficient in Shoham's personality thoery, who were requested to rate each sentence on a seven-point scale, with one representing the most participant sentence and seven the most separant possible.

b) *Reliability of the Questionnaire.* Based on the statistical analysis of the judgement stage (see Results) a questionnaire was accompanied by a five-point scale in which -2 meant completely out of character; -1, not very characteristic; 0, don't know; 1, true to a certain extent; and 2, absolutely true. The questionnaire was administered to 271 subjects, 238 of whom were students (humanities 100, law 128, and theatre and cinema 10) and 33 of whom were not. Sex was recorded as male in 130 subjects and female in 138; 3 subjects did not indicate their sex. Ages ranged from 18 to 50, with an average of 24 years.

c) *Validity Measurement.* The reliability measurement stage yielded a questionnaire of 36 items which were arranged in the same order as in the reliability questionnaire. The characteristics represented on this questionnaire were: passive/active, high/low sensitivity to pain, augmentor/reducer, tolerance/intolerance of ideational ambiguity, moral/sanction orientation, low/high level of risk-taking, outer/inner orientation, conformity/non-conformity, submissiveness/aggressiveness, social involvement/retreat, resignation/achievement, fatalism/combativeness, social mobility/ static social positon.

Subjects were asked to grade themselves on each statement on a five-point scale similar to that used at the reliablity stage. Two groups of subjects were tested; a separant group of 46 doctors (39 male and 7 female) from three hospitals in the centre of Israel. Doctors were chosen because they are, as a rule, very ambitious, they believe in science, and they have the ability to solve problems by manipulation of the environment. They seek power and position, and value quick and efficient decisions.

The participant group consisted of 42 subjects (22 male and 20 female), all inhabitants of a Moshav in the North of Israel which applies Gurdhieff's philosophy of life to everyday living. The Moshav inhabitants were extremely participant, since they anchored on contemplation and renounced many of the usual achievement motives prevalent in western society.

RESULTS

a) *Judging Stage*

The distribution and mode of scores given to each statement on the separant-participant continuum were measured. Statements judged on more than four consecutive levels and whose standard deviation was greater than 1.3 were rejected, and 71 questions representing 25 characteristics were accepted.

The characteristics represented were:

Moral/sanction orientation (M/S O), five statements
Social mobility/ stable social position (M/S S), five statements
Stimulus hunger/ aversion (H/A S), four statements
High/ low sensitivity to pain (H/ L P), four statements
Augmentor/ reducer (A/R), four statements
Active/ passive (A/P), four statements
Conservative/ progress-oriented (C/P O), four statements
Submissive/ aggressive (S/A), four statements
High/ low vulnerability to sensory deprivation (H/L SD), three statements
High/ low sensitivity (H/L S), three statements
Tolerance/ intolerance of objective ambiguity (T/IT OA), three statements
Resignation/ achievement (R/A), three statements
Non-conformist/ conformist (NC/C), three statements
Tendency to mysticism/ science (M/S), three statements
Social involvement/ retreat (I/R S), three statements
Field dependence/ independence (D/I F), two statements
Tolerance/ intolerance of ideational ambiguity (T/IT IA), two statements
Inner/ outer directed (I/O D), two statements
High/ low risk taking (H/L R), two statements
Symbolic/ tool orientation (S/ T O), two statements
Intropunitive/ extrapunitive (I/ E), one statement
Anchoring on revelation/ activist ideology (R/ A I), one statement
Time/ timeless orientation (T/ T O), one statement

74

Isolated/ group performer (I/ G P), one statement

Fatalism/ combativeness (F/ C), no statements

b) *Reliability of questionnaire*

1. Reliability measures of the 71 statement questionnaire yielded an alpha value of 0.67. Item analysis did not indicate an item as dissimiliar.

2. Factor analysis of the 71 items, once limiting the number of factors to 25 and once without limiting the number of factors, did not yield any clear-cut factors. This result could indicate a similarity of content.

3. Reliability measures of each of the characteristics separately (rather than the 15 characteristics represented by at least three statements) showed alpha (a) coefficients of between 0.18 to 0.72. Results are shown in table 2. Only characteristics whose=coefficients were above 0.2 were retained. Two characteristics, hunger or aversion to stimuli (*highest a poss* =0.18) and high/low sensory threshold (*highest a poss* =0.18) were excluded from later analysis due to the low a coefficients.

4. A factor analysis of the remaining 13 characteristics and the other 10 characteristics on which reliability could not be checked was undertaken. Results are shown in tables 3 and 4. Factor one (explaining 66 per cent of the common variance) included 13 characteristics with weighting of more than 0.23. The reliability of these 13 characteristics is 0.91, and item analysis indicated that the exclusion of no item would raise the a value. The characteristics represented are fatalism/ combativeness; risk taking; submissive/ aggressive; social involvement/ retreat; sensitivity to pain; reducer/ augmentor; ideational ambiguity; inner/ outer directedness; social mobility; resignation/ achievement; sanction/ moral orientation; conformity/non conformity; active/passive.

c) *Validity Meaurements*

A one-way analysis of variance between the two groups on the total score and 13 characteristics was performed. Results (see table 5) showed the separant group to have a significantly higher total score ($P \leq 0.04$) than the participant group. On ten of the 13 characteristics the separant group had a significantly higher average than the participant group:

F.C ($P \leq 0.01$); S/A ($P \leq 0.05$); I/R S ($P \leq 0.02$); H/LP ($P \leq 0.04$);
R/A ($P \leq 0.03$); I/O D ($P \leq 0.01$); M/S S ($P \leq 0.04$); R/A ($P \leq 0.01$);
NC/C ($P \leq 0.01$); A/P($P \leq 0.01$); (see table 6)

For two characteristics (H/L R and T/IT IA) no significant differences were found between the two groups. For a third characteristic (M/S O) no difference in the direction of the hypothesis was found between the two groups.

75

In order to evaluate the 'clean' influence of the 13 characteristics when controlling for sex, age and total score, a regression analysis was performed (see table 6). Age was not found to differentiate between the two groups, sex was found to have a certain influence (0.20) and the total score was shown to be the most influential (0.58) in explaining the difference between the two groups.

Table 1. *Descriptive data on questions judges agreed upon*

Characteristics	Question number	SD	Mode*
Active/passive	56	0.5	2.6
	94	0.44	5.8
	123	0.44	5.8
	134	0.83	6.2
Hunger for / aversion	49	0.5	2.6
to stimuli	82	0.44	5.8
	60	0.44	5.1
	130	0.5	5.3
High/low vulnerability	16	1.3	6.0
to sensory deprivation	23	1.3	2.0
	107	0.54	1.6
High/low sensitivity to	26	0	3.0
pain	30	0.4	3.1
	75	0.44	3.1
	113	0.54	2.3
High/low sensory	84	0.54	2.6
threshold	131	0.89	5.7
	142	0.83	5.7
Reducer/augmentor	8	0.54	2.6
	18	0.8	6.2
	86	0.54	6.3
	133	0.7	4
Group/isolate	81	0.5	5.6
performers	39	0.8	5.7
Field dependence/	146	0.54	5.3
independence			
Tolerance/intolerance	21	0.5	5.3
of objective ambiguity	53	0.5	5.6
	70	0.8	5.7
Tolerance / intolerance	85	2.7	5.7
of ideational ambiguity	110	0.54	2.3
Extrapunitiveness /	143	0.83	5.2
intropunitiveness			

Table 1 (continued)

Characteristics	Question number	SD	Mode
Sanction / moral	7	0.89	3.6
orientation	15	0.5	5.6
	28	0.3	3.0
	45	0.8	5.7
	101	0.89	2.6
High/low risk taking	128	0.7	6.0
	144	0.54	2.3
Other directed / inner	9	0.7	6.0
directed	36	0.8	4.7
Non-conformity /	62	0.54	5.6
conformity	91	0.83	6.2
	17	0.89	2.7
Fatalism /	54	1.6	1.7
combativeness	150	1.3	2.3
Social mobility /	19	0.89	5.6
stationary social	22	0.89	5.6
position	59	0.89	4.7
	125	0.54	5.3
	127	0.7	6.0
Anchoring on revelation / activist ideology	32	0.89	2.3
Time / Timeless orientation	126	0.54	6.3
Resignation /	12	0.8	1.75
achievement	65	0.8	6.2
Symbol tool	79	0.7	2.0
orientation	119	1.3	4.6
Conservative / progress	89	0.83	3.2
orientated	92	0.83	5.7
	122	0.44	2.8
	148	0.54	2.3
Tendency to mysticism	27	0.8	1.7
/ science	80	0.8	1.7
	129	0.5	2.3
Aggressivity /	58	0.8	6.2
submissiveness	63	0.8	1.7
	73	0.44	2.8
	120	1.0	6.0
Social involvement	14	0.89	2.6
/retreat	34	0.5	2.3
	109	0.44	2.1

*High mode value indicates a separant tendency and a low mode value, a participant tendency)

DISCUSSION

The final result of this study is a reliable and valid instrument for testing the placement of the individual personality type on the participation and separation continuum, and also for ascertaining the potency of the tantalic process and the tantalic system-in balance of the individual.

The instrument has a high reliability (=0.91) and is valid, because it differentiates significantly between a group characterised as extremely particpant and groups characterised as extremely separant. The 36 items were distributed into 13 scales of pairs of parameters as follows. (The item numbers in parenthesis indicate the position of the item on the final questionnaire).

Table 2, *Reliability results for 15 characteristics* (n=271)

Characteristics		Item Number	If Item omitted
Active / passive	0.59	55	0.63
		66	0.38
		75	0.54
		35	0.49
Hunger for / aversion to stimuli	0.06	38	0.18
		47	0.09
		32	0.10
		72	0.03
High / low vulnerability to sensory deprivation	0.08	22	0.19
		57	0.28
		17	0.49
High / low sensitivity to pain	0.39	43	0.38
		23	0.27
		26	0.42
		61	0.22
High / low sensory threshold	0.06	49	0.05
		76	0.00
		73	0.18
Augmentor / reducer	0.24	74	0.03
		12	0.16
		18	0.32
		51	0.25
Tolerance / intolerance of objective ambiguity	0.43	41	0.18
		20	0.04
		34	0.67
Moral / sanction orientation	0.63	56	0.52
		31	0.57
		16	0.59
		25	0.58
		11	0.62

Table 2 (continued)

Characteristics		Item Number	If Item Omitted
Non-conformity / conformity	0.40	53	0.36
		62	0.39
		39	0.16
Social mobility / stationary social position	0.55	67	0.41
		21	0.52
		37	0.59
		69	0.51
		19	0.44
Resignation / achievement	0.25	82	0.01
		48	0.06
		14	0.47
Tendency towards mysticism / science	0.57	45	0.36
		24	0.24
		71	0.72
Submissive /aggressive	0.44	64	0.60
		36	0.34
		42	0.33
		40	0.27

Fatalism/ a tendency to fight one's fate - two items (13 and 35)

Risk taking - two items (31 and 35)

Aggression/submission - three items (15,17,18)

Withdrawal/social involvement -two items (4,10)

High/ low sensitivity to pain - three items (8,19,26)

Augmentors/reducers - three items (2,22,32)

Tolerance/intolerance of ideational ambiguity - two items (21,25)

Internal/external orientation - two items (3, 11)

Social mobility/stationary social position - four items (6,7,29,30)

Resignation/achievement - two items (20,36)

Moral/sanction orientation - five items (1,5,9,12,24)

Non-conformity/conformity - three items (16,23,27)

Passive/active - three items (14,28,33)

The results of the intercorrelation of the means of the 13 parameters comply with Eysenck's statement that the parameters which describe the personality of a person have to be intercorrelated. Measurement of the differences in each parameter between the groups revealed that there were three parameters--risk taking, tolerance/intolerance of ideational ambiguity, and moral/sanction orientation--that did not distinguish significantly between the participant and separant groups. However, it was decided to retain them in the final version of the questionnaire, because of their possible contribution to the total differentiation between the groups.

It should be stressed that the questionnaire does not measure the tendency of a given individual in either direction for any one parameter. Our theory is based on a dialectical continuum of participation and separation and on the general direction towards separation participation, potency and balance of the Tantalus Ratio; these factors are measured by the questionnaire. Breakdown of the questionnaire into parts and analysis of the responses for each parameter would yield false results and false information about the core personality, since they would have been taken out of context.

In order to place a person on the participant/separant continuum or, in other words, to characterise a person as a participant or separant type, we have to add up the total responses on the 36 scales of parameters. The mean score determines his position. A score of three or more signifies a separant type, whereas a score of below three indicates a participant type.

The potency of the individual's Tantalus Ratio is theoretically proportional to his polarity on various scales. Hence, to glean the potency of the Tantalus Ratio from the questionnaire, we have to calculate the total variance of his responses. The greater the variance, the higher the potency of the Tantalus Ratio.

Table 3. *Factor structure after Kaisser rotation*

Characteristic	Factor					
	1	2	3	4	5	6
Fatalism	0.60	0.28	0.08	0.56	0.15	0.03
Risk taking	0.63	0.13	0.00	0.03	0.07	0.06
Symbolic / tool orientation	0.13	0.18	0.74	0.11	0.10	0.26
Tendency towards mysticism / science	0.07	0.38	0.28	0.28	0.13	0.09
Submission / aggression	0.65	0.14	0.24	0.16	0.06	0.02
Social involvement / retreatism	0.26	0.37	0.50	0.05	0.36	0.08
High / low vulnerability to sensing deprivation	0.12	0.23	0.68	0.00	0.16	0.01
Sensitive to pain	0.44	0.14	0.52	0.05	0.14	0.04
Reducer / augmentor	0.47	0.51	0.31	0.05	0.17	0.01
Field dependence / independence	0.07	0.53	0.00	0.19	0.08	0.28
Tolerance / intolerance of objective ambiguity	0.11	0.13	0.30	0.06	0.23	0.26
Tolerance / intolerance of ideational ambiguity	0.23	0.65	0.39	0.02	0.11	0.08
	0.28					
	0.59	0.46	0.19	0.05	0.23	0.09

Table 3 (continued)

Characteristic	Factor 1	2	3	4	5	6
Other- / self-directed						
Social mobility / stationary social position		0.46	0.07	0.14	0.00	0.18
Resignation / achievement	0.42	0.43	0.05	0.51	0.04	0.19
Sanction / moral orientation	0.46	0.45	0.28	0.00	0.08	0.13
Non-conformity / conformity	0.42	0.52	0.21	0.12	0.05	0.09
Active / passive	0.60	0.19	0.40	0.10	0.15	0.02
Conservative / progress orientation	0.16	0.61	0.50	0.17	0.12	0.03
Extrapunitive / intrapunitive	0.14	0.01	0.18	0.00	0.05	0.26
Group / isolated performer	0.03	0.00	0.00	0.09	0.58	0.04
Anchoring on revelation / activist ideology	0.00	0.03	0.00	0.28	0.13	0.05
Time / timeless orientation	0.12	0.05	0.01	0.00	0.01	0.23

Table 4. *Eigenvalue and percentage of common variance explained by factors*

Factor	Eigenvalue	Per cent of total variance
1	7.86	66.2
2	1.33	11.3
3	0.82	7.0
4	0.80	6.8
5	0.54	4.6
6	0.50	4.2

Table 5. *One-way analysis between separant (n=49) and participant (n=42) groups on Total and characteristic scores.*

Variable	d.f.	F	$P \leq$
Total score	90	64.7	0.0001
Fatalism/ combativeness	90	10.6	0.001
Risk taking	90	0.083	0.77
Submission/ aggression	90	3.7	0.05
Social involvement/ retreat	90	5.0	0.02
Sensitivity to pain	90	4.1	0.04
Reducer/ augmentor	90	4.8	0.03
Tolerance/ intolerance of ideational ambiguity	90	0.038	0.84
Inner/ outer directed	90	18.8	0.0001
Social mobility/ stationary social position	90	4.2	0.04
Resignation/ achievement	90	82.5	0.0001
Moral/ sanction orientation	90	0.24	0.61
Non-conformist/ conformist	90	16.5	0.0001
Active/ passive	90	26.7	0.0001

81

Table 6. *Influence of independent variables on division into separant and participant groups*

Independent variable	Coefficient	Significant P≤	R
Sex	0.21	0.025	0.20
Age	-0.14	0.835	0.09
Total score	0.60	0.001	0.58

The system in balance of the Tanatalus Ratio of the individual can be seen in the questionnaire as a tendency towards the centre. As our scales each have six points, a mean score of 3 represents the maximum possible balance. We have to point out that measurement of the balance is meaningful only if we take account of the potency of the Tantalus Ratio.

We could envisage two people, both of whom might have a balanced core personality, but one could have a minimum Tantalus Ratio, signifying a low 'life drive', whereas the second could have a maximum Tantalus Ratio, and be full of life drive. Hence, the dialectics of the Tantalus Ratio cause individuals to balance their core personality in different ways determined by the way their personalities are skewed. We assume that social characteristics will also balance their core structure in different ways.

Analysis of variance of the measurement of the difference between the participant and separant groups revealed interesting findings. The mean results reveal not only a significant difference between the groups, but also a tendency in the expected direction of the participant groups in the participant direction and the separant group in the separant direction. The two groups can balance each other, because their distances from the centre of the scale are almost equal. This symmetry sometimes manifests itself in people who maintain their system in balance by belonging to two different value circles. An instance of this, as related to our research samples, is a doctor who joins the Gurdieff circle.

In the process of validation, we ascertained whether the questionnaire differentiated between a participant and separant group. This validation analysis, which showed that our questionnaire did indeed differentiate between the two groups, revealed another interesting finding. Shoham (1977) hypothesised that the separant type had a higher Tantalus Ratio potency than the participant type, and a higher total variance was in fact observed in the separant research group (although this was not significant) than in the participant group. This suggests that potency of the Tantalus Ratio was higher for the group of doctors than for the group of Gurdieff disciples. The fact that the differences were not significant means that the hypothesis was not proved, but it showed a possible direction for its vindication.

In conclusion, this study reconstructed an instrument measuring participation and separation, in order to ascertain the personality types according to Shoham's personality theory. This is a unique study, in that it constructed a measurement instrument for a wide personality theory, which enables it to be applied successfully to empirical studies. The theory and instrument are now linked together, and we see many opportunities for adapting the questionnaire to many languages in addition to Hebrew, for investigation of cross-cultural differences and the universality of the theory.

References

Block, J. (1977), 'Advancing the Psychology of Personality: Paradigmatic Shift or Improving the Quality of Research', D. Magnusson & NS.Endler, (Eds.), *Personality at the Crossroads: Current Issues in International Psychology*, pp.37-63.

Eysenck, H.J. & S.B.G. Eysenck (1969), *Personality Structure and Measurement*, London: Routledge and Kegan Paul Ltd.

Eysenck, H.J. (1964), *Crime and Personality*, Boston: Houghton Mifflin.

Fairbairn, W.R.D. (1957), *Psychoanalytic Sudies of the Personality*, London:Tavistock, p.47.

Graves, R. (1955), *The Greek Myths (Vol. 2)*, Harmondsworth, England: Penguin.

Itri, A. & W. Collino (1964), 'Personality and Depersonalization Under Sensory Deprivation Percept', *Motor Skills*, Vol.115, pp.659-60.

Shoham, S.G. (1977), *The Myth of Tantalus*, St. Lucia, Australia: Queensland University Press.

Witkin, H. A., R.B. Dyk, H.F. Paterson et al (1962), *Psychological differentation*, New York: John Wiley & Sons Inc.

5 The Family Parameters of Violent Prisoners

R. Abba b. Kahana said: No philosophers have arisen among the nations to equal Balaam and Abnimos, the weaver. They said to them, 'Can we attack this people?' They replied, 'Go to their house of assembly. If the children are chirping there with their voices, you will not be able to destroy this people, but, if not, then you will, for their fathers made them rely upon this saying: 'the voice is that of Jacob; the hands are those of Esau.' When the voice of Jacob is heard in their houses of assembly and of study, then the hands of Esau are powerless; but when no voice chirps there, then the hands of Esau can act.

Lamentations Raba Introduction, 2, on Genesis XXVII, 22.

METHODOLOGY

The major theoretical approaches in criminology justify the view that family structure and family relationships may have a significant effect upon individuals' antisocial tendencies. The study reported in the present paper was conducted in an attempt to explain that the criminal offences, and particularly criminal violence, among a sample of 60 violent and 60 non-violent prisoners with reference to their attachment to the family, were inversely related to impulsive violence, and that the offspring of parents who were described as non-punitive, planned their violent behaviour.

Independent Variables

A number of indices representing different aspects of family life were constructed from a questionnaire dealing with family background. The questionnaire dealt with the division of household responsibilities (e.g., income, shopping, playing with the children) between the parents. The indices were compiled from scores representing the distribution of household duties. For example, a point was added to the index of 'father dominance' for each task performed by the father. The scores of these indices ranged between 0 and 3. Indices of punitive behaviour were built up in a similar manner. Indices of agreement-disagreement were constructed from questions dealing with disagreement between the parents, between the parents and the school, and between the parents and the subject. An index of the subject's attachment to his family was constructed from questions dealing with the subject's current relationship with his parents. The most positive response to each of several questions dealing with the closeness of the subject's current relationship with his parents received a point on the index. Similarly, an index of attachment to friends outside prison was constructed from questions concerning visits and correspondence with friends.

Each subject was given a number of psychological tests: Cattell's Personality Inventory (CAQ), Zuckerman's Sensation Seeking Scale (SSS), and a risk taking scale (Shoham et al., 1976). While these variables are not utilised in the present analysis, we considered them significant tools for interpretation of the associations that might be found between independent and dependent variables.

FINDINGS

The first procedure involved the following steps: a matrix of intercorrelation coefficients was calculated pairwise, using BMDP's all value method (Dixon et al., 1979). These coefficients were then used in regression analyses. Four multiple regression analyses were calculated, one for each dependent variable. Each regression was calculated in two steps: in the first, variables describing family interactions were introduced; in the second step, the respondent's age and education were added to the equation. This procedure has one major advantage: it uses the greatest possible amount of information available for estimation of the correlation coefficients. The major disadvantage is that the estimated correlation and regression coefficients may be biased, since missing information may characterise specific types of subjects.

The second procedure followed Cohen's (1973) recommendations; missing values were replaced by means, and a set of dummy variables was created. These variables were scored 1 whenever a mean replaced a missing value and otherwise, 0. This set of dummy variables was introduced into the regression equations after the two regression steps described above. The change in R^2 obtained in this step may serve as an indicator of the association between availability of the data and the dependent variables. This procedure yields unbiased estimates of the regression coefficients and was therefore considered preferable to the first one. Its major disadvantage is that it tends to reduce the variances as well as the number of degrees of freedom. Consequently, it may be conservative whenever results are assessed by their statistical significance. The following results are all based on this second analytic procedure, yet they are all consistent with results obtained by the first procedure.

85

A summary of the results of four multiple regression analyses is presented in table 1 below. These analyses refer to a selected group of variables. Preliminary analyses indicated that communications with the social system outside the prison and parental disagreements in childhood had no significant effect; consequently, these variables were dropped from the analysis.

The influence of each of the variables may be assessed by two criteria: the simplest and the most common is the significance of the coefficient. This is the most conventional criterion, but since the sample is not representative of a particular population, it is doubtful whether inferential statistics would be meaningful. Another problem with this criterion is that because of our analytic procedure the inferences would be highly conservative. The second criterion is the proportion of the variance of the dependent variables explained by each of the independent variables.

Table 1 summarises the four regressions. Using the two above-mentioned criteria, the most significant variable is attachment to the present family. This variable alone accounts for over 2.5 per cent of the variance of each of the dependent variables. It is inversely associated with the number of offences and the impulsiveness of the violent offences. This finding may suggest that attachment to significant others has an inhibitory, restraining effect (Hirschi, 1969).

The other significant variables are the age and the educational attainment of the subject. Age has a positive effect upon the number of violent offences. This is probably because criminal records accumulate slowly and it takes years for a long record to be established. The direct association of age with impulsive violence and its inverse association with planned violence are congruent with the notion that older violent offenders are often persons who have been labelled because of a single violent explosion, usually in a family quarrel. The negative effect of education on the number of offences is probably a reflection of the well-known inverse association between official crime and socio-economic status.

Table 1. *Multiple regression analyses: standardised regression coefficients*

Step		All offences	Violent offences	Impulsive violence	Planned violence
1.	Father's dominance	-0.04	-0.17	-0.10	0.15
	Mother's dominance	0.05	- 0.14	0.04	- 0.08
	Impunitive parents	0.24	- 0.27	-0.02	0.21**
	Attachment to family	0.28*	0.03	- 0.27	- 0.03

Table 1 (continued)

Step		All Offences	Violent offences	Impulsive violence	Planned violence
2.	Age	0.06	0.02	_0.19_	0.10
	Education	- 0.32**	- 0.23*	0.06	0.03
3.	Missing Data	0.02	0.01	0.02	0.13
	R^2	0.17	0.13	0.22	0.44
		104	97	52	44

Variables explaining more than 2 per cent of the variance are underlined

* $p < .05$

**$p < .01$

Another variable whose influence is clear is the lack of punishment in childhood. This variable has a markedly positive effect upon planned violence. Surprisingly, however, it is inversely, though only mildly, associated with the number of offences. Of the two parental dominance indices, only maternal domination has a significant effect if it is positively associated with the premeditation of violence, and to a lower extent, with impulsivity.

Of the findings concerning each dependent variable, the most noticeable is that the independent variables explain a significant proportion of the two measures of the type of violence, while the number of offences and the number of violent offences have a rather low R^2. In other words, the independent variables seem to explain the type of violence, but not violence proneness. This finding seems to lend some construct validity to our measures of the type of violence.

Situationally, impulsive violence is significantly influenced by the current family relationships, which explain 7 per cent of the variance. The consistently negative effect suggests that strong family relationships serve as an inhibiting factor against this type of violence. Another significant factor is age: this type of violence characterises older offenders and those whose general educational level is low. As for family relationships in childhood, paternal influence has a weak inhibiting effect and permissiveness is positively related to impulsive violence. Thus the image of a typical impulsive offender may be construed as that of an older person who is detached from his family and whose parents were permissive during his childhood.

Maternal dominance seems to have a positive effect on the level of impulsivity in violence. However, this effect emerges only when the dummy variables indicating availability of information are introduced into the equation. There are thus consistent differences between subjects with a full set of data and those with missing values. Therefore, it is difficult to draw a valid conclusion about the influence of this variable.

The level of planned violence (or plannedness) is most strongly related to parental permissiveness; this variable alone explains 26 per cent of the variance. Both maternal dominance and current family ties have positive effects, each adding about 6 per cent to the explained variance. Altogether, the independent variables explain 42 per cent of the variance, and the availability of full data adds only 3 per cent. Thus, there are no significant differences between subjects with and those without missing values.

DISCUSSION

The major finding is that, contrary to our hypotheses, the independent variables have very little to do with the amount of violence or offensive behaviour. On the other hand, they seem to offer a rather good explanation for the type of violence the subjects have engaged in. Although in discussions of violence a distinction is often made between premeditated and impulsive behaviour, we are not aware of any attempts to distinguish empirically between the two. Moreover, our preliminary factor analyses suggest that these are not two extremities on a single continuum, but rather two independent dimensions.

More substantively, the findings seem to support two hypotheses. First, consistent with Hirschi's (1969) control theory, the current level of attachment to the family seems to be a crime- and violence-inhibiting mechanism. It is quite surprising, however, that this inhibitory effect applies to impulsive rather than planned violence. This present attachment seems to be more effective than childhood socialisation practices. However, the data allow an alternative explanation as well: it may be contended that questions concerning childhood socialisation are inherently less valid than questions concerning present behaviour. In any case, however, these findings lend some construct validity to the distinction between the types of violence.

The second major finding involves the analysis of planned violence. Quite clearly, this variable seems to be affected by childhood experiences (at least insofar as these experiences are reflected in present reports). Among these experiences, parental punitiveness has a particularly significant role. This finding seems to be quite consistent with those recorded in other studies (e.g., Gove and Crutchfield 1982; McCord, 1979). The present results, however, indicate that it is planned violence, rather than general aggression and antisocial behaviour, that is most influenced by this factor. Finally, a word of caution: given the small number of cases, the limited range of variation and the missing data problem, these findings should be considered very carefully before they are generalised more widely.

References

Black, D.J. & A.J. Reiss Jr (1970), 'Police Control of Juveniles', *American Sociological Review*, Vol.35, pp.63-77.

Cohen, J. & P. Cohen (1975), *Applied Multiple Regression & Correlation Analysis for he Behavioural Sciences*, Hillsdale, NJ: Erbaum.

Gove, R.W. & R.D. Crutchfield (1982), 'The Family and Juvenile Delinquency', *The Sociological Quarterly*, Vol.23, pp.301-19.

Hare, R.D. & D. Schallin (1978), *Psychopathic Behaviour: Approaches to Research*, Chichester: John Wiley & Sons Inc.

Hirschi, T. (1969), *Causes of Delinquency*. Berkeley: University of California Press.

Kornhauser, R. (1978), *Social Sources of Deliquency: An Appraisal of Analytic Models*, Chicago: Chicago University Press, p.85.

McCord, J. (1970), 'Some Child Rearing Antecedents of Criminal Behaviour in Adult Men', *Journal of Personality and Social Psychology*, Vol.37, pp.1477-86.

Parsons, T. (1947), 'Certain Primary Sources of Patterns and Aggression in the Social Structure of the Western World', *Psychiatry*, Vol.2, pp.167-81.

Rahav, G. (1983), 'Models of Delinquency', *International Journal of Group Tensions*, Vol.10, pp.61-72.

Rosen, L. (1970), 'The Broken Home and Male Delinquency', M.E. Wolfgang, E. Savitz & N. Johnson (Eds.), *The Sociology of Crime and Delinquency*, New York: John Wiley & Sons.

Sellin, T. & M.E. Wolfgang (1964), *The Measurement of Delinquency*, New York: John Wiley & Sons.

Shoham, S.G. (1964), 'Conflict Situations and Delinquent Solutions', *Journal of Social Psychiatry* , Vol.64, pp.85-215.

Shoham, S.G., N. Geva, R. Markowsky & N. Kaplinski (1976), 'Internalisation of Norms, Risk-Perception and Anxiety as Related to Driving Offences', *British Journal of Criminology*, Vol.16, p.2.

Sutherland, E.H. & D.R. Cressey (1960), *Criminology*, Philadelphia: Lippincott.

6 Multivariate Parameters of Violence

The evil inclination desires only that which is forbidden. R. Mena (on the Day of Atonement) went to visit R. Haggai,who was ill. R. Haggai said: 'I am thirsty' R. Mena said, 'Drink' Then he left him. After an hour he came again, and said, 'How about your thirst?' He said, 'no sooner had you permitted me to drink than the desire left me'.

Jerusalem Talmud, *Yoma* 43;b.

MULTIVARIATE ANALYSIS OF THE BIO-PSYCHO-SOCIAL CORRELATES OF VIOLENT PRISONERS

When the electrophysiological findings were linked by discriminant function analysis to the hormonal findings to differentiate between violent and non-violent prisoners, we found that the violent prisoners were distinguished from the non-violent ones by the standard deviation of theta waves and by the secretion of the prolactin hormone (see table 1).

Table 1. *Discriminant function analysis of neurological and endocrinological variables between violent and non-violent prisoners* (n=57)

Independent Variables	Standardised Coefficients
SD beta	0.79*
SD theta	0.38**
Luteinising hormone (LH)	0.49
Prolactive hormone (PRL)	0.29*
Wilks lambda	0.60
Canonical correlation	0.63

Table 1. (continued)

Group centroids:

Violent	0.82
Non-violent	0.79

P< 0.0001**
P< 0.05*

These results may be interpreted as meaning that theta waves signify a minor functional brain pathology, which could be related to some malfunctioning of the limbic system (Williams, 1969, Wieser, 1983). The fact that these theta waves are also related to a high variability of their energy, is linked to Shoham's theory on the disruption of the system imbalance of the personality which could be related, *inter alia*, to violent behaviour (Shoham, 1979). The excess secretion of the sex-related hormone prolactin manifests itself by lactation of the breast; in males, it could be related to blocked sexual activity in prison. However, it could also be related to the violence-based sexual display in males reported by ethologists; that is, the more violent a male is, the better are his chances to win fights over females and impregnate them. The sexual aspect of male violence may also be manifested by lactation of the breast.

Finally, excess prolactin might be evidence of a nervous imbalance gland dysfunction of the hypophyseal gland on the hypothalamus. Further research is needed to ascertain which of these hypotheses should be accepted.

The interrelationship between psychological and electro-physiological correlates of our research population examined via discriminant function analysis, showed the violent prisoners to have a higher standard deviation of theta energy, and to be more tense and bored (see table 2).

Table 2. *Discriminant function analysis of psychological and electro-physiological variables between violent and non-violent prisoners* (n=57)

Independent Variables	Standardised Coefficients
SD beta	0.68
SD theta	0.47**
CAQ boredom (D7)	0.57*
CAQ hypochondria (D1)	0.34
CAQ tenseness (Q4)	0.33*
Wilks lambda	0.61
Canonical correlation	0.63

Table 2. (continued)

Group Centroids:

Violent	0.81
Non-violent	0.78

*p<0.05
**p<0.001

We have already commented on the standard deviation of theta wave energy. The tenseness and boredom of violent prisoners may be linked to our previous findings that violent prisoners are more hungry for stimuli. As the prison environment provides few outlets for this stimulus hunger, violent prisoners display tenseness and boredom.

The interrelationship between psychological and hormonal variables are shown in table 3, which shows that the violent prisoners were high in hypochondria, tenseness, prolactin and testosterone. Yet, only the hypochondria variable was found to be significantly higher amongst the violent prisoners, the other three variables being on the border of significance. We have already commented on the significance of the tenseness and sexually-based secretion of hormones of the violent prisoners. As for the higher hypochondria of the violent prisoners, the explanation could be as follows: Violent prisoners are tense because of their lack of sexual activity and their unrelinquished hunger for stimuli. In the confined space of prison, this makes them feel unwell and imagine all kinds of physical disabilities.

Table 3. *Discriminant function analysis of psychological and hormonal variables between violent and non-violent prisoners.*

Independent Variable	Standardised Coefficients
Testosterone	0.44*
Prolactin hormone	0.52*
Hypochondria (D1)	0.49**
Tenseness (Q4)	0.51*
Wilke's lambda	0.61
Canonical correlation	0.63
Groups centroids	
Violent	0.4
Non-violent	0.13

P<0.05*
P<0.01**

In the discriminant function analysis between the violent and the non-violent prisoners in relation to their original family dynamics and their attitudes toward authority, the following variables were included: mother's dominance, father's dominance, impunitive parents, attachment to family and the scale signifying an expectation of a negative attitude towards authority figures and prison rules (see table 4).

The results show that the violent prisoners were characterised by a closer relationship with their original family and a negative attitude towards authority and prison rules, whereas the non-violent prisoners were characterised by higher maternal dominance and impunitive parents. In other words, amongst violent prisoners, reinforcement and protection from their original family, coupled with a negative attitude towards the wider normative authorities of law enforcement agencies would be conducive to violent behaviour. On the other hand, the non-violent offenders whose criminal activity is more geared towards lucrative gain are more dominated by the mother and lack the normative punitive and restraining attitude of the father.

Table 4. *Discriminant function analysis of family, dynamic variables and attitudes toward authority between violent and non-violent prisoners*

Independent Variables	Standard Coefficients
Dominance by mother	0.46*
Impunitive parents	0.71**
Link with the family	0.38*
Attitude towards authority	0.81**
Wilke's lambda	0.71
Canonical correlation	0.50
Group centroids:	
Violent group	0.41
Non-violent group	0.50

$$P<0.050$$
$$P<0.01**$$

According to Shoham's theory *Sex as Bait* (Shoham, 1982), the mother's dominance manifests itself more in the separant adjustment and instrumental manipulation of one's environment. Hence, when this pragmatic object manipulation is not coupled with properly directed paternal, normative restraints, violent behaviour is more likely.

A discriminant factor analysis between the violent and non-violent prisoners utilising all four groups of independent parameters (see table 5) showed the following characteristics to be significantly discriminating: mother's dominance, negative societal attitude towards prison personnel, close relations to original family members and a high standard deviation of the energy of slow brain waves. Thus, to the family parameters and social attitude scale which we had described as characterising the violent prisoners in the previous section, our present multivariate analysis added a neurophysiological parameter which signifies an unstable dynamic of the brain activity.

The profile of the violent prisoner according to our bio-psycho-social aetiological hierarchy may be as follows. On the bio-physiological level, they display diffuse and alternating energy of theta waves in response to random photic stimulation and a significantly high secretion of prolactin hormone. On the psychological level, the violent prisoners are *tense, bored* and *hypochondrical*. On the familial and social level the violent prisoners were close to their original family and had a negative attitude towards normative authority.

Table 5. *Discriminant function analysis of electro-physiological, hormonal, psychological, family and societal attitude of violent and non-violent prisoners.*

Independent variables	Standarised coefficients
Mother's dominance	0.59
Close relations to family members	0.43
Negative societal attitude towards prison personnel	0.58
SD theta	0.82
BRC	0.50
Wilke's lambda	0.510
Canonical correlation	0.70
Group centroids:	
Violent prisoners	0.82
Non-violent prisoners	0.09

$$**P<0.01$$
$$*P<0.05$$

This profile has relevance to the interdisciplinary conception of violent behaviour, insofar as each level could be related to other levels of analysis. The variations of the theta waves when evoked by photic stimulation are related to Shoham's personality theory which states, inter alia, that a wide range of personality disturbances may be expected if the personality's convectors are diffuse and do not achieve a system inbalance. The significantly higher level of prolactin, a sex related hormone, among the violent prisoners, may be linked to trends of thought in ethology and sociobiology which relate sex with violence as a mate selection mechanism and a courting behaviour. The more violent a male is, the more sexual prowess he is supposed to have and he would, therefore, be favoured by the female after having won a violent battle against other males.

The tenseness, hypochondria and boredom of violent prisoners may be related to the male adaptation to the prison setting, in which their violence has little or no outlet due to the repressive conditions within walls. The attachment of the violent prisoner to his original family might be related to his wish to revert back to the forgiving and sheltering bosom of the family fold, coupled with a hostility towards the normative system outside the family. This could be related to Shoham's theory concerning the normative separation process inherent in the Isaac Syndrome (Shoham, 1976). The violent prisoner, judging by his hostility towards the normative system, wishes to revert back to the fold of his original family, from which he was ejected by painful rites of passage. As his indoctrination seems to have failed and he is in obvious conflict with the normative system at large, he obviously aims to revert back to his original family fold in which he feels everything is permitted and forgiven.

DISCUSSION

We shall conduct our discussion of the results of our study according to the aetiological hierarchy we have presented in the introduction to this volume and in previous works (Shoham et al., 1987). We shall thus start with the biological factors, proceed with the personality parameters and end with the familial and societal correlates of violent prisoners.

Our findings about the fluctuating amplitude of 7-4 c/s waves driven by means of an unsynchronised photic stimulation in the impulsive violent prisoners group, indicates a limbic functional imbalance. This could be an empirical anchor to theoretical suggestions as to the possible link between limbic functional imbalance and impulsive violence (Wieser, 1983). Also, the diffusion and fluctuation of the energy of 7-4 c/s waves are linked to Shoham's theory as to the connection between the disruption of the system imbalance of the core personality and some functional personality disorders. In this sense, the fluctuations of the 7-4 c/s brain waves are linked to a structural personality imbalance, which underlie a predispositon to violence.

Our findings concerning the link between prolactin and impulsive violence may be interpreted as follows: this sexual based hormone was found to increase with pituitary tumours, which were linked to male impotence. The sexual function of these subjects was restored by lowering prolactin levels. Hence, the high level of prolactin in our population of impulsive violent prisoners might be a balancing mechanism to reduce the sexual impulse which does not have a free outlet in prison. Thus, the more impulsive violent prisoners would be linked with a lower sexual activity. This interpretation is supported by the studies of Narabayashi et al. (1983) on the Kluver-Bucy Syndrome due to bi-temporal lobe excisions. The finding was an inverse relationship between violence and sexuality. Also, prolactin can produce impotence independent of its action on testosterone secretion. This is in line with our findings and could account partially for the fact that our violent prisoners displayed an increased level of prolactin independently of testoterone and LH. We are well aware of the established link in the professional literature between testosterone and violent behaviour.

Another possibility which has to be checked in further research is the link between the prolactin inhibitory factor and the dopaminergic pathway. It has been found that a decrease in dopaminergic activity is linked to an increase in prolactin secretion. The dopaminergic nuclei are part of the structure of the amygdaloid complex, which is known to be related to violence. Hence, the enforced check and decrease in the dopaminergic activity of the amygdaloid complex and a resultant increase in prolactin secretion could be linked to the lower impulsive violence of the prisoners due to their incarceration. The whole syndrome of separation which we have presented in the introduction to this volume as characterising the violent person might be linked to our findings concerning the personality of our violent prisoners. Their boredom is characteristic of their hunger for stimuli, field dependence, object relatedness and intolerance of objective ambiguity of the separant personality type. When our violent prisoner is naturally deprived of excessive stimuli, excitement and activities within prison, his immediate reaction will be boredom, unlike the participant type who is adverse to stimuli and hence, less likely to be bored.

This lack of external stimuli and activity would also prevent the violent separant prisoner from spending his inner energies and therefore generate internal tension within his personality. Finally, when the separant violent prisoner cannot direct his energies towards the objects in its surroundings, he tends to project his aggressive tendencies toward himself and relates all kinds of physical and mental diseases to himself. This has been observed with violent prisoners in solitary confinement, where there are almost no external stimuli and no other objects except their own bodies. They would injure themselves by placing burning cigarettes on their hands and chests in order to satisfy their hunger for stimuli, albeit painful. Others swallowed sharp metal objects and parts of cutlery in order to injure themselves internally.

It is suggested that these psychological and personality parameters, inferred from EEG data, may be linked to the limbic system. Tension and hypochondria are known to be related mainly to the amygdaloid complex and hippocampus, whereas boredom would be related to the frontal lobes of the brain (Narabayashi et al., 1963).

On the family level, the violent prisoners revealed closeness towards their original family. This shows an attachment to the family fold in which they are being sheltered and their misbehaviour is condoned. In other words, they were attracted to the permissiveness of their nuclear family before being exposed to the harshness of the world outside. This dynamic is in line with Shoham's model concerning social separation. This model envisages a painful transition from the forgiving family to the severe society at large, by means of formal and informal 'rites de passages'.

The seemingly maladjusted violent prisoner is not accepted by the professional criminal subculture which has little use for the impulsive violent offender. Therefore, he longs to revert back to the normatively cushioned family and to block out, so to speak, the depriving and depressing agencies of social control from his interactive surroundings. These tie up with the violent prisoners' negative attitude towards the agencies of social control: courts, the police, judges, and the prison authorities. The violent prisoner who ever clashes with the agencies of social control in a way which is illogical and incomprehensible to him, is both frightened and enraged at the normative system which seems ever to limit him and close him behind walls for reasons which are incomprehensible and unacceptable to him.

In conclusion, the following composite profile of the violent prisoner is obtained:

Alternating energy of photic driven theta in temporal lobes; high prolactin; boredom, tenseness and hypochondria; close relations to his immediate family; and negative attitudes towards normative authority. The significance of all these parameters and their interrelationsip have been discussed in the present study.

References

Adams, R.D. (1982), 'The Limbic Lobes and the Neurobiology of Emotion', *Text Book of Neurology*, pp. 381-2.
Allsop, J.F. (1965), in Eysenck, H.J. (1967), *The Biological Basis of Personality*, Springfield, Ill: Charles C. Thomas, p.99.

Black, D.J. & A.J. Reiss Jr (1970), 'Police Control of Juveniles', *American Sociological Review*, Vol.35, pp.63-77.

Budner, Stanley. (1962), 'Intolerance of Ambiguity as a Personality Variable', *Journal of Personality*, Vol.30, pp.29-50.

Cattell, R.B, M.W. Eber, & M.M. Tatsuoka (1970), *Handbook of the 16 Personality Factor Questionnaire*, Champaign, Ill. (CAQ). Institute for Personality and Ability Testing.

Christie, R, & F.L. Geis (1970), *Machiavellianism*, New York: Academic Press.

Cleaver, P.T, A.D. Mylonas & W.C. Reckless (1968), 'Gradients in Attitudes Towards Law, Courts and Police', *Social Forces*, Vol.2 (Winter), pp.29-48.

Ellingson, R.Y. (1954-55), 'The incidence of E.E.G. Abnormality Among Patients with Mental Disorders of Apparently Non-organic Origin: A Critical Review', *American Journal of Psychiatry*, Vol.111, p.263.

Eysenck, H.J. (1967), *The Biological Basis of Personality*, Springfield, Ill; Charles C. Thomas, p.36-7.

Gibbs, F.A., B.K. Bagchi & W. Bloomberg (1945), 'Electro-encephalographic Study of Criminals', *American Journal of Psychiatry*, Vol.102, pp.294-8.

Gibson, H.B. (1961), *Manual of the Gibson Spiral Maze*, (2nd ed) Kent, Britain: Hodder and Stoughton.

Gove, R.W. & R.H. Crutchfield (1982), 'The Family and Juvenile Delinquency', *The Sociological Quarterly*, Vol.23, pp.30-319.

Grossman, C. (1954), 'Laminar Cortical Blocking and its Relation to Episodic Aggressive Outbursts', *Arch Neurol. Psychiatr*, Vol.71, p.576.

Herrmann, W.M. & R.C. Beach (1976), 'Psychotropic Effects of Androgens: A Review of Clinical Observations and New Human Experimental Findings', *Pharmakopsych*, Vol.9, pp.205-19.

Hill, D. & W.W. Sargent (1943), 'A Case of Matricide', *Lancet*, Vol.1, pp.526-7.

Hirschi, T. (1969), *Causes of Delinquency*, Berkeley: University of California Press.

Irwin, J. & D. Cressey (1962), 'Thieves, Convicts and the Inmate Culture', *Social Problems*. pp.142-55.

Irwin, J. (1970), *The Felon*, Englewood Cliffs, NJ: Prentice-Hall.

Kagan, J., B. Roseman, D. Day, J. Albert, & W. Phillips (1970), 'Information Processing in the Child's Significance of Analytic and Reflective Attitudes', *Psychological Monographs*, Vol.78, (1-whole No. 578).

Kornhauser, R. (1978), *Social Sources of Delinquency: An Appraisal of Analytic Models*, Chicago: Chicago University Press.

Lairy, G.C. (1964), 'Quelques Remarques sur le Probleme EEG. Psychologie du Comportement EEG Clin, *Neurophysiol*, Vol.16, pp.130-5.

Lane, P.J. (1978), 'Annotated Bibliography of the Overcontrolled-Undercontrolled Assaultive Personality Literature and the Overcontrolled-Hostility (0-4) scale of the MMPI', *JSAS Catalog of Selected Documents in Psychology* (JSAS ms. No. 1790).

Levenson, H. (1973), 'Perceived Parental Antecedents of Internal Powerful Others and Chance Locus of Control Orientations', *Developmental Psychology*, Vol.9, pp.260-5.

Megargee, E.I. (1966), 'Undercontrolled and Overcontrolled Personality Types in Extreme Antisocial Aggression', *Psychological Monographs*, (3, Whole No. 611).

Megargee, E.I. (1982), 'Psychological Determinants and Correlates of Criminal Violence', M.E. Wolfgang & N.A. Weiner, (Eds.), *Criminal Violence*, Beverly Hills London/New Delhi: Sage Publications, pp. 81-160.

Murray, M.A. (1938), *Explorations in Personality*, New York: Oxford University Press. (TAT: Thematic Apperception Test).

Narabayashi, H.T., Y. Nagao, M. Saito, M. Yosluda & M. Nagahota (1963), 'Stereotaxic Amygdalectomy for Behaviour Disorders', *Arch. Neurol J.*, pp.9-16.

Parsons, T. (1947), 'Certain Primary Sources of Patterns and Aggression in the Social Structure of the Western World', *Psychiatry,* Vol.2, pp.167-81.

Persky, H., K.D. Smith, & G.K. Basu (1971), 'Relation of Psychologic Measures of Aggression and Hostility to Testosterone Production in Man', *Psychosom. Med.,* Vol.32, pp.265-77.

Quay, H.C. (1956), 'Psychopathic Personality as Pathological Stimulation Seeking', *American Journal of Psychiatry,* Vol.122, pp.180-3.

Rahav, G. (1983), 'Models of Delinquency', *International Journal of Group Tensions,* Vol.10, pp.61-72.

Rosen, L. (1970), 'The Broken Home and Male Delinquency', M.E. Wolfgang, E. Savitz & N. Johnson (Eds.), *The Sociology of Crime and Delinquency,* New York: John Wiley & Sons Inc.

Saul, L.J., H. Dans & P.A. David (1949), 'Psychologic Correlations with the Electroencephalogram', *Psychsom. Med. H.,* p.361.

Schalling, D. & R.D. Hare. (Eds.), (1978), *Psychopathic Behaviour: Approach to Research,* New York: John Wiley & Sons Inc.

Sellin, T. & M.E. Wolfgang (1964), *The Measurement of Delinquency,* New York: John Wiley & Sons Inc.

Shoham, S.G. (1964), 'Conflict Situations and Delinquent Solutions', *The Journal of Social Psychology,* New York: The Journal Press, Vol. 64. pp.185-215.

Shoham, S.G. (1983), 'Isaac Syndrome', *Revue de Droit Penal et Criminologie,* The American Image. Vol.33, p.4, (Winter 1976).

Shoham, S.G. (1982), *Eve, Casanova and Don Juan: Love as Bait,* Tel Aviv: Ramot, (Hebrew); Queensland:University of Queensland Press, (English) 1983, Paris:L'Age D'Homme (French), 1992.

Stumpf, W.E. & M. Sar (1976), 'Steroid Hormone Target Sites in the Brain: The Differential Distribution of Estrogen, Progestin, Androgen and Glucocortiscosteroid', *J. Steroid Biochem,* Vol.7, pp.1163-70.

Sutherland, E.H. & D.R. Cressey (1960), *Criminology,* Philadelphia: Lippincott.

Wieser, H.G. (1983),'Depth Recorded Limbic Seizures and Psychopathology, Neuroscience', *Biobehavioural Reviews,* Vol.7, pp.427-40.

Williams, D.P. (1941), 'The Significance of an Abnormal Electro-Encephalogram', *J. Neurol. Psychiat,* Vol.4, pp.257-68.

Williams, D. (1969),'Neural Factors Related to Habitual Aggression', *Brain,* Vol.92, pp. 503-20.

Wilkinson, K. (1974), 'The Broken Family and Juvenile Delinquency Scientific Explanation or Ideology'? *Social Problems,* pp.726-39.

Zimmerman, I.D., K. Isaacs (1975), 'A Possible Effect of Testosterone on the Adenosine 3-5 Cyclic Monophosphate Levels in Rat Cerebral Cortex: A Brief Noted', *Mechanisms of Aging and Development,* Vol.4, pp.215-9.

Zuckerman, M., E.A. Krolin & I. Zoob (1964), 'Development of Sensation Seeking Scale', *Journal of Consulting Psychology,* Vol.28, No.61 pp. 477-82.

7   The Situational Analysis of Violence

A drunken husband, beating his wife in their kitchen, gave her a butcher's knife and dared her to use it on him. She claimed that if he struck her once more, she would use the knife. He slapped her face and she stabbed him to death.

Marvin E. Wolfgang, Homicide

INTRODUCTION

This example, cited by Wolfgang (1967), describes the last phase of a dyadic relationship between husband and wife, which culminated in violent death. Most of the attempts to explain murder would aim at finding some specific factors which single out the slayer from other human beings. The biologists would try to find some physiological irregularities, abnormal blood chemistry, or the recently popular Xyy chromosome theory, claiming that the murderer is a real 'he-man'. Psychoanalysts would look for unresolved oral, anal or Oedipal complexes. Sociologists would pursue their perennial quest for correlations between murder, 'bad' homes, 'bad' schools and 'bad' neighbourhoods. These types of explanations are 'genetic' or 'historical'. We propose to examine the feasibility of a situational explanation of murder. Such an explanation would consider murder as a direct sequel to an escalation of tension, culminating in the violent act. This bifurcation in the causal analysis has already been pointed out by Sutherland:

> Scientific explanations of criminal behaviour may be stated either in terms of the processes which are operating at the moment of the occurrence of the crime or in terms of the processes operating in the earlier history of the criminal. In the first case, the explanation may be called 'mechanistic,' 'situational' or 'dynamic', in the second 'historical' or 'genetic'... Criminological explanations of the

mechanistic type have thus far been notably unsuccessful, perhaps largely because they have been formulated in connection with the attempt to isolate personal and social pathologies among criminals. Work from this point of view has, at best, resulted in the conclusion that the immediate determinants of criminal behaviour lie in the person-situation complex (Sutherland and Cressey, 1966).

This study attempts to present a model for explaining the violent act within the situational matrix of the criminal-victim relationship.

In some types of violence, personality and demographic factors would be relevant as predisposing factors. Apart from the physiological factors predisposing to 'low boiling points', some measurable personality traits may also contribute to violence-proneness. The introversion-extraversion continuum as studied primarily by Eysenck (1964) might indicate the initial probability of involvement in an escalatory interaction leading to violence. We may envision a Maine farmer whose inner-directedness is so firm that any infringement upon his internalised standards would confront him with a private purgatory. On the other hand, he would very rarely interpret communications transmitted by others to be provocations, as they are by definition extraneous to his internal controls.

Predispositon to violence, as gleaned from various studies, may eventually be expressed as probability profiles. These would point out the low or high chances of an individual, displaying a given set of characteristics, to commit a violent act. However, the actual sequence of events precipitating the violence, would in some cases take the form of a causal chain of interaction between criminal and victim. This communication pattern could be ignited on the spot by the exposure to a compromising situation, e.g. the ever-loving wife and her lover in the husband's nuptial double-bed. Words hurled with obvious intent to offend would have the effect of switching 'ego' action to a different cognitive level, i.e., 'he would see red'. Other expressions may have this 'triggering off' effect on 'ego' because he defines them subjectively as humiliating, due to personality peculiarities of his own. The word 'bugger' thrown at a latent homosexual or an expression questioning the virility of a man who has anxieties about his potency, may have the same effect. The conventional form of an offensive gesture, such as the twisting of a moustache and the emission of a snore in the presence of a devout Moslem, may have an even stronger escalatory effect. Such an exhange of words and gestures would not trigger off immediate arousal to another cognitive level but, depending on the reaction, may gradually lead to the 'point of no return of violence.

THE SITUATIONAL MODEL

The structure of the relationships, which we hypothesise as determining acts of violence, would be as follows:

1. 'Alter' transmits to 'ego' a pattern of communication, which is overtly or latently provoking.
2. The narrowing of the range of non-violent reaction leads 'ego' swiftly and inexorably to a 'point of no return' where the violent solution becomes highly probable.
3. In the course of the interaction, 'ego' makes an outward commitment to 'alter' or a relevant other, to commit the act of violence. This would further accelerate the generation of tension.
4. The violent act would be the cathartic release of this tension.
5. It would be followed by a sense of fulfilment or homeostatic contentedness.

1. The Provoking Communication

The offender may be exposed to words, gestures or actions, which are culturally defined as provoking, e.g. gestures of obscenity which are performed by different fingers in different cultures. The communication pattern may also be provoking within the specific context of interaction between the offender and the victim, such as reference to some very touchy personal episodes or vulnerable character traits known only or primarily to the other partner in the dyad. Finally, there may be words or acts neutral to 'alter' but *interpreted* as offensive by 'ego.' This could occur in the confrontation of individuals from different cultures. We admit that a violent reaction, or one that may further accelerate the violent interchange occurs, where sublimation has not been possible, in a small percentage of cases only; but these are the ones which we are trying to study. We shall first dwell on the types of non-violent reactions.

2. The Alternatives to Violent Reactions

As we have assumed that the 'point of no return' involves the narrowing of the range of reactions to those which lead to an escalation towards violence, we may proceed by eliminating the non-violent alternative reactions. It is evident that the dynamics of the interaction are not one-directional towards violence, and the various forms of perception are not exclusive of each other. One form is the *twisting of the incoming perception* to fit 'ego's' previously internalised stances, which can be analysed in the following categories:

a) *Selective perception*, which is not a 'face-saving' mechanism as described by Goffman, but a non-awareness of the provoking communication. This may happen when the communication seems so painful that its perception is evaded in self-defence.

b) *The differentiation process* is another technique for utilising some demographic or social-stratification characteristics of the provoker so as to avoid taking offence, such as 'he is only a child', 'what can you expect of a woman?', 'these bums just have to be lewd and dirty-mouthed', or 'I shall not lower myself to his level by answering him'. The best illustration of this premise is in O. Henry's 'The Coming-out of Maggie', where Dempsey Donovan, the Irishman, finds out that his opponent, O'Sullivan, is nothing but a Dago in disguise: 'and then Dempsey looked at O'Sullivan without anger, as one looks at a stray dog, and nodded his head in the direction of the door. 'The back stairs, Guiseppi,' he said, briefly. 'Somebody'll pitch your hat down after you'. This differentiation process might also guard against taking offence even if the provoker is in a position of authority. Elia Kazan's *America, America*, and the numerous instances depicted in the novels of Kazantzakis describe the Greek as disregarding the insults hurled at him, because a Barbarian Turk can never hurt the serene inner dignity of a Greek.

c) Finally, there are techniques for *explaining away* provoking behaviour. A prostitute interviewed in one of our previous studies related how her boyfriend had had sexual intercourse with a new girl in her presence. She did not mind, she said, because 'The new girl had to be "broken in" for business', while she herself was the only true love of her pimp.

The above are examples of perceptual twists of the provocative communication which do not reach 'ego', because he either evades or misinterprets it so that it loses its offensive sting. An alternative reaction which would also amount to a non-violent solution, is the *docile acceptance of the offending label*. This would occur, for instance, when a member of a minority group is caught in a cycle of self-hatred and as a result is induced to accept the derogatory tags by which he is labelled by a member of the elite reference-group. The white-orientated negro has accepted *faute-de-mieux* many of the offensive remarks hurled at him as the interpretation of the reality of his situation. His strong other-orientation makes him feel that the white man's derogatory epitaphs have more than a core of truth to them. The Algerian colon, the *pied-noir*, had regarded himself as the representative and protector of French culture in the Maghreb.

Therefore, when forced to emigrate to the 'mother country', he could not dismiss the snubs and insults of the Parisians, who had been his culture-idols all his years in Algiers, as totally unfounded. The provocative transmission by 'alter' would be absorbed, therefore, by 'ego', and not countered with an escalatory reaction.

When neither of these two techniques are used in diverting 'egos' reaction to a non-violent solution, a third line of defence, consisting of corrective techniques, similar to Goffman's 'face-saving' mechanisms (Goffman, 1967) might occur. A common technique of avoidance is 'ego's pretending' not to notice the provocation. At a later stage 'ego' may give 'alter' a chance to apologise, admit a mistake of identity, or dismiss the provocation as a joke. Another corrective technique is the time-honoured Christian offering of the other cheek. A modern counterpart of this is Albert, in Jules Pfeiffer's *Little Murders*, humming quietly while being dealt murderous blows by his assailants. Finally, the corrective technique could involve a passive attitude towards 'alters' provocation because 'ego' has found secret and devious ways of retaliation, which are deeply satisfying to him. Malaparte aptly illustrates this through his outwardly docile Neapolitans, who manage to outsmart their conquerors by cunningly hilarious means.

When all the defence lines and corrective techniques cannot prevent an escalatory exchange, the next stage would take the form of a 'one-upmanship': 'ego' would react with words and gestures, which would again narrow 'alter's' range of reactions to further provocations, and ultimately to violence. It is, of course, feasible that either party to this repartee may decide to withdraw at even an advanced stage of the escalatory interaction. However, withdrawing with righteous indignation, and postponing action with a threat is not necessarily an end to the escalatory interchange, as hypothesised by Goffman (1967). This huff and puff, 'show you later' withdrawal may quite possibly be taken up by either party when time and place permit.

3. *The Outward Commitment*

The self-definition of being in an escalatory process leading to violence, may be enhanced by 'ego's' outward commitment. He may announce before an audience, that 'alter's' behaviour leaves him no choice but to retaliate. This outside commitment would serve as a complementary booster to 'ego's' self-defined inner commitment to violence. The compelling force of the outside commitment to make the promise good, would depend on the interrelationship between 'ego' and his audience. The prestige, authority or any other normative pressure of the audience may be so formidable that 'ego' may have practically no alternative other than committing the act of violence or some other act leading to it. It is possible, however, that a casual or chance link between 'ego' and his audience may permit a quick or quiet withdrawal after the magnanimous commitment is made.

In many cultures so much poise and theatrical stance are invested in the articulation of a threat or a gesture precipitating violence, that a subsequent action becomes superfluous. The word, the stance, or the gesture itself has a tension-releasing effect on 'ego' and his audience. In most cases, however, neither would 'ego' be willing to withdraw nor would 'alter' and the audience let him withdraw from the escalatory interaction leading towards violence.

4. *The Violent Act*

The eruption of violence as the convergence of the inter-actional *danse macabre* which culminates into a critical mass of the violent act.

5. *The Cathartic Release of Tension Consequent to the Act of Violence*

When the escalatory interchange reaches its peak, 'ego's' self-definiton of being at a 'point of no return' leads his outside commitment to erupt in a release of violence similar to that of a critical mass. This has been witnessed by a large number of police officers who received the confessions of husbands and wives who had killed their mates. Such killers display a genuine air of homeostatic contentedness.

MacDonald cites a case which illustrates this tension-releasing sense of fulfilment felt by a murderer: 'A young soldier calmly informed a fellow soldier that he was going to kill an NCO. He shot the NCO and returned to his barracks where he announced: 'Mission accomplished, mind at ease' (6). Jean Genet lends a Satanic hue to his description of the sense of fulfilment and accomplishment accompanying the act of murder. According to Genet (7), murder should be performed by the kind of 'noble gesture' by the priests of Molloch, who should be solemn, as in a black mass. It should be a ceremony, a rite of hatred. The sense of fulfilment following the act of murder stems also from the pollution 'gained' by it. This being the final and irremediable 'badness', the murderer has passed the 'point of no return' of social damnation.

This sense of fulfilment is eventually disrupted, when 'ego' is confronted with such harsh realitites as trial for murder, prison, the electric chair or the hangman's noose. However, immediately after the violent act, both 'ego's' organism and his personality regain a measure of equilibrium, since the escalatory exhange has accumulated so much pent-up aggressivity. This cathartic effect has been recorded in many cases of aggressive behaviour, especially gang warfare, 'blood revenge' or in long-standing feuds.

Following the above descriptive treatment of the situational escalation towards violence, we now present in concise form our conceptual scheme as related to a system of research hypotheses.

THE CYCLES OF VIOLENCE

The various types of interaction described above can be analysed as cycles of stimulus-response. A chain of cycles accelerates towards violence in the form of a positive feedback cycle which culminates in the blowing of a fuse, i.e., the violent act. When the interaction does not end in violence, the interchange may be likened to a negative feedback cycle. It should be pointed out that such acts may be further analysed into meaningful typologies and the interaction can be related both to the involved and the passive actors. The following paradigm may be a useful framework for a typology of the differential perception of stimuli and the corresponding reactions towards violence, for each given cycle.

Figure 1. *Differential perceptions and reactions towards violence or non-violence for each cycle of interaction*

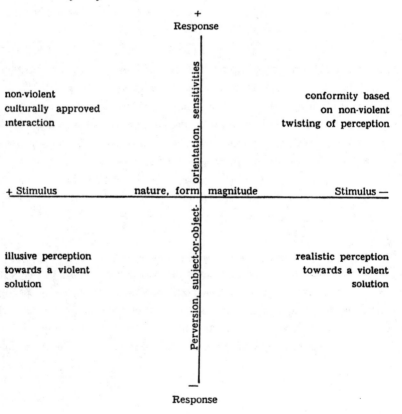

The axes of the paradigm represent the classical stimulus-response relationship. Stimuli may be either neutral or intentional. It may be pointed out that even at this stage the neutral stimulus is not detached from the probable reaction. The fact that a neutral stimulus appears in our paradigm of violence suggests the possibility that the perception of this stimulus might not be at all neutral. In other words, the stimulus specified as neutral is expected not to be perceived as such by the violence-prone reacting 'alter'.

The interrelationship between the stimulus and its perception by 'alter' may be described by the four property spaces around the intersection of the axes. Of these, only two are relevant to our present context. These are the violent-realistic perception of the stimulus and the illusive-violent one. These may be arranged at the extreme planes of a space in a scalogram, utilising the Guttman-Lingol technique. Schematically, the hypothetical factors which would be linked to the movements on this continuum, or to the nature of the planes in the scalogram, might be as follows:

Table 1. *Schematic presentation of a cycle of violence*

Nature of stimulus	Form of stimulus	Magnitude of stimulus
Intentional + neutral 0 intentional -	physical mimicry, gesture verbal	according to objective grading
Perception of stimulus	Orientation of Perception	Sensitivity
towards differentiation towards conformity	object orientation subject orientation	body, self-image family, social

The main vectors portray the nature of stimuli as related to the perception of these stimuli. A positive stimulus would mean that 'alter' relates to 'ego' in a cordial or any other culturally approved manner. The positive perception of these positive stimuli would not, of course, result in violence, e.g., neighbourly exchanges of 'good morning' and ritualistic predictions on the weather. If the stimulus is negative and the perception of it by 'alter' is either neutral or positive, 'alter' performs some perceptual *jonglerie*, which amounts to explaining away the offensive nature of the stimulus, e.g. when a gracious lady mutters to herself that this coarse and vulgar type cannot possibly hurt her feelings. A positive stimulus when perceived as violent, would be related to

107

an illusive perception by 'ego', of 'alter's' intention, e.g. a benign smile by a lad at a passing beauty may be perceived by her as an offensive leer which calls for a violent reaction. The predisposition towards violence can be measured by some standard instruments for perceptual twisting, e.g. the Petrie Augmentor and Reducer (Petrie, 1968). Another possiblity may be the negative perception of a negative, i.e. offensive stimulus. This is, of course, the realistic perception of a fist in the eye as being what it is meant to be. It should be stressed that the decision on the nature of a stimulus, as well as on the nature of a response to a stimulus with a positive, neutral or negative grading, permits a wide range of stimuli ranking vis-á-vis perceptual ranking. The dichotomy of violent and non-violent solutions is clearly apparent in our scheme, so that the cycle of interaction which constitutes an acceleration towards a violent solution, is only displayed in the lower half of our paradigm.

Other components which may be correlated with our main axes are: the magnitude of stimuli would be ranked on the stimuli-axis, according to an objective violence-prone stimuli typology. The form of the stimulus could be physical (i.e. actual assault or other physical contact performed by 'alter' on 'ego'), gesture, mimicry or other stances which are culturally defined as offensive, and verbal insults or provocations. These forms of stimuli cannot be ranked, because the magnitude for the first form might be the amount of force used as related to the physical perception of pain by 'ego'. The second may be related to a typology of gestures as related to the magnitude of obscenity or offensiveness as defined in a given culture. The third, verbal form of provocation could be ranked not only by the offensive content of the words, but also by their pitch and volume.

The variables which relate to the perception axis are linked to the twisting of incoming perception, so that it better fits 'ego's' previous normative internalisation (Shoham, 1968). This involves the various defence-mechanisms, differentiation techniques and other processes of 'explaining-away', which we have already discussed above. These, as well as 'egos' tendency to conform, are measurable personality dimensions: the higher 'ego's' tendency to conform or twist incoming perception in order to achieve congruity, the lower are the chances of violence.

Another dimension which has been utilised by many behavioural scientists in many contexts is the basic continuum of a subject-based, as opposed to an object-based, orientation of 'ego.' This personality typology has been extensively documented by Eysenck and his followers, who offer us a detailed scaling inventory for measuring these polar traits. Our hypothesis in the present context is that the subject-orientated 'ego' would be more realistic in his perception of these stimuli.

Finally, the perception axis should be related to 'ego's' sensitivity towards his body, his self-concept and various social institutions. These sensitivities, which should, of course, be determined individually for each case, would link 'ego's' perception of 'alter's' stimulus to his actual behaviour. The reaction of 'ego,' following his perception of 'alters' stimulus, is the link between one cycle and the other. This reaction would determine 'ego's' future behaviour--whether it would escalate towards violence or de-escalate away from it.

THE DYADIC INTERACTION PROCESS, ANALYZED IN TERMS OF STIMULUS, PERCEPTION, DEFINITION OF THE SITUATION AND RESPONSE

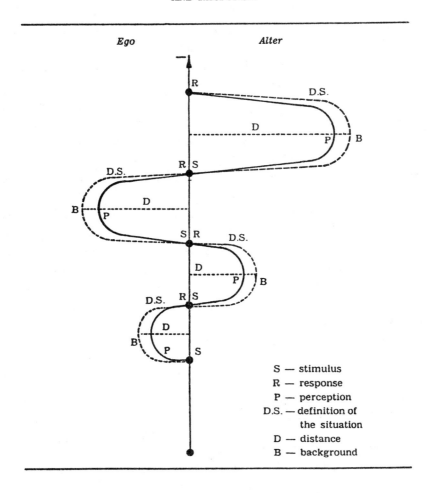

S — stimulus
R — response
P — perception
D.S. — definition of
the situation
D — distance
B — background

THE ESCALATION

The research model proposes to analyse the different steps of interaction towards violence, as the interrelationships among the stimuli by 'ego', the perception of it by 'alter', and 'egos' reaction, within the context of the general situational model of violence. This model synchronises the various cycles into a continuous chain.

The vertical line represents the objective ranking of stimuli and responses (from neutral to negative) according to the average severity of the provocation they present to individuals in a given representative sample of the population.

On this line, the first stimulus will be the trigger and the last response-the violent outbreak.

The model represents the interaction between 'ego' and 'alter'. The spiral curve delineates the dyadic process of interaction. Each loop stands for one cycle. 'Ego' perceives the stimulus by 'alter', and when he reacts his response becomes the stimulus for 'alter' in the second cycle, which 'alter' is supposed to perceive and react to in turn. In the case of escalation towards violence, the distance between the subjective perception and the objectively ranked stimulus increases with each cycle. For analytical purposes we shall differentiate the process into two dimensions, represented in our model by the spiral curve and its shadow. The first dimension, the spiral line itself, is the process of perception of the stimulus. This perception is deepened, is interwoven with, and at times is perverted by the person's background and personality which constitute the second dimension--the shadow of the line. The outcome of these two dimensions is the definition of the situation which comprises the actor's perception of the stimulus, the various factors which tend to augment or reduce the provocative meaning of the stimulus, and the sensitivities which we have described previously when the actor relates the stimuli to himself. This definition of the situation includes also the individual proneness to react violently as measured by some biological factors, e.g., the amount of alcohol in his blood or a hypoglycemic condition, the degree of anxiety, fear and central nervous system excitation or other aggressivity traits which may be measured by various personality inventories and projective techniques.

The definiton of the situation is described by MacIver (1964) as a process of 'dynamic assessment' which includes 3 stages:

1) A choice between alternatives which is made by the actor, based on his salient values and psychological needs in the given situation.

2) With the decision, 'certain external factors' are selectively rearranged and given subjective significance. This dynamic assessment brings the external world selectively into the subjective realm'.

3) Finally all the factors which belong 'to different orders of reality are determining conscious behaviour and are brought into a single order'. The single order is the definition of the situation directing and determining the response of the actor, which closes the cycle.

The responses are also scaled objectively for severity, in the same manner in which we have ranked the stimuli. The responses may also be physical, verbal or by gesture. Their ranking is carried out in relation to their cultural significance and legal severity as determined by the courts. It can be assumed that the stimulus response relationship could be predicted. Deviations from this prediction may then be used as a hypothetical indicator for distorted perception and an illusory definition of the situation by the *dramatis-personae* of the situational dyad of violence.

References

Eysenck, H.J. (1964), *Crime and Personality,* London: Routledge & K. Paul.
Genet, J. (1964), *Our Lady of the Flowers,* New York: Bantam Books.
Goffman, E. (1967), *Interaction Ritual: Essays in Face-to-Face Behaviour,* Chicago: Aldine.
Lamberti, J., N. Blackman, & J. Weiss, 'The Sudden Murderer', M.E. Wolfgang, op.cit., pp.179 et seq.
MacDonald, 'The Threat to Kill', M.E. Wolfgang, op. cit., p.104.
MacIver, R. (1964), 'Subjective Meaning in Social Situations', L. Coser & B. Rosenberg, (Eds.), *Sociological Theory,* (2nd Ed.), New York: Macmillan, pp. 252-7.
Petrie, A. (1968), *Individuality in Pain and Suffering,* Chicago: University of Chicago Press.
Shoham, S. G. (1973), *The Society and the Absurd,* Oxford:Basil Blackwell.
Sutherland, E.H. & D.R. Cressey (1966), *Principles of Crimnology,* 7th Ed, Philadelphia: J.B. Lippincott.
Walker, D., 'Rights in Conflict', *Reports Submitted by the Chicago Study Team of the National Commission on the Causes and Prevention of Violence, Nov. 1968.*
Wolfgang, M.E. (1967), *Studies in Homicide,* New York: Harper & Row, p.73.

8 The Cycles of Interaction in Violence

They had already had too much to drink and wanted a meal. But it was Christmas Eve and the restaurant was full. They were turned away, but on insisting, were thrown out. They in turn kicked the owner's wife, who was pregnant. The owner, a frail fair-haired young man, grabbed a gun and fired. The bullet lodged in the man's right temple. His head rolled over and rested on the wound. Drunk with alcohol and terror, his friends began to dance around the dead body.

Albert Camus, *Notebooks, 1935-1942*

INTRODUCTION

In this chapter we shall deal with the situational aspects of violence, suggesting that a violent act may be best explained and understood by regarding the act as an escalating series of stimulus-response interactions between two persons. The basic unit of such a series is the cycle which is described and explained. A scale for measuring the intensity of the cycle is constructed, and its reliability and objectivity is tested and proved. Methods of data collection and processing for constructing and using the scale are described, as well as the applicability of the scale to different cultures. The scale is used to verify the suggested hypotheses that the intensity of stimulus decides the form taken by the interaction, and that the escalation towards violence occurs more rapidly when the provocative intensity is high.

The theoretical framework of the situational aspects of violence has already been presented in two articles (1), which consider that the biological, psychoanalytical and sociological aspects of violence are less relevant to the explanation of violence than the actual chain of events leading up to the violent act. The authors do not deny that the genetic and historical aspects are relevant in that they can be used to provide a generalised explanation of violence in terms of probability. However, these explanations do have an exclusionary aspect, in that they explain violent acts only to the extent that a predispositon may exist.

The situational aspect of violence, on the other hand, applies to all individuals, whether predisposed or not, and furthermore, allows the complete explanation of violent acts from the initial provocation through to the final eruption of violence. In other words, the situational explanation begins where the genetic and historical explanations leave off.

The study of violence as a situational phenomenon contained in an interactional matrix of alter and ego has several important connotations. The first, obviously, is to add a new dimension to our understanding of violent acts. Second, it has important legal connotations. If a violent act is accepted as the inevitable result of a series of escalating stimulus-response cycles leading to a 'point of no return', the overall importance of *mens rea* and criminal responsibility as conceived by the criminal law may be left open to doubt, as the question whether it is ego or alter who inflicts the final (legally-defined) violent blow is seen to be solely a result of the structure of the situation. Third, there are preventive connotations. Once the perspective is placed on the situational aspect, the position of contributory factors (such as availability of weapons, use of alcohol, etc.) becomes clear, and preventive policies with regard to these factors may be implemented.

The main hypothesis of the study is that the outbreak of violence is the result of a series of interactions, called cycles, between ego and alter. Each cycle consists of stimulus and response, and given favourable circumstances, will effect a new cycle with a higher level of provocation and consequent reaction, until a 'point of no return' is reached, after which the eventual eruption of violence is inevitable.

The following points are relevant to the primary description of our premise.

1. Subjective perception of stimulus: The stimulus may be either positive (provocative) or negative (non-provocative). The perception may be either realistic or non-realistic. The manner of perception of the stimulus may affect:

2. Corrective techniques, leading either to escalation of violence (in the case where a stimulus is perceived, either realistically or non-realistically, as provocative) or away from violence (in the case where the stimlulus is perceived, realistically or non-realistically, as non-provocative). (2)

3. Form taken by the cycles: In the event of violence, this is seen as a causal chain of interaction between ego and alter. The form of the cycles will be effected to varying degrees by:

4. Content of the cycle: This involves the degree of provocation, objective and perceived, contained in the stimulus. The provocation may take the form of an action, gesture or verbal expression, and may have varying degrees of effect, in the light of specific cultural or personal connotations.

The interactional nature of these four factors, and their mutual effect on the nature of the cycle, can be represented diagramatically, as in figure 1. (3)

Figure 1.

	Negative Response	
Non-violent culturally approved interaction		Conformity based on non-violent twisting of perception
Negative Stimulus		Positive Stimulus
Illusive perception towards a violent solution		Realistic perception towards a violent solution
	Positive Response	

The Aims and Hypotheses of the Study

The aim of the study is the examination of the actual process of eruption of the violent act. We have, therefore, not taken into consideration the predisposition to violence as measured by biological and personality variables. The practice of 'holding the level of analysis constant' is generally accepted in criminological and sociological research.(4) This process may well have its disadvantages, but in the present study, we felt that the interactional dynamics of violence have enough independent processes to warrant their separate treatment.

The study, therefore, concentrates on a stimulus-response interaction, and examines the nature of the provocation, the nature of the reaction, and the relationship between the two factors. These three components constitute one cycle, and each cycle acts as stimulus to the subsequent one.

A full scale study of violence should include not only a study of the escalatory processes leading towards an eruption of violence (that is, verbal communication, gestures, and mutually-understood symbols), but also a study of the factors which are linked to the avoidance of violence. The non-violent sequel to a tension-laden interaction may be explained using the cognitive dissonance and balance models in social psychology. (5) It is feasible that homeostatic and congruity mechanisms may

114

induce the actors to solve their dispute in a non-violent way. The present study, however, confines itself only to those interactions which escalate towards violence.

Similarly, many violent situations involve more than the two principle actors. Observers, both non-participant and participant, often play a part, even to the extent of an all-out brawl. Our theoretical model, however, involves the conception of violence as a dyadic type of interaction between ego and alter, or two groups in a dyadic interrelationship, and the present study, therefore, confines itself to an examination of the dyadic interaction which escalates towards violence. This interaction takes the form of cycles, and our hypotheses are based on the assumption that the interaction towards violence takes the form of an escalating series of stimulus-response cycles.

The Hypotheses

1. The nature of the response is in direct relation to the nature, both form and content-wise, of the stimulus, so that the possible number of responses, and hence cycles, arising from a specific stimulus, is limited.

2. The intensity of the interaction is inversely proportional to the number of cycles leading towards violence: that is, the lower the intensity of the interaction, the greater is the number of cycles leading to violence, and the higher the intensity, the lower is the number of cycles leading to violence.

THE RESEARCH DESIGN

Methodological Problems

The nature of the phenomenon under study does not allow a full-scale investigation based on observational techniques only, for two reasons. First, the outbreak of violence cannot be predicted, so that the amount of time and manpower involved in the observation of violence in the field would simply be economically impractical. Second, and perhaps more importantly, we felt that there are significant personality differences between those individuals who take part in acts of violence in observable situations, and those who do not, so that the results obtained from observational techniques alone would not pertain to a representative population sample.

In order to overcome these problems and to cover the field completely, we chose the following four methods of research:

Content analysis of court records

Content analysis of fictional accounts of violence

Role-playing
Observation

Data Collection
1. Content analysis of court records
The obvious problem connected with this method is that the information provided by the opposing sides is not always objective, for obvious reasons. We therefore concentrated on the evidence of objective witnesses (bystanders and police) and found that it was indeed possible to obtain the sequential order of events from these witnesses. An unexpected problem which arose during the collection of data was connected with the court's purpose of excluding all irrelevant facts. The problem was that many facts which were irrelevant for legal purposes, were vital for our purpose. The average number of acts recorded per case was 5 (that is, 3 cycles--see figure 4) which does not represent a total sequence. We were therefore not able to include all these data in every phase of the processing. All cases of offences against the person appearing in the Tel Aviv Magistrate's court during 1969 were recorded.

2. Content analysis of fictional accounts of violence
The basic assumption underlying our use of this method was that fiction is a true, albeit dramatic, reflection of reality. Naturally, fiction making use of violence for purposes of exploitation (violence for violence's sake), such as detective and war stories, was expressly excluded. The data was collected by university students taking courses in Hebrew and English literature. The students were asked to provide selections describing violent interactions, but were not informed of the purpose behind the request. We examined the selections provided, and excluded those which did not represent a detailed and sequential description of events which could be translated into terms of stimulus-response cycles.

3. Role-playing
The use of role-playing in psychological research and therapy is based on the assumption that the actor's subjective perception of the given situation results in his acting out his own problems through the media of the given situation, so that the behaviour enacted in the role-playing is, in fact, true or 'natural' behaviour. This being the case, the use of this method is highly suitable for our study.

This assumption was sustained by the results obtained. We used four potential violence-provoking situations, which we took from the fictional accounts mentioned above, and used two groups of actors. One group comprised university students

116

studying drama, and the other, a group of working-class adolescents from interstitial areas (6).

The intellectual and cultural gap between the two groups was illustrated by the results. The role-playing arising out of the same given situation was markedly different in content for the two separate groups. However, the content of the reactions of the individual members within each separate group was similar. These results also tend to support our assumption that the enactment reflects real life. For example, one situation involved a wife who was obliged to support the family because her husband refused to work. She returns from a hard day's work, prepared to begin the chores of housework, and is enraged at her husband's demand that she make him a cup of coffee. The content of the average university 'wife's' reaction was something like this--'Oh, when will you finally take a job and stop making excuses that every job you're offered doesn't suit you'! The average slum 'wife's' reaction, on the other hand, was markedly different in content--'I'm fed up with you! You spend the whole day hanging around with her, and doing the bars with your mates. You'd rather play snooker than work!'

Because none of the participants was informed of the purpose of the research, there were many instances of enactments resulting in peaceful solutions. These instances were not used in the final analysis.

4. Observation

Workers dealing with 'marginal youth' from all over Israel were contacted and asked to describe instances of violence, both physical and verbal, in which they had been involved or which they had observed. Once again, the workers were not informed of the purpose and nature of the research, so that many observations were not suitable, either because they involved more than two participants, or because the description was incomplete and unable to be translated into terms of stimulus-response cycles. These instances were not used in the final analysis.

All material collected by these four methods was arranged in the form of simple sentences, in sequential order for each case, each sentence representing a single act.

The Research Instrument

Our principal problem was to find a standard and objective measure of stimulus intensity. The problem was further complicated by the unlimited number of possible stimuli. The obvious measure of stimulus intensity is reaction. The fact that reaction is culture-controlled was proved by our tentative attempt to produce a rating scale. We gave a number of provocative statements to a group of students and to a group of working-class adolescents from interstitial areas to rate the stimulus intensity, and found a marked difference in total results between the two groups.

In order to find a measure of stimulus intensity which would not be distorted by personal/cultural/ethnic variables, we first took 80 potential stimuli, in the form of single sentences.

The stimuli were presented to a grading group of 8 working-class adolescents from interstitital areas. They were asked to rate each sentence subjectively according to their perception of its provocative content, using 7 possible degrees of intensity, from 0-6. We then selected those items for which the degree of agreement was largest, and constructed a scale of 6 grades of intensity, from 0-5 (7). A concise and precise verbal description of each grade of intensity was a literal impossiblity, so that the final scale consisted of the six degrees of intensity, each degree being exemplified by several stimulus-sentences (see table 1).

Table 1. *Subjective Grading Scale* (reduced version)

Intensity Level	Stimuli
1.	-She stood between him and the shelf and wouldn't let him go to it. -She asked him to leave her alone. -He asked the policewoman to let him off.
2.	-The inspector came by and moved his motorcycle. -The clerk didn't react at all. -She doesn't deserve higher grades.
3.	-I'll call the landlord. -Watch out, I've got ten buddies and after the movie we'll beat you up. -He cursed the driver coming opposite him.
4.	-He said to the inspector, 'You lousy bastard, why did you move the motorcycle'?
5.	-You think everyone's a whore like you. -Give me back all the money I've paid, and I'll teach you good and proper, I'll bash your head in (tenant to landlord). -He raised his hand and slapped her.

Once the scale was constructed, it was used in the following way. A new list of stimulus-sentences was prepared, and given to the subjects, together with the scale. The subjects were asked to rate each item objectively, according to the item in the scale that it resembled most closely. For example, if the list were to contain an item stating 'she picked up the rolling pin and hit him with it,' it would be judged most similar to the scale item 'he raised his hand and slapped her,' and would therefore be given a rating of 5. The grading was, therefore, in accordance with the degree of similarity between the sentences and not in accordance with the perceived provocative content, and may be referred to as objective grading.

The objectivity and validity of the scale was then tested. First, a small group of adults, all of middle-class status but of different ethnic origins and ages, rated a set of 80 stimuli by the above mentioned method, comparing the stimuli to those of the subjective scale. The degree of intra-group agreement was between 85-90, and the disagreements were of no more than one degree. We can conclude, therefore, that the rating system is objective, in so far as the results were uniform and did not reflect cultural or age differences of the members of the group. Members of this group continued to work for the project, grading all the data collected by the four methods described above.

In order to test the validity of the scale, the same set of stimuli which had been given to the middle-class group was given to a group of working-class adolescents. This group was asked to grade the stimuli according to the subjective method used by the original grading group, whom they resembled. The degree of intra-group agreement was high. Total scores for both the middle-class and working-class groups were obtained, taking average scores on items where disagreement existed. A comparison of the total scores for both groups revealed 80 per cent agreement. Inter-group differences on specific items was mostly of one point only, and none were more than two points. This comparison demonstrated that the objective grading of the middle-class group equalled the subjective grading of the working-class group and thus demonstrated the validity of the scale as a measurement of the provocative intensity of the stimuli.

We would like to mention at this point the reason why the basis of our scale was the subjective perception of a working-class group. The adolescents who made up the group were mostly first generation Israelis whose parents had come from underdeveloped countries and had made their homes in the semi-slums, or interstitial areas close to Tel Aviv. The adolescents who made up the grading group were, to some degree, more upwardly mobile than their parents, most of them having at least some years of secondary education, and some degree of success in the army and/or at work. However, they still attract the label of 'marginal' or 'underprivileged' youth and do exhibit a degree of resentment usually found amongst youth of this type. Their environment, in particular, ensured a fair amount of contact, both participant and non-participant, with violence, and we assumed that their perception of the stimuli would be typical of the social group where violent interactions are most prevalent.

The reason why we did not use the same group to grade the collected data was the simple and practical one that the group was not prepared to continue their cooperation beyond the point where the situation was no longer interesting. Once the novelty value had worn off, the job of grading the collected data was seen, and quite rightly so, as a lengthy and tedious task. This task was carried out, as mentioned previously, by members of the middle-class group who had carried out the grading for the objectivity testing.

The construction and use of the grading scale as described above is a reliable way to obtain an objective rating of perceived intensity of provocation. It can be applied to different sub-groups belonging to the same broad social group as the original grading group. The applicability or non-applicability of the scale to different sub-groups is easily seen by comparing the total objective score of the different sub-groups to that of the subjective score of the original grading group, as we did in our validity check. Should the degree of disagreement indicate that the cultural differences between the two groups are too great to allow the application of the scale, a new scale can be constructed using a more suitable grading group.

DATA PROCESSING

Defining the Cycle

As mentioned above (see section I), the cycle is seen as a unit in a chain of action in which the first stimulus is the 'trigger' and the last response is the violent action. For this purpose, we have construed the cycle as a matrix of three interrelated actions, representing the interaction between ego and alter. The response arising out of the first stimulus also acts as stimulus for the following reaction and is represented as Rs. This matrix may be represented diagramatically as follows:

Table 2. *One Cycle in Terms of Stimulus-Response*

Action Number	Type of Action	Actor	Reactor
1	S	Ego	Alter
2	Rs	Alter	Ego
3	R	Ego	

When the final reaction is no longer perceived as stimulus, (either because of corrective techniques used by the reactor or because the reaction was the final act), the cycle ends.

In real life situations, the action continues for more than one cycle, until the final reaction is no longer perceived as stimulus. A series of five actions may be represented diagramatically (see table 3). The division of the same series into cycles is shown in table 4. Generally accepted psychological theory usually represents such actions as made up of stimulus-response pairs. Our representation using cycles of three actions (stimulus-response/stimulus-response) is simply a different way of construing the usual S-R pairs. The advantage of our conception is that the cycle describes the continuity of the action, making the interdependent relationships of all the actions clear. Table 4 shows how the effect of the first action continues to influence the cycle to the final action.

Table 3. *Series of five actions showing interrelationship between stimulus-response*

Action Number	Type of Action	Actor	Reactor
1	S	Ego	Alter
2	Rs	Alter	Ego
3	Rs	Ego	Alter
4	Rs	Alter	Ego
5	R	Ego	—

Table 4. *Series of five actions represented by cycles*

No. of Action	1	2	3	4	5
Cycle 1	S	Rs	R		
Cycle 2		S	Rs	R	
Cycle 3			S	Rs	R
Actor	Alter	Ego	Alter	Ego	Alter

First Hypotheses

Our first hypothesis was that the number of cycles arising out of an initial response is limited. According to this hypothesis, the diagrammatic representation of a chain (ref. table 3) should change in form according to the degree of intensity of the stimulus. Figure 1 is a graphical representation of a cycle of violence, presented for didactic purposes only, in order to illustrate how the effect of stimulus intensity may be represented.

Figure 1 demonstrates that the deciding factor for the form of the escalatory process is not the actual degree of intensity of stimulus, but rather the difference in intensity between S, Rs, and R. In other words, the escalation towards violence may be described and measured in terms of the discrepancy of intensity of interaction.

Figure 2. *Chain of Interaction Showing Assumed Effect of Stimulus Intensity*

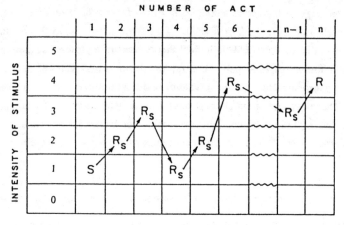

Thus, once all the actions had been graded, the cycles were grouped according to patterns. For example, the following 3 cycles all formed the same pattern:

Table 5.

S	Rs	R
3	2	4
4	3	6
2	1	3
a+1	a	a+2

For the sake of convenience, we recorded each pattern in terms of a=0, where 'a' represents the lowest intensity in the cycle, and all the cycles having the same pattern were grouped together.

Second Hypothesis

Our second hypothesis was that the number of cycles leading to the final act is inversely related to the intensity of stimulus. We were not able to use simple correlation techniques in order to demonstrate the relationship between the total number of acts and their intensity, because the form of the total interaction is not necessarily a simple linear escalation, but may well take a more complicated form, depending on the intensity of any given stimulus (ref. fig 1). In order to process the data, we used a regression formula which introduces the dynamic form taken by the escalation. The following formula was used:

122

$$Y=b_0+b_1 X+b_2 x_2$$

The line drawn from this equation using the customary regression formula has the property that the sum of squares of vertical deviations of observations from this line is smaller than the corresponding sum of squares of deviations from any other line. This formula was computed for each cycle, where b_0= mean intensity of total interactions of the cycles; b_1= the gradient (that is, the expression of the linear relationship between the intensity of each act and its sequential number); b_2 expresses the non-linear connection between these factors. In other words, the formula expresses the relationship between the intensity and the sequential number of the acts in the interaction.

RESULTS

First Hypothesis
The results of the data processing were divided into four groups according to the method of data collection used, and data for the four groups were divided according to the number of patterns formed. The results are presented in Graph Number 1.

Graph 1 shows us that the greatest intensity difference between acts was from 0-3. Thus, the number of possible patterns was 81 (4 grades of intensity combined with 3 possible positions). Of these 81 possible patterns, only 18 were found to appear more than four times. This is a small number of patterns in relation to the number of possible patterns, and we may therefore conclude that the frequency is not random, and that there are deciding factors. We also found that the frequency of the patterns within the four groups was similar, indicating that the deciding factor is the same for all four methods of data collection.

Graph 1.

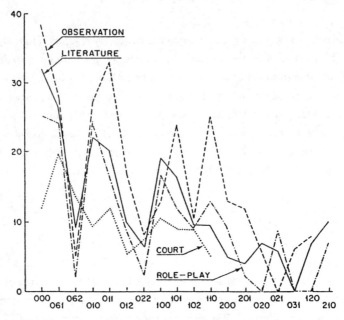

The pattern appearing most often was that of three actions on the same level of intensity, that is:

S	Rs	R
0	0	0

The second, third and fourth most frequent patterns were 001, 010, and 011. This supports the hypothesis that the governing factor is the initial stimulus intensity.

These results support the hypothesis that the number of possible cycles is limited, and is related to the stimulus intensity.

Second Hypothesis

As mentioned above, the data collection from court hearings did not provide a sufficient number of acts to enable the use of the regression analysis, and therefore computations were made for three methods only.

During computation, we found that b_2 (which expresses the non-linear connection between the sequential number of the action and its intensity) was not significant, and therefore the following formula was used:

$$Y = b_0 + b_1 x$$

The results found for the three methods are seen in graphs 2 (fictional accounts of violence), 3 (role-playing), and 4 (observations). Graphs 3 and 4 showed a clear trend in the expected direction. The lower the intensity of interaction, the lower the gradient (representing the total number of acts), and the higher the intensity, the higher the gradient. This trend may be seen by the marked connection between b_0 and b_1.

In other words, the results of role-playing and observational techniques tended to prove the inverse relationship between the degree of intensity of the action and the total number of acts, as suggested in the hypothesis.

Graph 2

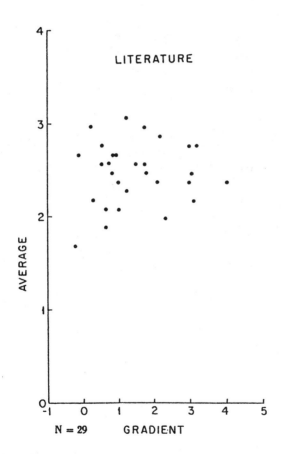

Graph 3

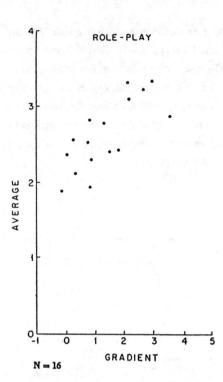

ROLE-PLAY

AVERAGE

GRADIENT

N = 16

Graph 4

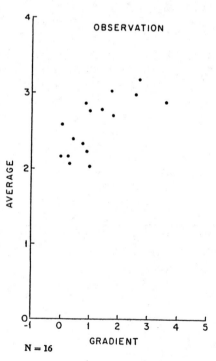

OBSERVATION

AVERAGE

GRADIENT

N = 16

126

The results obtained from the fictional accounts of violence (see Graph 2) did not support the hypothesis. There are several possible reasons. First, it is possible that our scale was not suitable for the contents of the accounts, as they represent a wide variety of cultures. Second, it is quite feasible that the accounts included only those acts perceived by the author to represent reality, and that in real life, other acts would be included. The possibility that the accounts did not represent a random sample of interactions must also be taken into account.

The results obtained from fictional accounts, while not supporting the hypothesis, are not sufficiently conclusive to disprove it completely. In fact, the results did show a superficial trend in the expected direction.

Discussion

This study is only the beginning of the empirical verification of the intricate and vast field of the situational aspects of violence. We have established that the situational interaction of violence may indeed be quantified and measured, and have devised a measuring instrument. The cyclic conception of the escalation towards violence has been shown to be tenable, and we have also demonstrated that the escalation towards violence is related to the perceived intensity of the initial provocation. Finally, we have shown that there is a distinct relationship between the number of cycles, the intensity of the interaction, and the escalation towards violence. When the intensity is high, the number of cycles is less and the duration of the interaction is shorter. Per contra, when the intensity is low, the number of cycles is larger and the duration of interaction longer. We realise that our measures may be crude, and that their application to different cultural settings may involve the drawing-up of new scales. However, the first step in the investigation of the situational aspects of violence has been made, and any further contemplated research may do well to take our study as a base and a first stepping-stone.

References

Banitt, R., S. Katznelson & S. Streit (1970), 'The Situational Aspects of Violence-
    A Research Model', S.G.Shoham (Ed.), *Israel Studies in
    Criminology*, Tel Aviv: Gomeh Publishing House, Vol.1, pp.241-58.
Brown, R. W. (1965), 'The Principle of Consistency', *Social Psychology*, New
    York: Free Press, Chapter 12.
Goffman, E. (1967), 'Interaction Ritual', *Face to Face Behaviour*, Chicago:
    Aldine.
Shoham, S. G. (1972), 'Points of No Return:Some Situational Aspects of Violence',
Rolland S. Parker (Ed.), *The Emotional Stress of War, Violence and Peace*,
    Pittsburgh:Stanwick House, Inc.
Sutherland and Cassey (1966), *Principles of Criminology*, New York:
    J.B.Lippincott, 7th Ed.

9 Sexual Violence

The sexual instinct. What is this instinct? On the one hand it is the ultimate expression of nature and on the other, the blind force which demands the total subjection of human beings, even at the price of their destruction.

Albert Camus, *The Rebel*

INTRODUCTION

In this chapter, we attempt to apply the concepts of interdisciplinarity to the study of rape and examine the ways in which we have developed the aetiological hierarchy, in relation to the study of violence relating to the aetiology of rape.

We also examine the feasibility of applying some of the aspects of our personality theory to the study of rape. A theoretical scheme is then presented and the relevant research findings are related to it. This chapter examines somatic factors and personality variables as predisposing agents to rape. Sociocultural backgrounds are also examined as independent variables within the situational context of relationship between the rapist and his victim. The construction of an interdisciplinary model of sexual violence has to take into account two preliminary issues: first, the existing empirical data are often problematic from the methodological point of view and far from being satisfactory materially; second, rape has become one of the main bases of feminist ideology. As for the first issue, it might be sufficient to cite the reviews of some of the most often cited studies of rape: 'The book is annoyingly flawed... by some questionable methodology. The author also espouses a now-controversial theory of victim precipitation regarding rape' (Chappell and Fogarty, 1971:2). Other reviewers (Gagnon and Reiss, 1971) offer the following comments:

Figures in tables are transposed and columns fail to add to the sum reported...the author fails to warn readers that police data must be handled with consummate caution. He notes that some police records were missing for the years he investigated, and he does not include episodes that were 'unfounded', though it is incontrovertible that many cases thrown out by the police are actual instances of criminal rape, 'unfounded' because the officers are prejudiced against the victim (or for the offender) or, probably more likely, because they do not believe a conviction or guilty plea will be forthcoming if the offender is apprehended. The author offers no clue as to the number of cases dropped from this study cohort (p.20).

Another much relied-on study has earned the following remarks:

In addition to its lack of scientific utility, the volume is tasteless...in its attempts at humor. The story of a woman who is raped while circulating a petition is given comic relief by noting that the records did not show whether or not the offender signed her petition...In large measure the author reinforces...misconceptions about rape, feeds societal fantasies through his handling of case materials, and generally obscures and distorts any understanding of sex offense behavior (Gagnon, 1971:20).

There are, of course, some excellent studies in the field, but it is a problem if two of the most relied-on empirical studies on the subject are poorly thought of by their peers. As for the issue of feminist ideology and rape, let me state at the outset that I am a staunch feminist. I believe that women in human society have been and are discriminated against in many areas of life and that most of the goals espoused by the feminist movement are struggles for just causes. I am also not a salon feminist paying lip service to the movement without doing anything about it. I voted in the last elections in Israel for a small party that had as one of its major goals equal rights for women. However, ideology and science do not mix well. That was shown in the Soviet Union: after Stalin proclaimed that Lysenko was right in holding that acquired traits can be inherited, a disastrous decline in Soviet biology ensued. It was also apparent in the so-called New Criminology movement, in which Marxist ideology was interpreted as opposing measurement and observation and in which the study of crime was supplemented with or substituted by slogan shouting. It is also apparent in the present area of concern, in which feminist ideology adopts bad research because it happens to agree with feminist beliefs or supports irrational and exaggerated claims in instances where properly measured facts and rational deductions are needed.

However, before delving into this issue more deeply, an even more basic issue must be addressed: the fact that rape is a blanket concept including many different types of behaviour that hardly have any common denominator.

A TYPOLOGY OF RAPES, RAPISTS, AND THEIR VICTIMS

The legal tag of rape is quite meaningless when applied to the various types of behaviour that constitute the legal offence. This is why many researchers of sexual violence have tried to devise typologies of rape that would serve as the dependent variables of their studies. Cohen et al. (1974), for instance, presented three categories for describing rape acts: (1) rape with an aggressive aim, in which the rape serves to humiliate, degrade, and defile the victim; (2) rape with a sexual aim, in which aggression is used primarily in the service of a sexual wish; and (3) rape with a combined aim of sex and aggression with a strong sadistic component. Burgess and Holmstrom (1974) distinguish between the sudden attack of a 'blitz' rape and 'confidence' rapes, in which the assailant works his way into the confidence of the victim prior to the attack. Bromberg and Coyle (1974) present five categories of rapists as follows:

> The immature adolescent rapist, who is worried about his sexual inadequacy; the gang rapist, whose motivation is more for status among his peers than for sexual satisfaction; the adult rapist, with sadistic tendencies; the lonely rapist, with low self-esteem and hate towards the world in general; and the despoiler, who cannot tolerate feminine beauty and is driven to destroy it. The rapist dreams of being a compelling lover but ends up a destroyer (p. 25).

Gibbens, Way, and Soothill (1977) offered a three-part classification of rapists as paedophiliacs, aggressive individuals, and a residual category of 'others'. Gebhard (1965) and his associates offered another three-part classification of rapists. The first group are statistically normal individuals who simply misjudged the situation. This is a rather small group. Numerically the largest group is the sociopaths. These are criminally inclined men who take what they want, whether money, material or women, and their sex offences are by-products of their general criminality. The third group, larger than the first but smaller than the second, are the rapists who suffer from

131

personality defects and stresses that ultimately erupt in a sexual offence. Finally, there are the homosexual rapes in or outside prison.

Obviously, there are hardly any behavioural traits common to a group rapist, a paedophiliac rapist, and a homosexual rapist. Yet, a behavioural homogeneity of the dependent variable is necessary in order to study its aetiology. The typologies mentioned and others similar to them are quite useful, but for the study of rape, a behavioural typology is needed, one that takes into account the act of rape, its perpetrator, and its victim. This kind of a typology has not yet been devised. Thus, the methodology used by Shoham, Rahav, and Guttman (1970) to construe a typology of offences, should be employed in devising a typology of rapes, to allow for their study as dependent variables in aetiological research. In order to delineate a range of offences with a sufficiently homogeneous behavioural basis to serve as dependent variables in research, an offence has been defined epistemologically as an act performed by an actor against an object protected by a legal norm. If this conception of an offence is applied to rape, the relevant components are (a) the legal norm proscribing rape; (b) the rapist, (c) the act of rape itself, and (d) the victim. These components are then classified as follows: characteristics of the rapist according to his social roles and position, age, ethnicity, and nature of involvement in the offence, that is, whether he was the planner or the actual rapist. If it was a group rape, was the actor one of the perpetrators or the leader? Was the rape premeditated or impulsive? Was the rapist under the influence of drugs or alcohol when committing the offence? As for the act of rape, there is a need to ascertain its motivation and whether it was committed repeatedly or as an isolated act. As for the victims, it is necessary to know their ages, ethnicity, social roles, positions, status in relation to the rapists, and their social proximity, ranging from strangers to family members. When the primary instruments have been devised, a sample of about 200 court files of convicted rapists should be classified and analysed according to the nonmetric scalogram analysis devised by Guttman (Shoham et al. 1970:47). The result would be clusters of profiles of the rapes, rapists, and victims, grouped together by a multivariate analysis. Such clusters would then constitute homogeneous types of behaviour to be taken as dependent variables in the aetiological studies of rape.

RAPE: A DASTARDLY FURTIVE USURPATION

Susan Brownmiller (1975), in her widely quoted *Against Our Will: Men, Women and Rape*, describes rape in this way:

Rape is the quintessential act by which a male demonstrates to a female...that she is conquered--vanquished--by his superior strength and power (p.49).

Rape is a dull, blunt, ugly act committed by punk kids, their cousins and older brothers, not by charming, witty, unscrupulous, heroic, sensual rakes, or by timid souls deprived of a 'normal' sexual outlet, or by super-menschen possessed of uncontrollable lust. And yet, on the shoulders of these unthinking, predictable, insensitive, violence-prone young men there rests an age-old burden that amounts to an historic mission: the perpetuation of male domination over women by force (pp. 208-209).

Man's discovery that his genitalia could serve as a weapon to generate fear must rank as one of the most important discoveries of prehistoric times, along with the use of fire and the first crude stone axe. From prehistoric times to the present, I believe, rape has played a critical function. It is nothing more or less than a conscious process of intimidation by which all men keep all women in a state of fear (p. 15).

This misogynist theory of rape is not accepted here. Rather, rape is related among other things to the sexual inadequacy of the rapist. It is related to his ontological inferiority. He usurps by furtive violence what he has no hope of gaining through dialogue, courtship, and love. Rape is not an act of power but of decrepit impotence. We shall try to substantiate these claims with the help of our theory of human personality presented elsewhere earlier in this book. For the sake of clarity and continuity, we shall reiterate and elaborate upon this theory here: the scaffolding of the personality core is structured in two vectors, participation and separation. By participation we mean the identification of ego with a person(s), an object, or a symbolic construct outside the self and the individual's striving to lose his or her separate identity by fusion with this other object or symbol. Separation is the opposite vector. These opposing vectors of unification-fusion and separation-isolation have been used as the main axis of this personality theory in conjunction with three major developmental phases. The first is the process of birth. The second is the crystallisation of an individual ego by the moulding of the 'ego boundaries'. The third phase, that of separation, is a corollary of socialisation, when one reaches one's 'ego identity' (Erickson, 1956). The strain to overcome the separating and dividing pressures never leaves the individual. The striving to partake in a pantheistic whole is ever present and takes many forms; if one avenue toward its realisation is blocked, it surges out from another channel. Actual participation is unattainable by definition. The objective impossiblity of participation is augmented by the countering separating vectors, both instinctual and interactive. At any given moment of a person's life, there is a disjuncture, a gap, between the desires for participation and the subjectively defined distance from the participatory aims. This gap has been denoted the Tantalus Ratio, which is the relationship between the longed-for participatory goal and the distance from it as perceived by ego (Shoham, 1979).

Another basic premise of the theory is the fixation of the separant and participant personality types. These are related to the crystallisation at later orality of a separate self out of the pantheistic mass of totality and early orality. This is the ontological base line by which the non-self (the object) defines the self. The coagulation of the self marks the cut-off for the most basic developmental dichotomy, from birth and early orality to the phase where the ego boundary is formed around the emerging individual separatum, and from later orality onwards. In the first phase, any fixation that might evolve, and thus imprint some character traits on the developing personality is not registered by a separate self capable of distinguishing between the objects that are the source of the fixation-causing trauma and the self as its recipient. The experiencing entity is a nondifferentiated pantheistic totality. On the other hand, if the traumatising fixation occurs at the later oral phase, after the objects have expelled the self from their togetherness by a depriving interaction with it, the self may well be in a position to attribute the cause of pain and deprivation to its proper source, that is the objects. Therefore, a personality typology is proposed that is anchored on this developmental dichotomy of pre-and post-differentation of the self, (see Money and Ehrhardt, 1972). The moulding process is the nature and severity of fixation, which in turn determines the placement of a given individual on the personality type continuum. The types themselves are fixated by developmental chronology, the participant at predifferentiated early orality, and the separant after the formation of the separate self. The participant core personality vector, however, operates with varying degrees of potency on both these personality types; but the quest for congruity manifests itself differently with each polar personality type. The participant aims to achieve congruity by defacing and annihilating the self, melting back, as it were, into the object and thereby achieving the pantheistic togetherness and nondifferentiation of early orality.

The separant type aims to achieve congruity by overpowering or swallowing the object. The congruity aims of the self-effacing participant have been denoted as exclusion. The object-devouring separant wishes to achieve congruity by inclusion, that is, incorporating the object in the outreaching self.

The attitude of parents, and especially the behaviour of the mother at early orality is crucial for the formation of gender identity (Money and Ehrhardt, 1972: 18-19). The emphatic relation between mother and child is so strong that the mother can often predict if and when the child is about to behave in a certain manner, for instance, throw up his food, burst into activity, cry, or laugh (MacFarlane, 1977). This creates a symbiotic cycle of dependencies, identities, and complementarities between mother and child, where one constantly reinforces the other. As for gender identity formation, the normal process at the oral phase of development is the female's identity with the mother and the male's complementarity with her. At the later socionormative phases of development, when the father becomes fully conspicuous as a socialising figure, the son identifies with him. These are the identification processes inherent in the social separation phase. Schematically, the identification and complementarity dynamics may be presented as in figure 1.

Figure 1.

The oral phase of development, with its temporal primacy and the dialectics of incestuous arousal and suppression, is, of course, more crucial in the crystallisation of gender self-concept. Consequently, the image of the father, as presented vicariously to the child by the mother, plays a more important role in the genesis of gender self-concept than the actual father. On the other hand, the complementarity and identity with the father at later social separation is bound to conflict with the initial processes of identification and complementarity with the mother at the child's oral phase of development. Consequently, gender identity is bound to undergo some changes at the social phase of separation and at puberty. Moreover, the attraction to and choice of mate are not determined by the simplistic rule of a girl seeking a mate who resembles her father and a boy looking for a wife like his mother. The positive correlation between identification with mother and feminine gender identity may be inferred from the following statement, based on a review of the literature, by Fisher (1973): 'A large majority of the studies have found that a girl's degree of femininity is positively related

135

to the perception of her mother as warm, nurturant or protective' (p. 104). The mother could not have been perceived as warm and protective without the daughter identifying with her.

It is hypothesised that the mother encourages the girl to identify with her from the very outset and that later many conflicts ensue bcause of the girl's stronger complementary links with her father. A mother may, however, encourage strong complementarity with her son, and yet when the time comes for him to identify with a male figure, many problems occur.

It is also hypothesised that the suppression of incestuous sex is more effective at early orality through identification than complementarity. The son is also sexually aroused much more by his mother than is the daughter by her mother.

Furthermore, the mother's heterosexual excitement while nursing her son would presumably be more intense than her sexual fantasies while nursing her daughter. Hence, the more direct transmission of sexual proscriptions by the mother to her daughter are more effectively internalised by the daughter. The boy, however, gets his sexual prohibitions reinforced later by the father, with whom he identifies at the phase of social separation. This coincides with the phase of the rites of passage and the surrogate sacrificial Isaac Syndrome of normative strictness. Consequently, the incestuous proscriptions towards the mother are sublimated through the identification with the father into absolute normative mandates. The mother, however, is still the symbol of normative forgiveness and, as elaborated later, the image of socially participant grace.

It is important to remember that at the oral phase of development, and especially at early orality, the father is present within the mother-child dyad through the vicarious representation by the mother.

The suppression of the father's sexuality, as represented by phallic images transmitted within the mother-daughter dyad, also operates on a basis of identification. Consequently, the incestuous proscriptions are directed towards all the males who are present in the immediate vicinity of the girl, and these naturally belong to the nuclear family. Other rules of extended forbidden mating outside the nuclear family are learned by socialisation and are as basic as those relating to the nuclear family that were ingrained at the oral phase of development. The males of the family present at this oral stage are included in the basic proscriptions of incest. But at the later stages of development, when the maturing girl is exposed to other males who were not present, and hence forbidden, by the post-oral proscription of incest, she would be sexually attracted to them. In like manner, the complementary relationships of the mother and boy result in a proscription of incestuous desire towards all females present physically

136

or symbolically within the family at the oral and post-oral phases of development, but when the boy matures and is exposed to other females outside his family, the oral and post-oral proscription does not apply and they become legitimate objects of his sexual desire.

The close mother-child relationship at orality, the different attitudes of parents towards their neonate boys and girls determined by culture, and the mother's encouraging of her daughter to identify with her and her son to complement her, make for effective dynamics of gender self-concept formation at the oral phase of the infant's development. It has also been noted that mothers display a softer, more feminine attitude towards daughters, whereas from about 7 weeks after birth, they display a harsher, more masculine, attitude towards boys and expect them to be tougher and therefore more independent (Friedman et al., 1974). Therefore the chances are greater that the boy is traumatised, and hence fixated, at early orality. The girl, on the other hand, is more likely to be traumatised by the contrast between the soft feminine attitude of the mother and her identification with her at early orality, and the harsh weaning processes of later orality. In addition, the girl at post-orality is likely to be exposed to the complementarity conflicts with her father, whereas the boy at post-orality is attuned to the less conflictual identification with his father. Also, the harsher and stricter suppression of the boy's sexual arousal by his mother at early orality makes for a greater likelihood of the boy's early oral traumatisation. Consequently, the girl is more likely to be later orally fixated and hence predisposed towards a separant personality core, whereas the boy, fixated at early orality, is more likely to be of a participant predisposition. The implications of this initial dimorphism are, of course, wide and far-reaching, both for personality development and the attitudes and behaviour related to gender identity. This developmental dynamic may be presented as related to sexual dimorphism and personality core in figure 2.

Figure 2. *Sexual Violence*

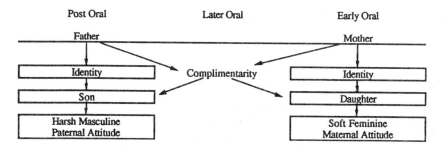

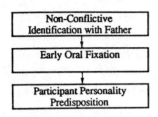

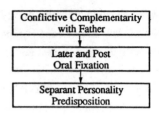

Suppression of the incestuous desires of the child at orality by the mother, serves not only as a means of legitimising the mother-child dyad, it serves also as a condition precedent for the normative acceptance sanctioned by transcendence and social approval of both mother and child.

This suppression purges the mother-son dyad of forbidden incestuous sex, so that the libido of the child is redirected towards approved objects. The deep primary importance of the suppression of the early oral incestous desires of children towards their mothers, as a condition precedent for their normative legitimisation within the family and outside it, may be inferred from the universality of curses, defamation, and swearing that derogate the mother's genitalia. In Arabic, the word *ard* denotes both the female genitals and the honour of the family.

An interim summary of the present premise points to the socio-normative importance of the suppression of incest within the oral mother-child dyad, not merely for the regulation of familial relationships, but also for the creation of a basis for socialisation and acculturation.

The implications of this conclusion are so vast and relate to so many frames of reference, focal interests, and areas of knowledge, that they are beyond the scope of this chapter. However, some attributes of these implications that have a general relevance to the present context are pointed out. The Freudian conception of the formation of the human family, and for that matter, the sustenance of human culture, as masterfully expounded in *Totem* and *Taboo* and other writings, is related to the suppression of the incestuous attraction towards the mother and the normative resolution of the Oedipal conflict with the father. This primal renunciation by the son of his instinctual drives and their sublimation into normatively accepted channels is ordained, directed, and carried out under the terms set out by the father and his abstraction, that is, the law and the normative system. One may have some wild, and at this stage, rather vague conjectures as to how this male chauvinist Freudian system would be affected by the present model, which posits the mother and not the father as the main suppressor of incest at the oral stage. The model thus sees the mother as the

138

prime initiator of human culture. It would be presumptuous to develop this theme more extensively in the present context.

It may be noted in conclusion that sex, or rather its suppression, has been chosen as a means of initiating culture, because of its infinitely wider maleability than the other basic drives. If one is deprived of food one dies, but the deprivation or blockage of some sexual manifestations creates culture. This of course, has been expounded by Freud. The innovation in the present work is that human culture has been initiated by the proscriptions of incest by the mother. Consequently, the mother, the woman, is the prime mover of human culture. She is the one who implants in her children the first seeds of the achievement motive epitomised by the *Yiddishe Mamma*, who emotionally blackmails her son to become a doctor, a lawyer, or a rabbi, and preferably all three simultaneously.

It was noted earlier that women tend to be later orally fixated and hence more separant. This again is developmentally appropriate: in the first year of life, the main problems of the infant relate to the need to learn to adjust to the objective environment and to reach a means of living with it. Consequently, the earlier separant directives of the mother and her instructions for acculturation are geared to the infant's needs. Later on, at the social phase of normative placement, the father introduces his more abstract and more normatively participant acculturation mandates. The mother, as the joke goes, deals with the small matters of culture--the way the children should be fed, dressed, and sheltered, whereas she leaves to her husband the grand issues of culture-- the nature of God, the essence of morality, and whether humans are endowed with free will or spurred by strict determinism.

The male also tends to be more participant biologically, because he is programmed to enter the female and cause his heritage to be absorbed by the female ovum, which biologically swallows the sperm and hence is more separant. The boy is more likely to be early orally fixated and consequently to be more participant as a result, and the girl is more likely to be later orally fixated and to be more separant in her personality core structure. However, this situation involves probabilities and continua so that the biological participant predisposition might be changed in form and intensity, or even set off entirely by a later oral fixation and a separant Sisyphean cultural imprint. On the other hand, the separant predisposition of a girl might be changed by a participant early oral fixation and Tantalic (participant) cultural imprint. (For a full exposition of the separant and participant core personality dynamics and the Sisyphean and Tantalic cultural imprints, see Shoham, 1979: chaps. 1-3).

However, some biological facts and processes linked to sexual dimorphism are related to the predisposing base line of separation and participation. First, males of most animal species take the initiative in courting (Michelmore, 1964), and the whole process of sexual reproduction entails the movement of the sperm towards the relatively stationary ovum, which absorbs it. The sperm's goal of being absorbed by the ovum is therefore biologically participant, whereas the ovum's quest to absorb and swallow the sperm is biologically separant.

Erickson (1951) has stated this premise figuratively as follows: 'Sex differences...seem to parallel the morphology of genital differentiation itself; in the male, an external organ, erectible and intrusive in character, serving the channelisation of mobile sperm cells; internal organs in the female with vestibular access, leading to statically expectant ova' (p. 69). Cultural studies of dreams in tribal societies, as well as some projective investigations and semantic differential analyses of groups in occidental societies, revealed that the self-concepts of males and females are related to the functional attributes of their genitalia (Erickson, 1951:70-71). Males saw themselves as moving and penetrating spaces, which in the present context would mean that they projected their participant aim of entering and being enclosed or absorbed, whereas females saw themselves as stationary and open to absorb, very much in line with the separant swallowing and engulfing nature of the vagina and ovum. The basic separant nature of women has also emerged from studies summarised by Fisher (1973), according to which they tend to feel that they are 'left by love objects who go off 'there' and leave her 'here.' The love object has motility and leaves but she has to stay where she is and therefore, finds herself alone' (p. 71). The separant elements here are that women saw themselves as stationary in relation to the moving objects and that their anxiety was centred on objects leaving them, contrary to their Sisyphean aim to incorporate and control the unruly objects. Other findings show that girls and women seem to be more sure of, more content with, and less anxious about their bodies than boys and men (Pitcher and Prelinger, 1963). This not only disclaims any support for the penis envy that Freud and some of his disciples imputed to women, but also sustains the contention here that woman has a clearer and stronger body image than man because of her later oral separant fixation. Women therefore have a more concrete image of their surrounding objects, which readily contrasts with their clearer image of the boundaries of their bodies. This makes for a more realistic and pragmatic conception of objects and people by the woman than by the early orally fixated, more participant man.

The greater likelihood of boys being early orally fixated has been explained as related to the mother's harsher, more manly treatment, and expectations of her infant son. The male child is therefore more likely to be traumatized at early orality. The mother identifies more with her infant daughter and hence allows her more attachment and proximity with less likelihood of fixation at early orality. The likelihood of a later oral fixation of the infant daughter is greater because the transition from the close identification with the mother to the harsh disengagement of weaning is more traumatising. The basic biological predisposition is thus linked to separation and participation and to the developmental fixations at early and later orality, which makes for the greater likelihood of an abstract, contemplative, idea-and self-anchored male and an object-bound, more actively pragmatic female.

The second biological premise that contributes to greater object-manipulating separatism of the female of the species are her pregnancies, childbirth, and the immediate need to control, arrange, and organise her own and her offspring's proximate environment to ensure shelter, protection, and nourishment to other neonates. This basic biological difference between woman and man, which has the widest of psychological and social implications, forfeits any claim for the equality between the social roles of the sexes by whomever it is made--be it feminists, communists, or the Israeli kibbutz movement. The following is an apt reaction of a Czech woman parachutist when asked about the equality of sex roles in her country:

> Our parachutes are the same as theirs, we jump from the same planes, we've got guts, and our performance isn't much different from the men's, but that's where emancipation ends. I'm married, I'm employed, and I have a daughter. And a granny. If I couldn't say 'granny keep an eye on her' my sporting career would be at an end (Weitz, 1977:210).

There is, therefore, an initially more marked biopsychological separant potential of the female. She is more attuned to the pragmatic manipulation of her objective environment, linked to her child bearing and rearing functions. The male, on the other hand, is more biologically participant, seeking to enter, be engulfed, and be absorbed.

The biopsychological predisposition to gender identity is reinforced and finalised by socialisation, and especially by the interaction of children with their parents. This has been aptly phrased by Diamond (1965) as follows:

> Sexual behaviour of an individual, and thus gender role, are not neutral and without initial direction at birth. Nevertheless, sexual predisposition is only a potentiality, setting limits to a pattern that is greatly modifiable by ontogenetic experiences. Life experiences most likely act to differentiate and direct a flexible sexual disposition and to mold the prenatal organization until an

environmentally, socially and culturally acceptable gender role is formulated and established (p. 147).

As mentioned earlier, the nonverbal empathy and cues by the mother transmitted to the child and the selective reactions of the latter to the mother's cues, constitute a major dynamic for the determination of the child's gender identity. The sex of rearing is therefore the finalising constitutive determinant of gender identity, whereas the biological sex is only a predisposing basis for it.

Mothers are, more often than not, culturally conditioned to treat their female infants in a softer, more affectionate way than their male infants. This presumably anticipates the tougher and manly roles of the male infant in society. The males are therefore trained earlier to distal behaviour, that is, to less proximal attachment to mother, whereas the infant daughter's more proximal attachment to mother is tolerated (Goldberg and Lewis, 1969) and quite often encouraged until the phase of weaning. This again helps to explain not only the greater likelihood of the male infant to be early orally fixated, but also the male's subsequently participant hardship to cope with his objective and human environment. Consequently, the male is bound to be more irritable, frustrated and hence more aggressive towards his environment (Friedman et al., 1974:72). The female infant, on the other hand, has an immediate, direct, empathetic, and identification-based smooth socialisation into the female role by the mother, who is likely to be more separant herself. Consequently, this initial oral socialisation of the daughter by the mother, through a dyadic bond of empathy and identification, is likely even at this early stage to provide the girl with an initial separant predisposition. Moreover, after weaning and the postoral complementarity conflicts with the father, the girl is more likely to experience an object-bound fixation that augments her separant predispositon. This makes for the girl's more Sisyphean anchor on her environment and her ability to manipulate it to provide the basic needs of shelter and subsistence for herself and her offspring. Women are thus more attuned to object relationships, and to other people and 'more finely tuned to make adjustments to stimulus changes' (McClelland, 1964:176).

On the other hand, the male's greater Tantalic predispositon to seek abstractions, ideas, and transcendence through his inner self can be traced to his early oral complementarity-based conflicts with his mother and the fixation related to his traumatic treatment by her in both her assignment of more hardy, manly roles for him and her harsher suppression of his incestuous oral desires. This Tantalic predispositon makes for a more restless seeking of aims, goals, and ideals to which to subjugate himself.

This could be linked later on to the male's greater achievement orientation as well as to his greater adventurousness.

Of special importance are the findings, replicated by many researchers that women are more field dependent, that is, object dependent in their spatio-temporal orientations, whereas men are more field independent, that is, not dependent so much on their objective surroundings for their orientations and decision making. This has been paraphrased by McClelland (1964) as follows: 'Women are concerned with the context, men are forever trying to ignore it for the sake of something they can abstract from it' (p.181). This basic premise is linked to other findings, according to which women are more gregarious and more interested in their objective environment and in other people (McClelland, 1964:176). Women also display a higher verbal proficiency than men (Martin and Voorhees, 1975:55), and it has been shown elsewhere that language is more of a separant than a participant means of communication (Shoham, 1984).

Men, on the other hand, were found to be less concrete, more abstract, and also less adaptable to their environment (Friedman et al., 1974:158). It is of special interest to note that it has been verified empirically that field dependence is linked to the separant Sisyphean predisposition, whereas field independence is one of the characteristics of participant Tantalic types (Shoham et al., 1979). This provides another empirical anchor to the linkage of gender dimorphism to the separant-participant core continuum. The present premise may be summarised by recapitulating that woman is predisposed to be more Sisyphically separant and man more participantly Tantalic on all the three focal levels of biology, personality core and cultural imprints. Parental investment is defined by Trivers (1972) in the following way:

> Any investment by the parent in an individual offspring that increases the offspring's chance of surviving (and hence reproductive success) is at the cost of the parent's ability to invest in other offspring. So defined, parental investment includes the metabolic investment in the primary sex cells and refers to any investment (such as feeding or guarding the young) that benefits the young. It does not include effort expended in finding a member of the opposite sex or in subduing members of one's own sex in order to mate with a member of the opposite sex, since such effort does not affect the survival chances of the resulting offspring and is therefore not 'parental investment' (p. 139).

In most species (except in special cases), including humans, the parental investment of females from the size and number of their sex cells to their subsequent caring for the young, far exceeds the investment of the male. However, in some species males may build nests, brood eggs, and help feed and protect the young. In these species, the customary, more striking display features of the male and his more active courting behaviour is invested in the female (Trivers, 1972: 142-143). The general rule is that the gender that invests less actively, courts and runs after the gender that invests more in its parenthood. The latter, however, holds the prerogative of choosing a mate from the competing individuals of the opposite sex (Trivers, 1972: 173). Consequently, in most species, including humans, males compete for females, and females choose by various overt or covert techniques, their suitable mate. Trivers (1972), however, does not try to explain the deeper dynamics for parental investment and choice of mate. The parental investment premise can perhaps be linked with the core vector dynamics of separation and participation. Trivers points out that the pattern of relative parental investment is strongly linked to differentiation of mobile sex cells fertilising the immobile ones (p. 173). Precisely this differentiation is linked to the polar dynamics of core vectors as expounded earlier in this work. The more mobile and participant male sperm court and seek the immobile ovum to be absorbed by it. Hence, the less investing and more mobile participant male competes with other males for the selection and choice by the less mobile and more investing separant female. A core-programming dimension is thus added to the sociobiological premise of parental investment.

The male is so wasteful in his enormous number of spermatozoa, as compared to the limited number of the female's ova, that this in itself induces the less investing participant male's active search for the more investing separant female. The male thus seeks the adventures of courting, the competition with his peers over the female's favours, and the pleasures of mating, whereas the female is more interested in the attention, care, and protection that her potential mate can provide her and her offspring. This is the common model, but in cases where males have a larger role in nest building and offspring care the roles may be reversed, with females competing for the sexual favours of males (Wilson, 1976: 326). The interesting point, however, is that the male, having invested less in his amatory relationship, is ever tempted to leave the female he has just copulated with and seek a new adventure. The females, women inclusive, tend to be less promiscuous, however, because they look for a more lasting relationship. In some societies, copulation, especially the first one, is so preciously special that the worst sin or crime a virgin may commit is to have premarital sex. In these societies, she virtually forfeits her social positon, her future, and often, her life, along with her hymen. Consequently, females favour monogamy more than males, who are, even if they have to be, only reluctant monogamists. This sociobiological premise may be interpreted to mean that the more separant woman is programmed to seek a more steady relationship with a man on whom she can ever rely for support and protection for herself and her children. Man, on the other hand, is programmed to move and seek immersion into the archetypal mother-woman. Yet, this goal is never achieved, so that after one love affair and after one orgasm, he tends to seek in a tantalic manner more love affairs and different orgasms.

The participant males are more mobile, so that they may court the more stationary females with greater vigour; consequently, the males' metabolism is quicker (Trivers, 1972: 164). Females are not only less mobile, but also less spontaneous in their choice of mates. For the less investing male, the encounter might be just another passing amorous or sexual episode, but for the more investing female, her own and her children's socio-economic welfare is at stake. Of special relevance is the phenomenon of the female mouse aborting when exposed to the smell of a new male (Sadleir, 1967), meaning that a new and more vigorous master of the house has arrived who chased away the previous one, so that the female is ready to be impregnated by the new and obviously more successful mate and raise a family with him. Separant expediency, pragmatism, and quick adaptability is always advantageous for the female of the species, whenever the welfare of her family is concerned.

The separant choice of the female is based on her need for a strong and vigorous, that is genetically healthy, male, who is willing and able to care for her and her offspring. The female thus uses many manipulative devices to test her potential mate's suitability for his roles as familial protector and provider. She develops studied coyness and shyness, which induce the male to court more vigorously and persistently, so that he proves his 'honourable' intentions (Wilson, 1976: 320). For a woman, not to be promiscuous is to safeguard her greater parental investment. The male, on the other hand, does tend to be more promiscuous because of his greater participant mobility and lesser parental investment. This premise might also help explain the fact that most prostitutes are women; their higher parental investment and their greater separant interest in the establishment of a family and the rearing of children render them more reluctant to be promiscuous. Hence, they have to be induced by money and other remunerations to sell their sexual services. This might also be the reason for the stigma attached to prostitution, as women thereby debase their parental investment and act in a manner contrary to their separant core vector, which programmes them for motherhood and family formation. In like manner, rape is condemned and abhorred in part because it violates the possibility of the choice of a mate by the proper socionormative criteria.

Female is the superior gender, and females chase their male mates, who invest less in the perpetuation of the human race and culture. The rapist is therefore the unchosen, the reject, who robs and usurps what he could not achieve by normative avenues. Rape is not an act of power and dominion, but an act of powerless loneliness. Indeed West et al. (1978) report that the feeling of masculine inadequacy and insecurity were very prominent among all the rapists in their study (p.130). Violence in Hebrew אלימות stems from the same root as dumbness, אלם. When a man is pitifully inadequate in wooing, courting, dialogue, romance, and love, he resorts to the violence of rape. The atrocity of rape as conceived here is hence much deeper than presented by Brownmiller and others, because the rapist infringes on the dynamics of normative procreation and the maternal sublimatory bases of creativity and culture. Rapists are punished, not as Brownmiller claims, because they usurped the property of another male, but because they incurred the wrath of others by tarnishing the archetypal graces of woman and trampling over her generative powers of bearing evolutionarily adaptive offspring and spurring them to creativity. The woman's share in the formation of the human family, in the bearing and the rearing of the young, and in the initial propagation of culture is more crucial than the man's. She carries out these duties through a direct use of her sexual attributes, as well as through an intricate, elaborate, and gently balanced dynamic of sublimation. Her stakes in the family, her offspring, and their creative partaking in culture are hence much greater than man's. The rapist is a callous usurper who smashes, through his furtive robbery, the delicate potential of the victim's feminine grace. What he manages to steal is the broken, smashed, and trampled bud of a flower symbolising the sullied pain of the victim and the total waste to himself. This, it would appear, is the main reason why women are overwhelmingly the victims of rape. The thesis presented here may also serve as a predisposing base line for a model of the aetiology of rape. However, the structure of this model is quite elaborate, and in order to facilitate its presentation, the concept of the interdisciplinary aetiological hierarchy must be explained.

The interdisciplinary approach to the study of human behaviour is accepted by us, but random eclecticism is not. Although every manifestation of the human soma and psyche, as well as every human endeavour, is regarded as relevant to the understanding of the aetiology of behaviour, there is a method in our madness. It is, of course, necessary to study the relationship between a number of factors on one level of analysis with a given phenomenon, but as a partial process within a whole and not as an independent process. The overspecialised atomistic fallacy may claim that the genetic code determines sexual behaviour or that a high level of testosterone accounts for aggression in males. The synthetic holistic view, on the other hand, acknowledges the relevance of both genes and hormones, but only within the wider integrative context, which also includes personality parameters and cultural imprints. The core vectors of separation and participation may serve them as a dialectical scaffolding within which the various levels of observation may be integrated.

As we have stated in the introductory chapter, a rather strict determinism of human behaviour, which ranges within a configuration of somatic and environmental factors, is assumed. Four levels of interaction involved in the genesis of human behaviour, including sexual violence, are envisaged. These are the neural, the endocrinological, the personality structure, and the sociocultural imprints.

We have further mentioned in the introduction that the notion of levels is somewhat misleading, because the flow from one level to another is continuous and gradual, not discrete or divided by partitions or barriers. The order of these levels is determined by the hypothetical sequences in which behaviour is elicited. The hypothetical model, which is far from being conclusive or proven, is that impulses or stimuli are received by their nervous system through the senses and they generate arousal and activation of both neurological and neuroendocrinological systems. These impulses are sifted through and processed by the personality parameters of the specific individual; they are finally structured by some of the relevant sociocultural patterns of experience of this individual.

This aetiological hierarchy envisages such a complex configuration of factors inherent in human behaviour, that at any given moment a behaviour pattern of a given individual is bound to be unique. The probability that the configuration of factors within each level and between the four levels would be identical to the corresponding configuration of another person is so remote that it can be assumed to be non-existent.

Moreover, this extreme determinism of regarding human behaviour at a given point as determined by the sum total of a person's experience interacting with a biological potential just prior to this point, excludes the possibility that one pattern of behaviour at a given space-time junction will be identical to any other pattern of behaviour at another place and another time. The relationship between the various levels in generating behaviour is, of course, dynamic. In addition, there is a multiphasic relationship between each level and all the others, every level being linked simultaneously to all the other levels and being fed back by them.

The notion of a behavioural hierarchy tries to point out that for each pattern of behaviour, the relative contribution of each one of the levels is not equal. Yet, the relative preponderance and intensity of each level in the generation of a given pattern of behaviour determines the nature and form of this behaviour. Consequently, if it is possible to grade the relative contribution of each of these four levels to the resultant behaviour, the framework for understanding the contents and form of a given behaviour will be obtained.

However, even if one level might contribute more to the genesis of a given type of behaviour, there is no instance where the contribution of the other levels is totally lacking. The aetiological hierarchy aims to determine the relative preponderance and contribution of each of the various levels in the generation of a given pattern of behaviour, a goal that is quite hypothetical at the present state of our knowledge.

An apt example for the use of an aetiological hierarchy is the development of gender identity as displayed by Money and Ehrhardt (1972) in figure 3.

Figure 3 *Sexual Violence*

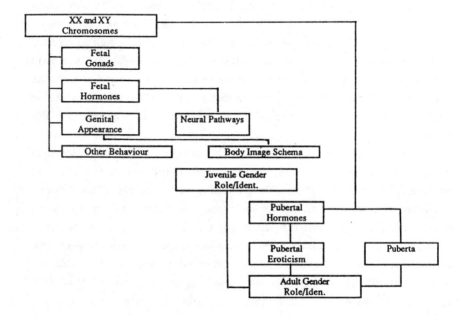

The genetic basis of gender is, of course, determined by chromosomes, but some abnormal karyotypes, such as the XYY, may predispose the 'he-male' to some extreme manifestations of masculinity. So, when given the right social context, he might end up either as a contestant for a Mr. Universe heavyweight wrestling championship or as an inmate in a maximum security prison for repeated violence.

Foetal hormones help fixate the sex so that a disturbance or anomaly at this stage might be related to hermaphroditism and its behaviour correlates later on. After birth, the attitudes of the mother or her surrogate towards the child would very much influence the child's behavioural gender identity. Dressing the boy as a girl, expecting him to behave contrary to his biological gender, and maintaining some skewed and

148

violent symbiotic relationship with the mother (or her surrogate) would predispose a child to transvestism, confusion of gender identity, and homosexuality (Shoham et al., 1978).

It should be stressed that this concept of aetiological hierarchy is related to a continuum ranging from the somatic and interactional, to the sociocultural factors of behaviour. Human behaviour may thus be likened to a play, where the various actors have different parts, some central to the whole play and others consisting of just a few lines or words. Yet each part is essential to the impact of the whole play because the assumption is that superfluous lines or dialogue should never have been included in the first place. And if a certain part is included, it must have--and does have--a necessary function.

It is now possible to turn to the topic and see how the aetiological hierarchy may be applied to the understanding of sexual violence. An appropriate place to start is the biological level, where the evidence is often contradictory and far from conclusive. For instance, no clear link has been established between rape and plasma testosterone level (Rada et al. 1976). However, if it is assumed for didactic purposes that the most violent rapists do exhibit high levels of plasma testosterone, why did personality and cultural factors not prevent the commission of rape, and how did situational factors facilitate it? In other words, if in this case biological factors explained the larger part of the variance, the contribution or lack of it by the other levels of analysis would still have to be accounted for.

As for the personality level, there are the following representative findings: rapists are plagued with doubts about their masculinity and have a sense of masculine inferiority (Halleck, 1971); they have a history of difficulties and problems in their heterosexual relationships; child molesters in particular have deviant sexual fantasies and are deviant in their sexual preferences (Henn et al., 1976); the rapist is less intelligent (Ruff et al., 1976), less aggressive, less independent, less motivated, less assured, less dominant, more needy heterosexually and more introspective (Fisher and Rivlin, 1971). This brings to the fore the contention that the rapist is the miserable misfit who has no chance of being chosen for a mate by the harbinger of grace, growth, and creativity. Hence, he furtively usurps in resentment and desperation the external semblance of a sex act. The rapist might aim to fly, but what he achieves is a pitiful jerk that hardly lifts him off the ground. The rapist's personal insecurity and sexual inadequacy has led Mackellar (1975) to comment that 'the man who rapes does so because he lacks a better means for making the point, 'I am a Man' (p. 67). One may add that the rapist uses the act of rape to shriek out his inadequacies. As has already been pointed out, violence may be related to the capacity for self-expression. The personal inadequacies of the rapist might help explain most of the variance of sexual perverts and lonely rapists. Social factors and facilitating situational factors such as drugs and alcohol might help explain the rest of the variance.

As for the sociocultural level of analysis, there is the macro-sociopolitical factor; in times of war, there is a higher incidence of rape by enemy soldiers, such as the rapes of European women by Soviet troops in World War II, the rapes of Angolan women by Cuban soldiers, and especially the rapes of tens of thousands of women in Bangladesh by invading Pakistani troops (Roy, 1975).

In a comparative study of the rate of rape in Los Angeles and Boston, it was found that the sexually more permissive city (Los Angeles) had higher rape rates (Chappell et al., 1971). In a study of rape among the Gusu of southwestern Kenya, it was found that the higher frequencies of rape were associated with (1) severe formal restrictions on the nonmarital relations of females, (2) moderately strong sexual inhibitions on the part of females, (3) economic or other barriers to marriage that prolong the bachelorhood of males, and (4) absence of physical segregation of the sexes (Levine, 1959). A study of rape in Denmark revealed that rape is more frequent in communities having a male surplus and that rapists are more likely to be from the lower social classes (Svalastoga, 1962).

There was no conclusive evidence as to the link between exposure to pornography and rape, but after the closing of brothels in Queensland, there was a 149 per cent increase in rape and attempted rape (Barber, 1969). These are some of the sociocultural factors that enhance or facilitate the commission of rapes. The claims by one sociologist (Amir, 1971) that 'the sociocultural framework precedes, and to a great extent, determines personality' and that 'understanding rapists' behaviour...implies understanding socialisation processes' are unwarranted. Sociocultural factors of rape combine with biopersonal ones in a configuration of predispositon that changes from one rapist to another. However, the biological, psychological, and social predisposition to rape needs the situational factors in order to erupt and change from a potentiality to an actuality. These are the situational factors of rape that are similar in their mechanism to the situational factors of violence presented elsewhere (Shoham et al., 1970). When the rapist meets his victim, there are some factors that enhance or facilitate the commission of rape and others that may impede or prevent it. Concern here is not with the discredited concept of the victim-precipitated rape, which depicts the victim as an accessory, or even initiator. Rather, our concern is with the accumulation of factors and the interchange of words, gestures, and acts beween rapist and victim that may lead to, or away from, rape. The use of alcohol and drugs has been found in many cases to lower normative controls and facilitate the commission of rape (West et al., 1978:82). Masculinity-proving rituals in stag parties, in dormitories and with some motorcycle gangs are situational states of mind that have facilitated gang rapes. Hitchhiking is also a compromising situational factor that raises the possibility for the commission of rape by a person who is biopersonally and socially predisposed to it.

The victim's behaviour may either enhance or impede the actual commission of rape. If a woman reacts violently to the abuses of her attacker, he might either let her go or be provoked to greater violence towards her. In a similar vein, if the attacked woman belittles her assailant's masculinity he might either be put off or his humiliation might push him to more bitter resentment, rage, and violence even if he is unable to consummate the sexual act. Some rape defence manuals advise victims to induce nausea or distaste in their assailant by the various excretions of their bodies. This might be effective with some rapists, and yet might heighten the excitement or increase the violence of some perverts. The gist of the contention here is therefore, that strategies for the prevention of rape and techniques for the treatment of rapists can be recommended only after a complete investigation of the biological, psychological, and social predispositions to rape and of the manner in which these factors interact in the actual situation of the sexual assault.

References

Amir, M. (1971), 'Forcible Rape', *Sexual Behavior.* Vol.1, No.8, pp. 25-36.

Barber, R.N. (1969), 'Prostitution and the Increasing Number of Convictions for Rape in Queensland', Australian & New Zealand. *Journal of Criminology*, Vol.2, pp.169-74.

Bromberg, W. & E. Coyle (1974), 'Rape: A Compulsion to Destroy', *Medical Insight* (April), Vols.21-22, pp.24-5.

Brownmiller, S. (1975), *Against Our Will: Men, Women and Rape*, New York: Simon and Schuster.

Burgess, A.W. & L.L. Holmstrom (1974), 'The Rapist's View of Rape', *Rape: Victim of Crisis*, Bowie, Md: Brady, pp.21-34.

Chappell, D. & F. Fogarty (1971), 'Forcible Rape', *Review of M. Amir's Patterns of Forcible Rape*, Chicago Law Enforcement Assistance Administration, p.2.

Chappell, D., G. Geis, S. Schafer, & L. Siegel (1971), 'Forcible Rape: A Comparative Study of Offenses Known to Police in Boston and Los Angeles', J.M. Henlin (Ed.), *Studies in the Sociology of Sex*, New York: Appleton, pp.169-90.

Cohen, M.L., R. Garofolo, R. Boulcher & T. Seghorn (1974), 'The Psychology of Rapists', *Seminars in Psychology*, Vol.3, No.3, pp.307-27.

Diamond, M. (1965), 'A Critical Evaluation of the Ontogeny of Human Sexual Behaviour', *Quarterly Review of Biology*, Vol.40, pp.147-75.

Erickson, E. (1956), 'The Problem of Identity', *Journal of the American Psychological Association*, Vol.4, pp.56-121.

Erickson, E.H. (1951), 'Sex Differences in the Play Configuration of Preadolescents', *American Journal of Orthopsychiatry*, Cited in S. Fisher, *The Female Orgasm*, New York: Basic Books, Vol.21, pp. 667-1592.

Fisher, G. & E. Rivlin (1971), 'Psychological Needs of Rapists', *British Journal of Criminology*, Vol.11, pp.182-5.

Fisher, S. (1970), *Body Experience in Fantasy and Behavior*, New York: Appleton-Century-Crofts.

Fisher, S. (1973), *The Female Orgasm*, New York: Basic Books.

Friedman, R., R.M. Richart, R.M.Wiele, & R.L. Vande (Eds.) (1974), *Sex Differences in Behavior*, New York: John Wiley & Son Inc.

Gagnon, J.H. (1977), Review of J.M. MacDonald's 'Rape Offenders and Their Victims', D. Chappell', R. Geis, & G. Geis (Eds.), *Forcible Rape: The Crime, the Victim, and the Offender*, New York: Columbia University Press, pp.12-13.

Gebhard, P.H.(1965), *Sex Offenders: An Analysis of Types*, New York: Harper & Row.

Gibbens, T.C.N., C.Way & K.L. Soothill (1977), 'Behavioural Types of Rape', *British Journal of Psychiatry*, Vol.130, pp.32-42.

Goldberg, S.& M. Lewis (1969), 'Play Behavior in the Year-Old Infant: Early Sex Differences', *Child Development*, Vol.40, pp.21-31.

Halleck S.L. (1971), *Psychiatry and the Dilemmas of Crime*, Los Angeles: University of California Press.

Henn F.A., M. Herjanic & R. H. Vaderpearl (1976), 'Forensic Psychiatry: Profiles of Two Types of Sex Offenders', *American Journal of Sex Offenders*, pp. 694-696.

Mackellar, J. (1975), *Rape! The Bait and the Trap*, New York: Crown Books.

Martin, M.K. & B. Voorhies (1975), *Female of the Species*, New York: Columbia University Press.

McClelland, D.C. (1964), 'Wanted: A New Self Image for Women', R.J. Lifton (Ed.), *The Women in America*, Boston: Houghton-Mifflin.

Michelmore, S. (1964). *Sexual Reproduction*, New York: Natural History Press.

Money, J. & A.A. Ehrhardt (1972), *Man and Woman, Boy and Girl*, Baltimore, Md: Johns Hopkins University Press.

Pitcher, E.G. & E.Prelinger (1972), *Children Tell Stories - An Analysis of Fantasy*, New York: International University Press.

Rada, R.T., D.R. Laws & R. Kellner (1976), 'Plasma Testosterone Levels in the Rapist'. *Psychosomatic Medicine*, Vol.38, No.4, pp.257-68.

Roy, K.K. (1975), 'Feelings and Attitudes of Raped Women of Bangladesh Toward Military Personnel of Pakistan', E. Viano (Ed.),*Victimology: A New Focus,* (Vol. 5), Lexington, Mass: Lexington Books, pp. 65-72.

Ruff, C.R., D.L. Templer & J.L. Ayers (1976), 'The Intelligence of Rapists', *Archives of Sexual Behavior*, Vol.5, No.4, pp.327-9.

Sadleir, R. (1967), *The Ecology of Reproduction in Wild and Domestic Mammals*, London: Methuen.

Shoham, S.G. (1983), *Eve, Casanova, and Don Juan: Love as Bait,* St. Lucia: Queensland University Press.

Shoham, S.G.(1979), *The Myth of Tantalus*, St. Lucia: Queensland University Press.

Shoham, S.G. (1984), *The Violence of Silence: The Impossibility of Dialogue*, London: Science Review Ltd.

Shoham, S.G., R. Banitt, S. Katznelson & S. Streit (1970), 'The Situational Aspects of Violence', S. Shoham (Ed.), *Israel Studies in Criminology*, Tel-Aviv: Gameh, pp. 242-58.

Shoham S.G., Y. Esformes, G.Rahav, R. Markovsky, N. Kaplinsky & B. Wolf (1980), 'Separant and Participant Personality Types of Suicides', *The Irish Jurist*, Vol.15, pp.99-110.

Shoham, S.G., G. Rahav & L. Guttman (1970), 'A Two Dimensional Space for Classifying Legal Offences', *Israel Studies in Criminology*, Vol. 1, pp.36-76.

Shoham, S.G., L. Weissbod, B. Gruber & Y.Stein (1978), 'Personality Core Dynamics and Predisposition Towards Homosexuality', *British Journal of Medical Psychology*, Vol. 51, pp.161-75.

Svalastoga, K. (1962), 'Rape and Social Structure', *Pacific Sociological Review*, Vol. 5, No.1, pp.48-53.

Trivers, R.L. (1972), 'Parental Investment and Selection', B. Campbell, (Ed.),*Sexual Selection and the Descent of Man, 1871-1971*, Chicago: Aldine, p.160.

Weitz, S. (1977), *Sex Roles*, New York: Oxford University Press.

West, D.J., C. Ray & F.L. Nichols (1978), *Understanding Sexual Attacks*, London: Heinemann.

10 Violent Drivers

The violent, the vain, the reckless, the vile, the impertinent and the bullies are ordained by scripture that the arms of the wicked shall be broken.

Derekh Eretz B.

INTRODUCTION

In this chapter, we shall present personality profiles of two types of recidivist traffic offenders. One is the 'anxious' traffic offender who imputes legitimacy to traffic norms, yet due to innate structural personality defects, he tends to enter into a state of anxiety when confronted with risky traffic situations or a traffic jam. The other type is the 'reckless' driver, who does not impute legitimacy to traffic norms, nor to other legal norms. From this personality theory, a number of hypotheses were derived and tested by means of multiple regression. Our ability to predict the number of traffic offences suggests that similar tools may be used by the traffic authorities and traffic courts.

As early as 1919, it was claimed by Greenwood and Wood (Shinar, 1978:30) that some people are more likely to cause road accidents than others. This propensity (accident-proneness) was studied by MacGier (Shinar, 1978:32).

Previously, we reported (Shoham et al., 1975,1976,1977) a number of variables were found to characterise traffic offenders. The main hypothesis posited in our previous research was that accident-proneness is not a characteristic of a certain personality type, but rather the behavioural expression of two different personality types. In the present research, we continued to investigate the previously mentioned variables, as well as additional factors--our aim being to establish such an optimal combination of variables as will enable the prediction of a certain driver's likelihood to get involved in an accident. The variables chosen for this study were those found, in earlier studies, to be related to traffic offences, as well as additional variables assumed to be of importance.

Our purpose was to find a combination of personality variables that would predict a given driver's proneness to traffic offences. We expect to find two types of traffic offenders with different profiles of the investigated variables. The variables studied in the past were as follows:

Anxiety - It is commonly accepted today that a person's anxiety level at a particular moment is affected by two components, (1) personality characteristics and (2) situational factors. We have tried to deal with the common product of these two, namely the anxiety aroused in subjects in driving situations. It was hypothesised (Shoham et al., 1977) that there is a non-linear relationship between one's level of anxiety and one's tendency towards involvement in traffic accidents and offences.

Internalisation of norms - This refers to the driver's attitude towards legally binding traffic norms. We differentiate between levels of internalisation, where at the highest level (moral orientation), the driver accepts the norms as obligatory commands, and at the lowest (sanction orientation), he will avoid offences only as long as he sees himself in danger of punishment. Our previous findings validated the existence of such a continuum of internalisation.

Risk taking - Specifically, the driver's willingness to take risks when driving.

Learning ability - We mean here the ability to learn a new mode of behaviour and at the same time to reject a previous one. Eysenck (1977:130) sees this distinction of 'conditionability' as the key to understanding a person's tendency towards conformity or non-conformity in every field. This characteristic is measured by the stepping-stone-maze test. This tool is used in measuring the learning abilities of brain-damaged people whose mental abilities are unimpaired, except for their ability to learn new behaviour.

The following are the additional variables assumed to be related to traffic offences:

Sensation seeking -Sensation seeking was studied by Zuckerman (1972:308-321), who saw it as a basic personality characteristic. The theoretical claim is that a person hungry for sensation will need many powerful stimuli in order to function optimally. Such a person, we assume, will not be easily conditioned and will therefore have difficulty internalising norms - which will, in turn, increase his tendency to break the law. The two personality types described in our previous research as highly accident-prone will be situated at the two extremes of this variable: either very low or very high.

Criminal offences -Usually, a distinction is made between traffic offences and other offences, assuming that traffic-law breaking has its own causes. In this research, we decided to ignore this distinction and use the subject's general criminal involvement as an independent variable.

In our preceding research, it became evident that a positive correlation existed between anxiety and the internalisation of traffic norms and that a negative correlation existed between internalisation of these norms and risk taking. This means that the deeper a person internalises traffic norms, the greater his anxiety about committing traffic offences. And the more a person internalises traffic norms, the less he is willing to take risks when driving. From these studies, it emerged that 33 per cent of all offenders were responsible for 53 per cent of the offences investigated, and the punishments imposed were by no means a deterrent factor (Shoham et al., 1976). This raised the hypothesis that there are two types of accident- and offence-prone drivers: the 'reckless' and the 'anxious' drivers.

1. The 'reckless' driver is characterised by a low level of learning ability, combined with high sensation seeking, low anxiety and high risk-taking levels. We hypothesise, following Cherno (1971), who found that psychopaths had a low ability for avoidance-learning, and Eysenck (1977: 130-32), that drivers who commit a greater number of offences have psychopathic personality tendencies. These tendencies will only allow a superficial internalisation of traffic norms (sanction orientation). If this hypothesis is correct, then these drivers suffer from sub-arousal, so that the threat of severe punishment is not liable to deter them, rather the opposite--it will raise their desired feeling of tension. This type is, presumably, the type that was first identified as a traffic offender with antisocial tendencies (Shinar, 1978: #65). The personality traits of this type make him liable for offences of many types, not only traffic offences (Eysenck, 1977: #130-32). Research comparing the involvement in road accidents of criminal offenders with a non-criminal population (Hariland and Wiessman, 1974, in Shinar, 1978: #32) showed that the involvement of the criminals was 3.25 times higher (and 19.5 times higher for fatal accidents!). In similar research on a smaller scale, Stein (1977) found, in Israel, a tendency for traffic offenders to have more criminal records than other drivers.

2. The second type of accident-prone driver is the 'anxious' one. He is characterised by high learning and conditioning abilities, and therefore by a low impulsivity level. His internalisation of norms is high, which will increase his anxiety when driving. His tendency for sensation seeking is low and he will therefore not take unnecessary risks. According to our hypothesis, this type will suffer from more strain and stress while driving. Previous researchers (MacMurray, 1970: in Shinar, 1978: #35) showed that these states of pressure increase his accident-proneness. Table 1 describes the two extreme accident-prone types:

Table 1.

Variable	'Reckless' drivers	'Anxious' drivers
Driving anxiety	low	high
Risk-taking when driving	high	low
Internalisation of norms	low	high
	(sanction orientation)	(moral orientation)
Conditioning ability	low	high
Impulsivity	high	low
Sensation seeking	high	low

A previous research paper on this subject examined two groups of traffic offenders (Shoham et al., 1974). One group consisted of 'reckless' drivers, characterised by sanction-orientation towards traffic norms, risk-taking tendencies, superficial internalisation of traffic norms and a low anxiety level. The second group included the 'anxious' drivers, characterised by high internalisation of traffic norms and a high anxiety level. The latter were found to have lower bio-psychogenic control over the basic mechanisms required for driving. Also, one should point out the significant negative correlation between internalisation of traffic norms and the tendency toward risk-taking found by Shoham in previous research (Shoham et al., 1977). As traffic norms are more deeply internalised (moral orientation), the desire for risk-taking decreased and vice versa--with the increase of sanction orientation towards traffic norms, the willingness for risk-taking increased and with it the readiness to break the law. In the present research, a correlation was found between high internalisation of traffic norms and anxiety. A driver who had internalised traffic norms more deeply showed signs of greater anxiety when driving. The extremely anxious driver accepts the normative system of traffic laws as the legitimate system and will generally be a law-abiding citizen in all fields, including traffic. This anxious driver is apt to mix emotions with his decisions and will become anxious in situations where he should decide quickly and almost instinctively. These conflicting pressures may produce in this driver an approach-avoidance conflict, resulting in confusion and loss of control, increasing his accident-proneness.

In summary, our research shows significant correlation between the above independent variables and traffic offences in general. A multiple regression analysis supported the hypothesis of two types of accident-prone drivers: the 'reckless' and the 'anxious', who have the traits we have outlined above. It must be mentioned that the present research is not only theoretical, but also has some practical implications. It can be used in predicting the 'criminality potential' of drivers in an effort to reduce the number of serious traffic offences and road accidents.

METHODOLOGY

Sample

Two groups of drivers were chosen, in order to increase the variance of the dependent variables. The first group consisted of 700 drivers who had been requested to participate in courses for corrective driving--that is, drivers who had committed a comparatively high number of offences of a relatively serious nature. Some of the drivers refused to fill out the questionnaires, or gave incomplete answers, so that the final sample comprised only 492 drivers.

The second group consisted of drivers who, to the best of our knowledge (or to that of their superiors), have never been requested to participate in a course for corrective driving. This group consisted of bus drivers whose clean records were vouched for by their company secretariat, drivers of a large industrial plant, volunteer drivers for the Association for Prevention of Accidents and student drivers. All the drivers were men, mostly adults (only 5.5 per cent were under the age of 20 and 36 per cent were aged 50 and over).

Measurement

Subjects were requested to fill out the following questionnaires:

1. A questionnaire of demographic details and other facts about themselves and their driving habits.
2. A questionnaire on internalisation of traffic norms. This questionnaire was constructed and validated in the previous stages of this research.
3. A questionnaire on risk-taking intended to examine the tendency for risk-taking when driving. This questionnaire was also constructed and validated by the authors (Shoham et al., 1976:142).
4. Gibson's Spiral Maze, which consists of a maze with a spiral shape, in which there are a number of dots representing obstacles. The subject has to draw a line from the center of the maze, finding his way out around the obstacles. This maze is intended to measure impulsiveness as opposed to self-control.
5. The Taylor Anxiety Scale, which measures psychosomatic signs of anxiety and for the purposes of this research, was adapted to a driving situation.
6. Zuckerman's Sensation Seeking Scale, which measures the need for sensory stimulation as against repulsion.
7. Barrat's Impulsivity Scale, which has three subscales: 'I am', 'I do', and 'I like', and measures the subject's tendency towards impulsive behaviour.

The tests were given to most of the subjects in groups that participated in courses for corrective driving and were completed at the site of the course. The bus drivers were summoned in groups of 10-20 over a period of about three months. The volunteer drivers completed the questionnaires at meetings held by the Association for Prevention of Accidents all over Israel, also in groups of 10-20. The students completed the questionnaires in the classrooms. In all cases, the questionnaires were administered in one session and in a constant sequence.

Also investigated were the number of traffic and other offences registered in the criminal register of the Israeli police. These data were examined only for drivers of the 'offenders' group, since only for this group was there information available that enabled us to obtain criminal records, if only in 196 cases. For the remaining cases it was impossible to identify the drivers' records with certainty.

FINDINGS

The technique used in the analysis of these data was mainly a series of multiple regression analyses. Table 2 presents the most important of these analyses. Examination of this table shows a distinct influence of the psychological variables examined (with the exception of risk taking) on the number of driving offences. Impulsiveness (as measured by the Barrat Scale and the Gibson Spiral Maze), internalisation of norms, anxiety and sensation seeking are all correlated with the tendency toward involvement in traffic offences. As for the theoretical model underlying this research, it is of special importance that in addition to their linear influence, these variables have a particularly strong effect when considering the statistical interaction between them.

The second column of table 2 presents the regression for prediction of traffic offences derived from the psychological variables, age and the criminal records of the driver. The multiple regression thus presented is not high (0.39) and none of the tests is of major statistical significance. However, when the interactions between the psychological variables (column 4) are added to these variables, the picture changes: the multiple regression coefficient rises to 0.65 and thus explains 42 per cent of the variance of the dependent variable. All the psychological variables examined (with the exception of risk taking) attained statistical significance in this formula. This proves to us the utmost importance of statistical interactions, such as the importance of a person scoring high on both internalisation of norms and anxiety, or high on sensation seeking and low on internalisation of norms. Theoretically, these interactions indicate the opposing types defined in the hypotheses.

The last two independent variables (anxiety and sensation seeking) have a similar theoretical significance. These variables are simply the squared value of the anxiety score and the squared value of the sensation seeking score. The presence of a squared element in the equation points to the fact that the correlation between anxiety and sensation seeking and the number of offences is not a linear one, but a curvilinear one.

Table 2. *Standard regression coefficients* (β) *for prediction of traffic offences*

Independent Variable	1	2	3	4
Age	0.06	0.07		
Body Offences	0.11	0.12*		0.10*
Property Offences	0.22*	0.21*		0.26*
Other Offences	0.15*	0.15*		0.03
Taylor's Anxiety Scale		-0.04	4.52*	-4.56
Gibson's Maze		-0.01	-0.10	0.11*
I like		-0.03	-2.89*	-3.19*
I am		-0.10	0.20*	0.17*
I do		0.03	1.20*	-1.21*
Risk Taking			0.03	0.04
Internalisation		-0.07	4.31*	4.65*
SSS		-0.05	1.67*	0.78*
SSS x Internalisation			0.18*	0.16*
Taylor x Internalisation			5.542*	5.61*
I like x Internalisation			3.48*	3.91*
Taylor x I like x I do			-0.56*	-0.52*
Taylor x I do x Intern			-2.26*	-2.17*
Taylor			1.49*	1.34*
SSS^2			1.60*	-0.76*
R	0.36	0.39	0.59	0.65
R^2	0.13	0.15	0.35	0.42

*$p<0.5$

Another interesting finding is the significance of criminal offences for prediction of traffic offences. Column 1 shows that from age and criminal offences alone, one can reach a prediction with a multiple regression coefficent of 0.36. The criminal offences are significant even after the psychological data of the offenders are controlled. Comparison of columns 3 (prediction using only the psychological variables) and 4 (psychological variables and offences) shows that the addition of the criminal offence data raised the multiple correlation coefficient from 0.59 to 0.65, which in turn, raised the percentage of explained variance from 35 per cent to 42 per cent.

These findings should, however, be considered with certain reservations. First, the criminal offences data were obtained only for 196 of the cases, and it is possible that this biases the sample significantly. Second, we assumed that the 'clean' drivers had no offences whatsoever. This assumption is probably inaccurate and artificially increases the variance of the dependent variable, which may increase the regression coefficients. Finally, it should be noted that two (2) of the equations presented in table 2 (columns 1, 2) produced very low regression coefficents and explain only 13 per cent and 15 per cent of the variance.

DISCUSSION

The findings of the present study, together with those of earlier studies, are consistent with the hypothesis of the existence of two types of traffic offenders, that is, two distinct combinations of personality traits which predict the proneness of drivers to traffic offences. The relevant variables (traits) are found in traffic offenders in certain statistical interactions. Consequently, linear combinations of variables (such as anxiety and sensation seeking) do not allow effective prediction of traffic offences. Rather, the proneness to traffic offences is a function of certain unique combinations formed by the variables.

On the basis of these findings, we will now turn to the two types of traffic offenders, the 'anxious' and 'reckless' drivers. A fair description of what happens on the road could be as follows: The driver who is anxious by nature and at the same time has a high level of internalisation of traffic norms, is likely to get trapped in a positive feedback cycle in which anxiety leads to confusion and a drop in activity due to the high internalisation of norms, which, in turn, will increase high anxiety about the possiblity of committing an offence. In this situation, the driver will become disorientated and will commit a traffic offence or cause an accident, through loss of control over himself and the car.

Impulsiveness also raises the likelihood of this kind of positive feedback mechanism, since it prevents the driver from overcoming his confusions. The result is a traffic offence or accident. Of special interest is the finding that each of the parameters can induce traffic offences.

As for the second type of traffic offender, the 'reckless' driver, we obtained a finding that is not only theoretically important but is also immediately applicable, namely that potential traffic offenders also tend to be potential criminal offenders in general. This means that we are able to predict potential traffic offences through detection of other criminal offences. This type of traffic offender shows low internalisation of traffic norms and a low anxiety level. He also shows, however, impulsiveness. Here we have the typical 'king of the road' syndrome - the driver who not only scorns all traffic laws but also the law itself. The important point here is that there is no pertinent correlation between traffic offences and violent offences. This syndrome expresses behaviour defying the legitimacy of the law in general and not of any particular norms.

It is also worth mentioning that in our previous research (Shoham et al., 1977), we proposed a similarity between the personality-attitudinal background of the 'reckless' traffic offender and the common criminal offender. Stein, in his research comparing traffic and criminal offenders, arrived at similar conclusions and did not find any significant differences between the two (Stein, 1977; see also Willett, 1964).

It should be stressed that from our findings, it appears that the impulsiveness found in both the 'anxious' drivers and the 'kings of the road' type has in itself no predictive value. Its value is in the interaction between impulsiveness and other variables and here, in different ways, we find that impulsiveness could be the cause for both 'anxious' traffic offences and 'reckless' ones.

The simplest predictive equation for the number of traffic offences is (traffic offences) = 1.474 - 0.002 (sensation seeking) - 0.0003 (internalisation of anxiety) + 0.3 ('I am') + 1.893 (property offences) + 1.684 (body offences) + 1.745 (other offences).

This formula is very easy to use, since it is based mainly on the subject's criminal record. However, table 3 below, presenting details of the regression analysis, shows that this formula explains only 14 per cent of the variance. Therefore, what was said before must be treated with great care--as only a first step towards a more exact examination of each case of any specific traffic offender on trial or under interrogation by the licensing authorities.

Table 3. *Regression analysis for the prediction of the number of traffic offences*

Variable	Regression Coefficient	B	P<
Sensation seeking	-0.0020	-0.03	0.65
Internalisation of anxiety	-0.0003	-0.03	0.60
'I am'	-0.3255	0.09	0.09
Property offences	1.8932	0.21	0.001
Body offences	1.6836	0.12	0.040
Other offences	1.7452	0.15	0.015
Constant	1.4741		

Table 3. (continued)

R^2	0.136

On the basis of the above findings and the prediction formula, it can be said that people with criminal records tend to break traffic laws more often than others. Hence, we would propose that the licensing and law-enforcing authorities take into consideration that certain traffic offenders also may have criminal records. We are fully aware of the many legal and ethical implications that this proposition will have, such as violation of privacy and problems of accessibility to previous records by the traffic authorities. But this may be unavoidable if we wish to create an efficient mechanism for the prediction of traffic offences, in an effort to effectively reduce the number of traffic offences and road accidents. The present research will, then, enable us to employ a fairly simple prediction system for the assessment of the risk involved in licensing a person to drive. This merely requires the testing of subjects by three brief questionnaires: the Taylor Anxiety Scale, specially translated and adapted for this research; the scale of internalisation of traffic norms; and two sub-scales of the Barrat Scale. Once again, questions will be raised as to if and where these scales should be used. Should the judge be supplied with this information in court, or should they be practically applied in the various licensing stages, or perhaps even at the stage when recidivist drivers attend courses for corrective driving? These are all questions the legislative, law enforcement and licensing authorities will have to consider.

References

Barrat, E.S. (1959), 'Anxiety and Impulsiveness Related to Psychomotor Efficiency', *Perceptual and Motor Skills*, Vol.4, pp.191-8.

Barrat, G.V., C.L. Thornton & P.A.Cabe (1969), 'Relation Between Embedded Figures Test Performance and Simulator Behaviour', *Journal of Applied Psychology*, Vol.53, pp.253-4.

Cherno, F.A. (1971), *Avoidance Learning Among Sociopathic, Normal and Neurotic Prisoners under Varied Conditions of Sensory Input*, Unpublished Doctoral thesis, University of Georgia.

Eysenck, H.J. (1977), *Crime and Personality (2nd Ed.)*, London: Routledge & Kegan Paul, pp. 130-132.

Gibson, H.B. (1961), *Manual of the Gibson Spiral Maze (2nd Ed.)*, Dunton Green, Kent, Britain: Hodder and Stoughton.

Shinar, D. (1978), *Psychology on the Road: The Human Factor in Traffic Safety*, New York: John Wiley & Son Inc.

Shoham, S.G., N. Geva, R. Markovski & N. Kaplinsky (1974), *Relationship Between Traffic Offences, Anxiety, Risk-Taking and Internalisation of Traffic Norms*, Tel Aviv University. Report to the Ministry of Transportation.

Shoham, S.G., N. Geva, R. Markovski & N. Kaplinsky (1976), 'Internalisation of Norms, Risk-Perception and Anxiety as Related to Driving Offences', *The British Journal of Criminology* , Vol.16, pp.142-55.

Shoham, S.G., G. Rahav, J. Blau, N. Kaplinsky, R. Markovski, Y. Shaked, Y. Stein, L. Weissbrod & B. Wolf (1977), *The Reckless and Anxious Drivers: Some Initial Parameters,* Tel Aviv University. Report to the Ministry of Transportation.

Stein, I. (1977), *Traffic Offenders and Criminal Offenders,* Unpublished Master's Thesis. Tel Aviv University: Faculty of Law.

Willett, T.C. (1964), *Criminals on the Road: A Study of Serious Motoring Offences and Those Who Commit Them,* London: Tavistock.

Zuckerman, M., A.N.Bone, R. Neary, D. Mangelsdorff, & B. Brustman (1972), 'What is the Sensation Seeker? Personality Trait and Experience Correlates of the Sensation Seeking Scales', *Journal of Consulting Psychology,* Vol.39, pp.308-21.

11 Inner Directed Violence

If I had been able to commit suicide and then see their (the friends') reaction, why, then the game would have been worth the candle. But the earth is dark, cher ami, the coffin thick and the shroud opaque.

Albert Camus, *The Fall*

INTRODUCTION

At the risk of being repetitious, we shall again recapitulate here the main outline of our personality theory. It would be superfluous to review in a research paper the various theories of suicide. Yet, we cannot possibly present our theory and its initial empirical anchors without mentioning some of the classic theories of suicide, which could be related, and more often contrasted, with our present approach.

However, before comparing our premises with those of others, we shall present the gist of our own theoretical expositions. Our main hypotheses in this chapter are based on some core personality parameters which we have presented elsewhere (Shoham, 1979). These core vectors were denoted by us as participation and separation. By participation we mean the identification of ego with a person(s), an object, or a symbolic construct outside oneself, and one's striving to lose one's separate identity by fusion with this other object or symbol. Separation, of course, is the opposite vector. We have used these opposing vectors of unification-fusion and separation-isolation as the main axis of our theory in conjunction with three major developmental phases. The first is the process of birth. The second is the crystallisation of an individual ego by the moulding of the 'ego boundary'. The third phase of separation is a corollary of socialisation when one reaches one's 'ego identity' (Erikson, 1956). The strain to overcome the separating and dividing pressures never leaves the human individual.

The striving to partake in a pantheistic whole is ever present and it takes many forms: if one avenue towards its realisation is blocked, it surges out from another channel. Actual participation is unattainable by definition. The objective impossibility of participation is augmented by the countering separating vectors, both instinctual and interactive. At any given moment of our lives there would be a disjuncture, a gap between our desires for participation and our subjectively defined distance from our participatory aims. We have denoted this gap the Tantalus Ratio, which is the relationship between the longed for participatory goal and the distance from it as perceived by ego (Shoham, 1979). These core vectors are related to the fixation of the separant and participant personality types. These in turn are related to the crystallisation at later orality of a separate self out of the pantheistic mass of totality at early orality. This is the ontological baseline by which the self is defined by the nonself, that is the object. The coagulation of the self marks the cuttting-off point for the most basic developmental dichotomy; from birth and early orality to the phase where the ego boundary is formed around the emerging individual separatum and from later orality onwards. In the first phase, any fixation that might happen, and imprint thereby, some character traits on the developing personality, is not registered by a separate self which is capable of discerning between the objects which are the source of the fixation-causing trauma and himself as its recipient. The experiencing entity at this stage is a non-differentiated pantheistic totality. On the other hand, if the traumatising fixation happens at the later oral phase after the objects have expelled the self from their togetherness by a depriving interaction with it, the self may well be in a position to attribute the cause of pain and deprivation to its proper source, i.e. the objects. We have proposed, therefore, a personality typology which is anchored on this developmental dichotomy of pre-and post-differentiation of the self (Shoham, 1979). The moulding process is the nature and severity of fixation which determines in turn, the placement of a given individual on the personality type continuum. However, the types themselves are fixated by developmental chronology: the *participant* at pre-differentiated early orality and the *separant* after the formation of the separate self. The participant core personality vector operates, however, with varying degrees of potency on both these personality types; but the quest for congruity manifests itself differently with each polar personality type. The participant aims to achieve congruity by defacing and annihilating himself, melting back, as it were, into the object, achieving thereby the pantheistic togetherness and non-differentiation of early orality.

The separant type aims to achieve congruity by overpowering or 'swallowing' the object. We have denoted the congruity aims of the self defacing participant as *exclusion*, whereas the object devouring separant wishes to achieve congruity by *inclusion*, that is incorporating the object in his outreaching self.

The parameters by which the participant and separant personality types are defined, are presented in the following chart:

PERSONALITY
Types, Dimensions and Traits

Separant		*Participant*
	Interactive Dimension	
Activist		*Quietist*
Stimulus Hunger		Stimulus Aversion
High vulnerability to		Low vulnerability to
sensory deprivation		sensory deprivation
Low sensitivity to pain		High sensitivity to pain
Reducer		Augmenter
	Ontological Dimension	
Object-inclusion		*Self*-exclusion
Group performer		Isolate performer
Field dependence		Field independence
Intolerant of objective ambiguity		Tolerant of objective ambiguity
Tolerant of ideational ambiguity		Intolerant of ideational ambiguity
	Normative Dimension	
Outwardly aggressive		*Inner Castigation*
Extrapunitve		Intropunitive
Sanction Orientation		Moral Orientation
High Risk Taker		Low Risk Taker
'Other-directed'		'Inner-directed'
Conformist		Non-conformist

The 'stimulus seeking' of the separant and the 'stimulus aversion' of the participant may be related to the ingenious experiments of Petrie. She found that introverts tended to subjectively increase the size of the stimuli (augmenters), whereas extraverts decreased it (reducers).   This, of course, is related to the 'stimulus hunger' of the extravert-reducers and the stimulus aversion of the introvert augmenters. She also re-established that augmenters (our participants) were more tolerant of sensory deprivation and naturally less tolerant of pain (Petrie, Collins and Solomon, 1960; Petrie, 1967). We are well aware that we are substituting Eysenck's introvert and extravert by our participant and separant, but we are concerned here with only two character traits, i.e. activity and excitability of the five which comprise his types. These two apply to our typology, whereas the others may not. We, therefore, thought it more appropriate to use our terminology instead of Eysenck's, which may cover more conceptual ground than we need.

The research findings we have surveyed provide an empirical anchor to the activity-quietist or the 'interactive' dimension of our typology. We shall proceed now to link some pertinent findings to our ontological dimension, which is the 'object-inclusion' of the separant and the 'self-exclusion' of the participant. We may recall that the separant aims at 'devouring' the object and incorporating it into himself, whereas the participant wishes to exclude, isolate himself and melt back into the object or the non-objective pre-awareness. Colquhoun and Corcoran have demonstrated that extraverts are better in groups (Colquhoun and Corcoran, 1964). Furneaux states 'it is entirely consistent with the known characteristics of the extravert to assert that he has a strong and continuing set (2) to attend to stimuli associated with the activities of other people, and that the situations which lead him to enter states of high drive are predominantly interpersonal in character' (Eysenck, 1967). This better performance of the extravert in group situations has been related to his stimulus hunger (Eysenck, 1967). We, however, hold that the higher motivation and drive in an interpersonal situation reported by Furneaux shows the dependence of the extravert-separant on the togetherness of the group. He functions better not *vis-à-vis* the others but *amidst* the others, within them and through them. The others thus serve as the necessary medium for the better performance of the separant because those others-objects are vital catalysers and as such, necessary components of his personality structure. Of even greater significance to our present premise are the findings which may allow us to link the separant (extravert) to a higher 'field dependence' than the participant (introvert), who would tend to be 'field independent'. These two concepts, as well as Witkin's *et al.* later studies on 'psychological differentiation', relate to the object, setting and environmental perception while performing a task. The 'field dependent' displays a low psychological differentiation because he is dependent in his performance on cues stemming from the overall gestalt and the background set of the situation. In other words, performance here is dependent on the configuration of the surrounding objects. On the other hand, the 'field independent' and the one who displays higher psychological differentiation relies on his own cognitive cues and not on the outward gestalt of the objects (Witkin et al., 1962).

It should be pointed out that Cohen and Silverman found that the field dependent, which like our separant is object dependent, was more vulnerable to sensory deprivation (Cohen and Silverman, 1963), which again is a major characteristic of the separant (extravert). As might have been expected, the separant's 'hunger' for stimuli made him less vulnerable to pain and more field-that is object-dependent.

We shall add here another trait for which we have not found, as yet, empirical evidence: we hypothesise that the separant is intolerant of objective ambiguity. He would grasp things, and situations which are clearly defined with boundaries. On the other hand, the participant would be tolerant of ambiguities relating to objects but he requires clear-cut abstractions. The objective haziness serves his quietist and mystical inclinations but he is intolerant of any ideational ambiguities which may blur his concern with unity and the ultimate reality beyond objective appearances.

The third normative dimension of our typology deals with the self-object relationships. We may recall that the participant type which has been fixated at non-differentiated early orality, tends to be a depressive 'bad me' surrounded by a good object, whereas the separant 'good me' is the outwardly aggressive 'good me' surrounded by a depriving object. Consequently, the participant would be 'intropunitive', the guilt-ridden self-blamer, whereas the separant would tend to be an 'extrapunitive' blamer of others. We shall proceed to enumerate some traits which we hypothesise as related to our present dimension, although no empirical evidence has been found as yet in support of this hypothesis. We hold that the participant tending to blame himself and consequently more ready to legitimise norms would be 'morally oriented', that is, he is internally controlled by the deeply internalised norms so that external repressive sanctions are unnecessary to secure compliance. Our hypothesis is based on Rommetveit's theory on the internalisation of social norms (see Thibaut, and Kelly 1959) and it differs from such expositions as Rotter's internal vs. external loci of normative control. Rotter imputes to his 'internal controller' a belief in his ability to manipulate the external world as well as to change the political system by involvement in social affairs (Rotter *et al.*, 1962). This characterises not our participant, but the diametrically opposite separant type. The latter would tend to be sanction oriented (Thibaut and Kelly, 1959), being outwardly aggressive, he would not tend to legitimise norms but would comply with them for fear of sanction only. Consequently, the separant would be a higher risk-taker than the participant as the separant tends to manipulate objects and operate through others. He tends to be other-directed as described by Riesman (Riesman, 1950). The other-directed has his normative antennae ever attuned to others and their approval. Consequently, he tends to be a conformist, in the sense of Crowne and Marlowe's approval motivation and need for affiliation (Crowne and Marlowe, 1960). It should be stressed that all the character traits we have mentioned above, both the hypothetical ones and those which have been empirically verified, are by no means an exhaustive list, but a mere illustration of measurable parameters to tie our theoretical dimensions and typologies to empirical anchors. They may also be useful indicators for the adequacy of our personality core vectors as the underlying sources for the various behavioural patterns and traits.

Our main hypothesis is that we could identify suicides by their personality parameters along a continuum between the separant and participant types as measured by the parameters we have presented above.

This would provide a dimension of suicide on the personality level which is not provided by sociological, socio-psychological and depth psychological expositions. Durkheim's three types of suicide (Durkheim, London, 1952), that is the anomic one relating to suicidal despair due to sudden social change, the egotistical suicide who retreats from society and his group because of conflicts and *ressentiment* grievances, and the altruistic suicide who sacrifices his life for the group, are all society-based premises which may contain explanations on a totally different level from the ones intended by us. Other sociological premises of suicide, some of them summarised by Alvarez in his *Savage God* (Alvarez, 1971) also operate on a group level and are related to socio-economic and other demographic factors to which we do not relate in the present study.

Psychoanalysts have dealt extensively with suicide from Freud himself (Freud, 1964), through Adler (Adler, 1967) and especially Wilhelm Stekel (Stekel, 1967). These studies emphasised the death drive inferiority, and guilt feelings, and identification with the dead to such an extent that the suicide wishes to join them. A contemporary classification of suicide has been presented by Schneidman (Schneidman, 1975), who analysed suicide notes and identified the following three types of suicide: egoistic, seen as an unresolved internal psychological conflict; dyadic, related to disappointment in the suicide's the 'significant others', and a generatic suicide, carried out by the alienated and lonely individual who dropped out of his various relationships with his environment.

In the course of presenting our findings, we shall point out the major differences between the current significant typologies of suicide and the ones presented by us.

METHODOLOGY

The Collection of Data

We have examined all the files of suicides in the five police stations of the central area of Israel (Gush Dan) for the years 1974-76. We have selected those cases that left suicide notes and for those who did (n=31), we have collected all the necessary demographic variables and contents-analysed the 31 suicide notes by the parameters

170

which we have specified above. The present study is, of course, an initial one because of the limited number of suicide notes, and our results should be a basis of a wider and deeper research. The protexts-analysis was carried out by judges who had carried out the collection of data. These were the five research assistants who are the co-authors of this study. They contents-analysed some suicide notes as a pre-test and then compared their judgments. Only when they reached a fair level of consensus did they contents-analyse the letters themselves. Finally, all the letters were analysed by all the research assistants participating in the study. The actual stages of analysis were as follows: the theoretical meaning of the various parameters were explained to and understood by the research assistants, then each assistant analysed some letters. The third stage was that the letters were exchanged and results examined, and in the fourth stage all the five assistants analysed all the letters together. This secured a high level of reliability of the contents-analysis and, indeed, when a reliability test was conducted after some weeks, it was found to be satisfactory. It should be stressed that various components of the suicide notes had more than one meaning, and the relative strength of each item was different. This is why we classified the power of each item as high or low and each component of the letter was analysed by all the various meanings it had according to the parameters we used for the contents-analysis. We thus accounted for both the intensity and quality of the statements in the suicide notes. After the content-analysis each letter was scored along the twelve parameters. The score range was between -2 and +2, expressing both intensity of expression and the parameters' direction--separant (plus sign) or participant (minus sign).

Analysis of Data

In the process of data analysis, we have employed, in two stages, two statistical techniques: factor analysis and cluster analysis. The purpose of the factor analysis was to organise the 12 parameters into broader constructs (factors). The cluster analysis was aimed at identifying clusters of suicides displaying specific configurations of factors.

Factor Analysis

The matrix of product-moment correlation coefficients between the 15 parameters was subjected to principal-component factor analysis, with orthogonal relations. Seven factors were identified, with eigenvalues greater than 1, explaining 79.2 per cent of the total variance. The factors structure is presented in the following table 1(only parameters with factor loading greater than 0.4 are presented).

171

Table 1. *Factor structure of 15 parameters*

Parameter	Factor Loading
Factor I: Object Vulnerability	
Low (high) sensitivity to pain	0.95
External (internal) control	-0.62
Stimulus hunger (aversion)	0.43
Factor II: Outward Aggression	
Extra (intra) punitiveness	0.75
High (low) vulnerability to sensory deprivation	0.63
Sanction (moral) orientation	0.50
Factor III: Ideological Orientation	
Tolerance (intolerance) of ideational ambiguity	0.97
Conformist (non-conformist)	-0.53
Factor IV: Deprivational Interaction	
High (low) risk taking	0.85
Field dependence (independence)	-0.61
Factor V: Interpersonal relationship	
Emotional Lability	0.75
Other (self) directed	0.40
Factor VI: Solidarity	
Group performer	0.76
Ressentiment	0.47
Factor VII: Object Perception	
Intolerance (tolerance) of objective ambiguity	0.76

FINDINGS

Factor analysis of the personality parameters

Factor I: Object Vulnerability - this factor includes the following parameters: high and low sensitivity to pain, stimulus hunger, stimulus aversion and external and internal control. It should be noted that with the first two parameters, only stimulus hunger and low sensitivity to pain had sufficient data. With the third parameter we see that contrary to expectations, the participant type was found to be internally controlled. This could be interpreted as follows: the participant pole had no data for stimulus aversion and high sensitivity to pain; therefore, any exposure to outside deprivational stimuli would be interpreted by the participant as being subject to forces over which he had no control. However, we do not have any explanation for the fact that contrary to our expectations, internal control turned out to belong to the separant part of our continuum.

Factor II: Outward Aggression - this second factor includes the following parameters; extra-intra-punitiveness, sanction and moral orientation, high and low vulnerability to sensory deprivation. This factor signifies the nature and intensity of the outward aggression felt by the subjects. Here the parameters came out as hypothesised by us *a priori* in our theoretical exposition.

Factor III: Ideological orientation - this factor contains two parameters. The first is intolerance of ideational ambiguity and the second conformity and non-conformity. The first parameter arranged itself in the factor according to our expectations. The second parameter, however, was reversed. The explanation for this is that the separant is not really concerned with ideas; he does not adhere unequivocally to one set of ideas or another. So he would tend not to commit himself ideologically and not care to conform to ideas when and if exposed to them. On the other hand, the participant is very much concerned with ideas and his conformity to them is a major concern for him.

Factor IV: Deprivational interaction with the object - this factor contains two parameters, high and low risk taking and field dependence and independence. The first parameter is in the right direction, but the second parameter is contrary to our *a priori* hypothesis and was reversed so that the separant was a high risk taker and field independent whereas the participant proved to be a low risk taker and field dependent. This seems to be reasonable because as far as risk taking in suicide is concerned, the separant high risk taker would utilise any means to carry out his suicide and to impress his audience, not caring very much about his behaviour. On the other hand, the participant low risk taker would be wary of disturbing his environment and would make sure that his actions as well as his mode of suicide would not disturb unduly the course of events in his environment and the structured routine of things and other people around him.

Factor V: Interpersonal relationship-this factor, which includes emotional liability and other directedness, came out according to our expectations.

Factor VI: Solidarity-this factor contains the parameters of group performing and the amount of *ressentiment*. The separant tends to be a high group performer and displays a high degree of *ressentiment*. The participant, on the other hand, is a low group performer and does not tend to blame the group for being let down. The direction of both these parameters was according to our expectations.

Factor VII: Object Perception-this factor contained one parameter only--intolerance and tolerance of objective ambiguity--and according to our expectations, the separant came out as intolerant of objective ambiguity and the participant, who is rather detached from his objective surroundings, proved to be tolerant of objective ambiguity.

Cluster analysis

Factor scores were computed by simply adding the scores of the parameters mostly contributing to the factor (table 1), after transforming the sign of parameters with negative factor loading.

Cluster analysis is a solution for finding homogeneous classes of objects, given a matrix of some measure of distance (or similarity) between objects. In our case, the objects are suicide notes presumably representing suicidal types.

The cluster analysis scheme used in the present study was the diameter method of Johnson (1967) and the measure of distance between pairs of objects (letters) was the Euclidian distance computed on the seven standardised factor scores.

The process of cluster analysis was repeated, and it was found that factor four did not differentiate between clusters. Therefore, the process of cluster analysis was repeated again, deleting factor four from the calculation of distances.

The second cluster analysis divided the 31 letters into four main clusters of size 11, 6, 5 and 4. The remaining 5 letters were organised into two 2-size clusters, and a single not-clustered object.

Table 2. *Mean factor scores of four suicidal cluster types*

Cluster (size)	I	II	III	IV	V	VI	VII
1 (1)	0.45	-0.10	1.10	0.72	0.64	1.10	1.90
2 (6)	-0.83	-3.67	-1.67	0.33	2.50	0.33	1.83
3 (1)	-4.50	-0.25	-2.25	0.50	4.50	2.75	2.50
4 (5)	-0.40	2.60	-0.40	1.00	3.20	2.80	0.80
Total mean sample	-0.42	-0.52	-0.58	0.68	2.26	1.87	1.52
S.D.	2.80	2.73	2.50	1.35	1.79	1.80	1.35

In order to identify the clusters, the means of each cluster in the seven factors were computed and contrasted with the final factor scores.

Cluster 1: This group is the accidiac suicide who is totally participant. He is morally oriented, he tends to accuse himself for his frustrations. He relates himself only minimally to outside experiences. He is unattached to his membership and reference groups and he rejects the values of the outside world because there is no point in being involved in them. The accidiac suicide is more than a retreatist because his non-involvement with the world is not because of a 'sour grapes' *ressentiment,* but because of a total lack of links with any of its values. His exit from the world is not dramatic and he does it without any fanfare. For example, in one of the suicide notes relating to this cluster, a suicide says, 'I do not blame anybody on my parting day'. And another one writes: 'Don't tell anybody about the whole thing, except for the legal authorities, don't even notify my husband and his relatives'.

This type does not employ the suicide as a kind of accounts settling with the here and now. His value-wise disjuncture from the world is total: he does not wish to impress anybody, least of all his family and the people around him. One suicide asks, for instance, not to divulge his name and to let people know that he died of a heart attack, and not by committing suicide. He leaves the world not in a rage of discontent but in utter realisation like Camus' Judge Penitent in *The Fall* (Camus, 1956) that his value system hovers on a totally different plane from people and objects in the world of social structures, appearances and norms of behaviour. One suicide states categorically, 'I am not interested in honour after death'. The accidiac suicide does not renounce the world, he just fades out of it.

Cluster 2: This cluster portrays the cowering suicide. He is characterised by a cringing away from the object and by an anxiety relating to outer stimulus, whatever their source. One note states, 'I am not responsible for what I am doing, I don't know what I am doing with my trembling hands, I am unable to do anything'. This type is very sensitive to pain. Many notes contain complaints about pain and the inability to cope with it. He is averse to stimuli yet controlled externally because the external stimuli and objects overwhelm him, and he has a feeling of being controlled by outside objects and environment to such an extent that he cannot cope. This type of object-cringing suicide is intolerant both of ideational and objective ambiguity because he is dismayed by whatever comes from outside. For instance, one suicide describes his mother in the following words: 'I must mention the old woman who is very far from being a mother and this is because of her many crimes against me'.

175

Although he tends to be conforming to the mandates that come from outside, he cannot cope with them because of his constant, anxiety-laden interaction with outside stimuli, norms and life in general. One of the suicides writes, 'Since the death of my husband, the loneliness and life in general has become unbearable'. He is not other - directed and he is not emotionally dependent on the outside, because he is disconnected from the objects around him. He did not achieve any link with the outside world to begin with or his relationship with his environment was so traumatic that he was afraid to reach out to objects and others irrespective of the latter's attitude towards him. One note states *inter alia* as follows: 'I blame my death on the income tax authorities, because of them I am sick, and my husband also is their victim, what do they want from our lives, two old and sick people'.

Incidentally, one of the notes of the suicides in this cluster feels so disconnected from his environment, even from his family, that he states as follows: 'I want to stress that I am ostracised by all my friends, even my family'. Moreover, this type is not only conflictive cringing from his surroundings, but also directs his family members to disconnect themselves from their own surroundings. Thus he tries to project his own cowering from the oppressive object and environment onto his family.

Cluster 3: This is the largest cluster. It appears that our research population is distributed normally with this cluster constituting its middle range. It is in the middle because it does not score either high or low on any of the factors. We may denote this as the cluster of 'the losers' who have been exposed to a failure experience: disenchanted lovers; elderly people who feel maltreated by their children; those who feel crushed by the indifference of others. This failure seems to be an unbridgeable gap between expectations and existing states of affairs stemming from both participant and separant premises. The following are instances illustrating this premise: 'I couldn't carry on life because of illness'; 'I decided to put a stop to this life in which so much cruelty from all directions impinged on me'; 'I never thought that life without my wife could be so pointless. I therefore decided to join her'.

An instance of an unbridgeable gap between expectations and reality is the following statement: 'I always tried to cling to life, but I realised that in order to keep alive I had to be a scoundrel'. Finally, the many instances of disappointed love can be symbolised by a young girl who had an affair with a married man who promised to marry her and did not fulfill his promise. Before committing suicide she wrote on the mirror in her room with lipstick: 'Monsieur, Madame, J'en ai marre' ('I'm fed up').

Cluster 4: This almost completely separant type might be denoted by us as the *ressentiment* suicide. This type of suicide is very much attached to his objective surroundings as well as to the relevant others. He is embedded in his group, other directed and extrapunitive. As one suicide states, 'A fulfilment of a dream of youth, no family, no obligations, you are totally free now, how does it feel, good luck'. He tends to accuse his surroundings for his failures and relates to his environment in a 'sour grapes', *ressentiment* attitude. The only exception that 'proves the rule' in this cluster is that he is low in intolerance of objective ambiguity. We hold this exception to be random and we cannot give an explanation for this. This type of suicide 'punishes' the vile and oppressing environment and others for treating him so badly. As one note says, 'My dear children, I have to go now, I have no means of livelihood left, I am sick, my insides are sick, I cannot take any medicine, so there is no other way, nobody can help me, miserably yours'. The *ressentiment* type of suicide has some elements of Durkheim's egotistical suicide (Durkheim, 1952), yet is more pronounced in his sour grapes revenge on his environment. One old woman writes for instance to her children: 'I have nowhere to live and I don't want to trouble you, so I have no other way'.

DISCUSSION

This is an initial study which tried to offer a new behavioural taxonomy of suicide and provide the typology with some empirical anchors. The main value of this initial study is in its linkage to a new personality theory and reliance on dynamics of some core personality vectors. It should be stressed that even after its further verification, this taxonomy relates to the personality of the suicide, and not to macro-sociological factors, or even to socio-psychological ones. The aetiological implications of this study are also confined to ontological and personality parameters. The relevance of this study is, therefore, to the personality level of the suicide, which could be linked eventually to the interactional and group levels of analysis.

References

Adler, A. (1967), *On Suicide,* P. Friedman, (Ed.), New York:
    International Universities Press.
Alvarez, A. (1971), *The Savage God,* London: Weidenfeld & Nicolson.
Cohen, S. & A.J. Silverman (1963), *Body and Field Perceptual Dimensions and
    Altered Sensory Environment,* Durham: Duke University Press.
Camus, A. (1956), *The Fall,* New York: Vintage Books.

Colquhoun, W.P., & D.W.J. Corocran (1964), 'The Effects of Time of Day and Social Isolation on the Relationship between Temperament and Performance', *British J. Soc. & Clin. Psychol*, Vol.3, No.93. pp.226-31.

Crowne, D.P. & D.A. Marlowe (1960), 'New Scale of Social Desirability Independent of Psychopathology', *J. Consult. Psycho*, Vol.24, pp.349-54.

Durkheim, E. (1952), *Suicide*, London: Kegan Paul.

Erikson, E. (1956), 'The Problem of Identity', *J. Amer. Psych. Ass.* No. 4.

Eysenck, H.J. (1967), *The Biological Basis of Personality*, Springfield, Ill: Charles C. Thomas.

Freud, S. (1964), 'Mourning and Melancholia' James Strachey et al. (Eds.),*Complete Psychological Works*, London: The Hogarth Press Vol. XIV, p. 252.

Johnson, S.C. (1967), 'Hierarchical Clustering Schemes', *Psychometrika*, Vol.32, No.3, pp. 241-53.

Petrie, A., W. Collins, & P. Solomon (1960), 'The Tolerance for Pain and for Sensory Deprivations', *Am. J. Psychol*, Vol.123, pp. 80-90.

Petrie, A. (1967), *Individuality in Pain and Suffering: The Reducer and Augmenter*, Chicago: University of Chicago Press, pp.138-40.

Riesman, D. (1950), *The Lonely Crowd*, New Hamphsire:Yale Univ. Press.

Rotter, J.B., M. Seeman & S. Liverant (1962), 'Internal v. External Control of Reinforcements: A Major Variable in Behaviour Theory', N.F. Washburne (Ed.), *Decisions, Values and Groups*, London: Pergamon Press Vol.2.

Schneidman, E. (1975), 'Classification of Suicidal Phenomena', S. Dinitz, Dynes & Clarke (Eds.), *Deviance*, N.Y: Oxford Univ. Press.

Shoham, S. G. (1979), *The Myth of Tantalus*, St. Lucia: Queensland U. Press.

Stekel, Wilhelm. (1967), article in *On Suicide*, P. Friedman (Ed.) .

Thibaut, J.W. & H.H. Kelly (1959), *The Social Psychology of Groups*, N.Y: John Wiley & Sons.

Witkin, H.A., R.B. Dyk, H.F. Faterson, D.R. Goodenough & S.A. Karp (1962), *Psychological Differentiation*, N.Y: John Wiley & Sons.

12 Macro Violence

Between the torturer and the tortured arises a kind of relationship. So long as the torture continues, the torturer has failed, and he recognizes an equality in the victim.

Graham Greene, *A Sort of Life*

INTRODUCTION

The Holocaust is the most confounding monstrosity in history. One can comprehend a pogrom or the killing of civilians in the heat of battle, but the slaughter of six million Jews, and many millions of non-Jews, in three years, by a factory production-line method, is incomprehensible.

Did the event redefine human depravity? Did it pulverise into insignificance all human values, norms and emotional attachments, friendships and loves? Or was it a re-enactment, on a grand scale, of the sacrificial passion of Isaac and Jesus Christ by the likes of Janusz Korczak--willing victims expiating some horrible sin of man and God? In the present state of our knowledge this is incomprehensible.

This chapter is an attempt to understand some central dynamics of the Holocaust. We must repeat the question that has been hurled out *ad nauseam*: How could the nation of Bach, Goethe, Schiller and Thomas Mann be responsible for Auschwitz? Moreover, every human being must grapple with the heavy burden of trying to come to terms with the Holocaust. Without such an attempt, the moral viability of man will always remain in question.

How could a culture which produced Goethe's *Faust*, Kant's *Critique of Pure Reason*, Beethoven's *Ninth Symphony*, and Rilke's *Duino Elegies* also have been responsible for the following, taken from documentary evidence. S.S. *Einsatzgruppen*, whose commanders included professors of aesthetics, ethics and law, a mayor and a priest, killed men, women and children by shooting them in trenches dug by the victims. When some of the Jews managed to escape, they were hunted down with dogs. The Nazis shot them like squires killing game. Gold teeth and fillings were torn from the victims' corpses. Their recta and vaginae were searched for 'treasures'. Lampshades were cured from their skins. Their hair was cut for industrial use, and one unsatisfied customer complained to the Auschwitz authorities that the hair should be sorted according to length to facilitate industrial processing, '*Ordnung Muss Sein*'! The fat from the victims' cremated bodies was collected and turned into soap stamped with R.J.F., *Reine Judisches Fett*. Babies were thrown into flames alive. If they cried or were noisy, they were torn from their mother's laps, their heads smashed against a wall and their corpses returned to their mothers. S.S. personnel in death camps enjoyed baths in water warmed by burning bodies. Teenage girls were made prostitutes for soldiers of the master race. They were classified as 'field whores' or 'for officers only', and their classification seared into their skin with hot iron stamps.

We believe that we can add a new vantage point to the current explanations of the Nazi regime and its extermination of European Jewry. We see the Nazi regime within the context of macro-criminology as a special case of our stigma and labelling theories (Shoham and Rahav, 1982). Furthermore, our theories on the main dialectics of human behavior (Shoham, 1982) are applicable to the mutually-dependent relationship between Germans and Jews, which was irrevocable by the Holocaust.

Finally, a personal note, which relates to the author's repression of the Holocaust for over a quarter of a century. Until 1973, youth in Israel cherished the image of the strong *Sabra*, the native Israeli, as the antithesis of the weak, downtrodden Diaspora Jew. The fighting Israelis were contrasted with the abject yielding of European Jewry to the murderous Nazis. However, after the Yom Kippur War of 1973, when Israelis reverted to the archetype of the Jewish victim, the author began a soul-searching study of the vast literature and sources on Nazi Germany and the Holocaust. A thoroughly new, macabre view was revealed to him, which has served as the basis for the present work.

Mosse has already pointed out the scant aetiological results yielded by years of research into the origins of Nazism and the Holocaust (Mosse, 1961). This may be due to the enormity of the events, which defy attempts at intellectual or rational analysis. Economic, political and social factors may contribute to, but cannot in themselves explain, complex social phenomena. At the risk of stating the obvious, we have to point out that no 'nothing but' explanations or, on the other hand, eclectic theories, can explain social and behavioural phenomena. Thus the theory favoured by Sartre and many others that the Nazis used the Jews as scapegoats might be incorporated into a more elaborate causal model, but in itself is of scant explanatory power.

Similarly, Hannah Arendt's *Banality of Evil* might indeed characterise some Nazis, but to anchor on it a whole theory of National-Socialism and the Holocaust is simplistic and shallow. To tag Hitler as a madman, psychopath, and sexual deviant explains, like all psychiatric tags, very little. Of more importance is to explain how this raving maniac almost succeeded in conquering the whole of Europe and winning the Second World War. Moreover, almost the entire German nation followed him.

Dissidence appeared only when it became obvious that he had failed to fulfil his megalomaniac promise to build the Thousand Year German Reich. The model we will construct will, therefore, be multifaceted. We shall point out some guiding clues as we go along, which will identify factors and trends to be incorporated in the model which we shall present at the end of the Introduction.

Our first clue presents itself in some of the more striking characteristics of Hitler and his henchmen. Hitler hated all laws, conventions and regulations. He usually found a way to ignore or evade norms, both secular and religious. His taste ran to Streicher's Stürmer, a rabid, anti-Semitic tabloid laced with soft pornography and political gossip, which he read from cover to cover. Any contemporary low-brow tabloid in London or New York would appear respectable by comparison. Hitler believed in the veracity of the Protocols of the Elders of Zion. He was superstitious and believed in the occult and astrology. He employed a quack doctor as his personal physician. He enjoyed playing cruel practical jokes on subordinates. The slow death by strangulation of the generals who had tried to assassinate him in the July 1944 plot was photographed for his sadistic enjoyment.

When Goering was arrested before the Nüremberg trials, he was found with two suitcases of paracodeine, an opiate drug to which he was addicted (Gilbert, 1961:17). Goering's graft, stealing, corruption and wholesale pilfering of art works were of such magnitude that he must rank among the greatest thieves in history. As there was no rule of law in Nazi Germany, he could get away with his colossal larcenies with impunity. It did not occur to him to conceal his activities. On the contrary, he was proud of them.

He used to receive guests at his palace, Karinhall, dressed as a drag-queen in velour togas, studded with outsize diamonds, sapphires and rubies. Then, like an overdressed Nero, he would exhibit the paintings looted from Europe's museums, which hung on the walls in three and four tiers, (Speer, 1970:255) without any attention to style, painter, school of art, or period.

Streicher was a dull-witted, ignorant pornographer. When undressed for a physical examination by his Nüremberg captors, he leered obscenely at the female Russian interpreter, exhibiting his genitals and urging her not to be 'afraid to see something nice' (Gilbert, 1961:15). He used to tell anybody who cared to listen about Goering's impotence, and when the two met, they often quarrelled like two fat butchers over a chunk of meat.

Joseph Goebbels, the club-footed, over-sexed Propaganda Minister, was also an *arbiter-elegantiarum* of the performing arts, especially cinema. Aspiring starlets looking for film roles knew that the most promising route to the realisation of their dreams was through the bedroom, or rather numerous bedrooms, of the Propaganda Minister. Thus they might be invited to his castle on *Schwanewerder*; his 'log cabin' at Lanke; upstairs at his own home, while his wife Magda helped the children with homework downstairs; or to his private rooms at the Propaganda Ministry. Visitors waiting in the reception room were assured by secretaries that 'the Minister will see you as soon as he finishes some urgent business he had to attend to' (Heiber, 1973:241).

How could a civilised and culturally sophisticated nation of 80 million accept, with almost no effective resistance, the absolute rule of a bunch of thugs? Nothing short of a type of religious frenzy could account for it. Uriel Tal has already pointed out the religious nature of the Nazi movement (Tal, 1980), but what kind of religion? We contend that Nazism, as a macro-criminological phenomenon, may be viewed as an example of black, or inverse, religiosity. Some crimes may be related to the inverse religious belief of a Jacob Frank who contended, 'to uphold the Torah is to infringe it'. Some esoteric religious sects claimed that in a world dominated by evil, one has to worship it in order to survive. A Jean Genet, for example, worshipped the trinity of homosexuality, theft and betrayal, and with it constructed a normative system diametrically opposed to bourgeois morality. For didactic purposes we may envisage the Nazi regime as a Frankist movement which seized power. Jacob Frank then becomes prophet and Fuehrer, with Al Capone-Goering, Genet-Roehm and Sade-Streicher as his aides. The rejection by the Nazis of the restraints of Jewish morality and laws made everything possible and permissible. The repression of Christian grace, compassion and mercy allowed S.S. death squads to commit wholesale murder. Without the constraints of Judaism and Christianity, the pagan *Furor Teutonicus* could reign unchecked, with Himmler, the arch-murderer, believing himself to be the incarnation of Henry the Fowler, the tenth century Saxon king. Goering, when drunk, also used to imagine himself as a Germanic tribal chieftain and jumped onto banquet tables and danced Teutonic war dances. Without laws and morals, the Nordic war gods reigned supreme. Only power counted and soldiers dying to further the Nazis' murderous aims would be resurrected in Valhalla.

GERMANY ARISE, JUDEA PERISH (DEUTSCHLAND ERWACHE, JUDAH VERECKE)

Most authorities agree that anti-Semitism was a central issue for the Nazis, more so than for any other movement, anywhere at any other time. Hannah Arendt goes further and states that it constituted the centre of Nazi ideology (Arendt, 1958:7). In France, while anti-Semitism was deeply rooted, it was mostly a means and not an end in itself. Even the Dreyfus Affair was instrumental in the struggle of the clerics and the army in the Third Republic against the republicans (Parkes, 1963:35-37). Nineteenth-century Russia was the most rabidly anti-Semitic country in Europe, but the Tzarist regime, the last absolutist monarchy in Europe, used anti-Semitism as a safety valve for the pent-up aggression of an oppressed populace (Cohn, 1972:38). In other cultures, anti-Semitism was instrumental in achieving political, social or religious goals.

Only in Nazi Germany was anti-Semitism, and later the destruction of Jews, a goal in itself, irrespective of its political, military or economic value. Indeed, the allotment of manpower, transportation and equipment for the Final Solution to the Jewish question took priority over the German war effort (Tal, 1979). In the spring of 1944, the German war machine was crumbling, but the death camps continued to operate full blast and the trains which transported the victims ran on schedule. Moreover, it seemed that the greater the defeats of the German army, the stronger the determination of the Nazis to implement the Final Solution to its gory end (Rosenfeld, 1955:9). Eichmann, at that time, bragged to his drinking partners that he would gladly jump into his grave when he knew that he had achieved the deaths of five million Jews. Hermann Goering, on learning during his captivity in Nüremberg that not all Hungarian Jews had been exterminated, said: 'Somebody in Hungary didn't do his job right'. Alan Bullock writes that hatred of Jews was the most sincere emotion Hitler felt (Bullock, 1962: 313, 397, 474, 673) and it was his constant obsession. His will and political testament, written before his suicide, accused the Jews of causing the war. In its last paragraph he wrote: 'Above all, I charge the leaders of the nation and those under them to scrupulous observance of the laws of race and to merciless opposition to the universal poisoner of all peoples, international Jewry' (Bullock, 1962:795). In his last moments Hitler saw as the most important task of his successors, the continuation of his frenzied fight against the Jews--six million of whom he knew to have perished already.

This obsession, shared by the Nazi hierarchy and openly or tacitly approved of by the vast majority of Germans, cannot be explained by psychiatric labels or by superficial personality factors or social forces. We claim, as a second clue for our model, that the anti-Semitism of the Nazis was related to the core dialectics of the German social character.

SOCIAL CHARACTER

When our core personality continuum is applied to the characteristics of groups or cultures, it relates to a social character. The family and other socialising agencies transmit the norms and values of the group, which the individual then internalises. It is important to note at the outset, however, that social character, as the composite portrait of a culture, is never pure. It portrays only essentials, not peripheral traits. One culture may absorb the social character of its conquerors. This social character may thence be classified along a continuum similar to our personality core continuum. The separant pole can be denoted as Sisyphean, after the Greek stone-manipulating Titan; we denote participant as Tantalic, after the stationary, inner-directed and abstract demi-god. Thus the social-character constitutes the cultural dimension of our personality continuum.

Patterns of Culture and Social Character

The classification of cultures along a continuum and their relationship to a given personality structure necessitate two basic assumptions. First, that cultures possess generalised traits that may be measured and ranked on a predetermined typology or scale. Second, that these traits could be related to the character of the individual. By adopting both these assumptions, we find ourselves in good or bad company, depending on taste or value judgement. Spengler and Toynbee have adhered to both these assumptions in their works on the growth and decline of cultures. Indeed, Spengler compares the ages of cultures to the ages of man: 'Every culture', he says, 'passes through the age phases of the individual man. Each has its childhood, youth, manhood and old age' (Spengler, 1954:107). Oswald Spengler and Arnold Toynbee thus introduced the dynamic temporal dimension to the study of culture.

184

The current anthropological conception of culture as the 'superorganic' (Kroeber, 1952) pattern of symbols, generated by the interaction of groups and individuals and transmitted by learning, lends itself to abstract classifications. The crucial question is, are the patterns Platonic ideals projected by the mind of the anthropologist onto the rarified ether of abstraction, or are they generalised descriptions of processes actually taking place in societies? If culture 'is what binds men together' and it does so by 'symbolating' human interaction, (R.Benedict cited by Kluckhohn, 1962:26) that is, by relating forms and appearances to qualities and attributes, then it already involves, by definition, the abstraction and ordering of 'Gestalts'. In other words, the processes of cultures are themselves manifested in arranged patterns. This may also be gleaned from some of the key concepts in the definition of culture. A symbol is a value-or meaning-laden sign; (L. White cited by Kluckhohn, 1962:52) and meanings and value judgments are readily expressed in generalised patterns. The 'superorganic' is manipulated by tools, and the means chosen to achieve cultural goals are regulated by norms. Yet rules and norms themselves are constructs that are choice objects for paradigms and classifications. *Prima facie*, therefore, we may accept the feasibility, contrary to the vehement objections of some ethnographers, of ordering cultures into generalised configurations and patterns, or to use Spengler's flowery language, of painting the portrait of a culture (See Spengler, 1954:Vol.1, p.101). Indeed, Ruth Benedict and her cultural-relativist colleagues have demonstrated how patterns may be identified by the direct observation of cultures. Furthermore, Claude Levi-Strauss and his structuralist school have shown that cultural processes in 'savage' societies are coincidental to the classificatory passage from things to symbols, notably the totemic generalisations from the concrete to the abstract (Levi-Strauss, 1966). The structuralists thus identify in societies not only patterns, but whole systems of functions underlying overt cultural processes. For Benedict, cultural patterns stem from 'unconscious canons of choice that develop within the culture...(Benedict, 1934:54) so that it selects some segment of the arc of possible human behaviour and, so far as it achieves integration, its institutions tend to further the expression of its selected segment and to inhibit opposite expressions'.

These habits, symbols, values, cultural goals and the means to achieve them, crystallise into 'total culture patterns' (Kocher, 1952:125-30) by which cultures may be identified. The ordering of cultural patterns into schemes, paradigms, continua and matrices may vary according to the purpose or theoretical orientation of the observer. There can be no universal criterion for measuring the validity of the classification of culture patterns. The value of a classification should be determined by the specific aims and needs of a given theoretical concern. This is aptly stated by Claude Levi-Strauss as follows:

> The real question is not whether the touch of a woodpecker's beak does in fact cure toothache. It is rather whether there is a point of view from which a woodpecker's beak and a man's tooth can be seen as 'going together' (the use of this congruity for therapeutic purposes being only one of its possible uses) and whether some initial order can be introduced into the universe by means of these groupings (Levi-Strauss, 1966:9).

We may thus observe in the literature, a vast array of classifications of cultures that serve an *ad hoc* aim of the researcher. On the micro level, we may find F.L.K. Hsu's classification of cultures by their dominant dyads. Japan, according to his criteria, is a father/son-dominated society, whereas American culture is dominated by the husband/wife-dyad (F.L.K. Hsu, 1969:86). On the macro level, Riesman and his associates identified the traditional, inner-directed societies within a scheme related to transitional growth and economic development (Riesman, Glazer Denney, 1953). The typology that is closest in its general objectives to our own, is of course, the one presented by Benedict, following Spengler's cultural relativism. The cultural-relativist method of identifying dominant social characters within a culture, which may be arranged between two poles of a continuum, suits our methodological purposes. By this method, we may characterise a culture according to its position on the continuum. This position is never static because it shifts with time and social change.

To, a social character does not consist of those peculiarities which differentiate people, but of 'that part of their character structure that is common to most members of the group' (Fromm, 1942:277). The social character is, therefore, a common attribute of individuals, ingrained in them by socialising agents, which display the characteristics of a culture. Riesman, who uses *mutatis mutandis*, Fromm's definition of social character, relies for the sources and genesis of this social character on Erikson who claims that 'Systems of child training...represent unconscious attempts at creating out of human raw material that configuration of attitudes which is the optimum under the tribes' particular natural conditions and economic-historic necessities' (cited in Riesman et al, 1953:19). Erikson's mesh of social Darwinism with Marxist material dialectics is too concrete and harsh in our view as an explanation for the volatile concept of social character. We prefer to see the social character as a 'collective representation' in the sense used by Levy-Bruhl, (Levy-Bruhl, 1966:3-5) of acts, symbols, and transitions from the concrete to the abstract displayed by groups in their interaction with the individuals which comprise them, or with other groups. This involves the transmission of the social character from the group to its young, and from generation to generation by a process of learning and socialisation, and not by heredity, as postulated by Jung (Jung, 1944:616). The social character is the psychological type of a character as displayed by a collectivity, and not by the individuals comprising it. Yet, when this social character is implanted in the individual by the group, it provides the necessary link between the phylogenetic and ontogenetic bases of the personality structure.

Activist and Quietist Cultures

Every classification fulfils the specific aims of a given theoretical structure. Our purpose is to determine the interrelationship of the Sisyphean-Tantalic personality type continuum with the separant-participant continuum of cultures. Consequently, we have to define our cultural continuum and describe the polarities of our social character, and this, to be sure, is no mean task. Recently, the author was sitting in one of the tavernas in the Plaka on the slope leading to the Acropolis overlooking the whole of Athens. He was reading Shestov's *Athens and Jerusalem* and was struck by the eloquent contrast between Socrates, 'the man who is led by reason alone', and the Biblical Psalmist who 'cries to the Lord out of the depths of human nothingness', (Shestov, 1968:61) which confronts the reason and fact-oriented Socratic Greeks with the intuition-outlook of the Biblical Jews, animated by faith and revelation. Yet, when he looked beyond the ruins of the Agora toward the horizon, he saw a striking similarity between the hills around Athens and the hills of Judaea around Jerusalem. The same scorching heat, the same bare rocks, the same cruelty of nature served as a physical setting for both the activist, object- manipulating, post-Socratic Greeks, and the quietist, contemplative and self-effacing Judaea of Ecclesiastes. The 'portrait of a culture', however, depicts only the predominant cultural traits and patterns; but every culture is perforce pluralistic and displays, to varying degrees, aspects of the opposite polar type as well. This is the main reason why a continuum is the most suitable means of describing the polarity and range of social characters. Also, some basic ideas and innovative modes of thought and observation, displaying either participant or separant attitudes, may or may not have been representative of a given society at a given time. In all likelihood, many great figures studied today with reverence, were eccentric recluses shunned by their contemporaries. We shall, therefore, use the ideas and insights of such thinkers to help us formulate our concepts; but for the description of cultures as separant or participant, we shall rely mainly on original documents.

The polarisation into Sisyphean-separant and Tantalic-participant social characters has influenced the *Weltanschauung* of observers from time immemorial. Parmenides founded the Eleatic School of Philosophy on the premise that reality is static. We have here the basic tenet of inaction common to the participant ideals of Taoism, Hinayana Buddhism, the Moslem Sufis and the quietist Hasidim. Heraclitus the Ephesean, on the other hand, postulated a universality of flux, the strife between opposites that sweeps everything into a dynamic flow of change. This is the basis of Hegelian dialectics, as well as of the Marxian creed of historical materialism, which postulates salvation through action. The first characteristic which distinguishes a separant culture is, therefore, an orientation toward action. The second contrast is between unity and plurality. The participant culture decrees that one has to rid one's thoughts of the illusory perceptions of the senses in order to reach the monistic wholeness behind the deceptions of plurality. Consequently, the Parmenidean sphere, representing all-present wholeness, is also the three-dimensional mandala that is the prevailing symbol of the Far Eastern participant cultures. The separant conception of reality follows Pythagoras, and of course Heraclitus, who saw the universe as ordered into measured pluralities that follow the universal formula of sequence and dynamic harmonies within interrelated boundaries. The third polarity contrasts the ideal of constancy in the participant cultures with the idea of relationship in the separant culture. If plurality is illusion and the veil of Maya and the sole reality is unity, then all relationships are also illusory, because unity cannot interact with itself. Moreover, for participant cultures, relationship is not only deceptive, but also the source of evil, sorrow and pain. For separant cultures, on the other hand, relations with space and time and with other human beings are the frame of reference of human life, and have to be coped with by integration, adjustment and solidarity. The fourth contrast relates to the emphasis of separant cultures on reason, on those formulae and models that explain man and his universe. The participant cultures tend to distrust and reject logic, relying more on intuition and revelation. Indeed, Spengler colours the following statement by a participant value judgment when he says: 'Reason, system and comprehension kill as they 'cognise'. That which is cognised becomes a rigid object capable of measurement and subdivision. Intuitive vision, on the other hand, incorporates the details in a living, inwardly felt unity' (Spengler, 1954. Vol.1:10).

The fifth polarity which we have found useful is that between the separant tool orientation, i.e., a culture geared toward the manipulation of objects and the participant symbol-oriented culture, in which ideas and belief systems are centred on inwardly-contemplating individuals immersed in 'doing their own thing'.

Our five polar characteristics of social character are summarised in figure 1. These patterns are by no means exhaustive, but rather illustrative. They point out the highlights of a given social character, but do not constitute a precise definition.

188

Figure 1. *Polar patterns of social character*

SEPARANT	PARTICIPANT
Object-manipulation	Self-manipulation
Reason	Intuition
Flux	Constancy
Action	Resignation
Plurality	Unity

Our use of a continuum to describe social characters means that no culture may be tagged by one definitive label. Consequently, in every participant social character there are separant patterns, and vice versa. In Judaism, for instance, *Yom Hakipurim*, the Day of Atonement, is a participant ritual in which the individual strives to partake of divinity through self-humiliation and effacement. *Yom Hapurim*, the feast celebrating the deliverance of the Jews from Haman, Ahasuerus' evil Wazir, is written in Hebrew like the Day of Atonement less one syllable: Ki. This led the Lurianic Kabbalists to link the two holidays: the Day of Atonement being Yom ki Purim. The lots cast by children and adults on the festival of Purim were compared with the lots of life and death cast by God on Yom Hakipurim, the Day of Atonement. And yet, Purim is a separant ritual of frenzy, in which individuals strive to reach each other through the ecstatic togetherness of wine, song and dance (Encyclopedia Judaica, 1971. Vol.13:1390). The pure separant or participant culture does not exist in reality, but the signs that indicate the presence of one or other type of social character may be arranged on several continua, representing various cultural areas.

At the separant extreme, we may place the northwestern European societies imbued with the Protestant ethic which burst forth in the full-blown flames of the 'American Dream'. On the participant pole we find cultures dominated by the Hinayana Buddhist doctrines of quietist self-annihilation.

It might well be that the separant-activist trends of northwestern European cultures have their origins in the ethos of the Germanic tribes who conquered their way across Europe, carrying Thor's hammer as a symbol of power. They even dispensed with the fear of the after-life by having Odin, the god of Battle, send his armour-clad Valkyries to carry slain warriors to eternal bliss in Valhalla. There is no doubt, however, that the concern with achievement, the manipulation by force of less powerful societies, and the scientific conquest of nature which marked the rise of northwestern European societies in the last centuries, were boosted by the Protestant ethic. A separant trend runs through Luther's sanctification of work as a sacred calling, Calvin's stress on achievement as proof of predestined worth, Hegel's doctrine of action as the necessary bridge between subject and object, and Marx's decree to harness all means of

189

production in order to mold man's (dialectical) future. The separant culture is Sisyphean because its aim of incorporating and controlling spatio-temporality within itself is unattainable. Hyperactivity often channels itself into routine and aimless ritualism, social engineering is more likely to lead to the social death of totalitarianism or the robotic zombies of 1984, and the scientific manipulation of matter seems to achieve the suffocation of air, the death of water and the perfection of artifacts for mass murder. Yet, the separant striving to reach Utopia through the dialectics of action is never-ending, like the pushing of the Sisyphean rock.

We may, at this stage, anticipate critical reactions to our focus on religion as an anchor for the identification of cultures along our continuum. However, this focus is warranted both by theoretical considerations and empirical findings. First, religious affiliation has been found to correlate with many attitudes and modes of behaviour, as well as with the structure and contents of social institutions (McClelland, 1961). Religion is a significant identification tag, although many other social institutions, norms and cultural goals are also relevant for our classification. Most, if not all, of our pairs of polar patterns are reflected in the religious doctrine of a given culture. Most of human history, to risk a sweeping generalisation, has been related, influenced and many times totally dominated by religion.

The 'uncharted region of human experience', to use Gilbert Murray's fortunate phrase, (Murray, 1955:4-5) is the domain of religion. Although the areas of our 'positive knowledge' are greatly expanding, most of the swift human journey from an involuntary beginning to an unknown end is governed by confusion and chaos. Consequently, religion has reigned supreme in human societies throughout history. Even Marxism has been denoted a 'secular religion', and Bertrand Russell has made the following ingenious analogies:

Yahweh =	Dialectical Materialism
The Messiah =	Marx
The Elect =	The Proletariat
The Church =	The Communist Party
The Second Coming =	The Revolution
Hell =	Punishment of Capitalist
The Millennium =	The Communist Commonwealth

(Russell, 1947:383)

Yet, if we try to place Communist China, the most ardent adherent of the Marxist secular religion, on our space continuum, we may decide that its position is not on the far separant pole, because it still retains some vestiges of the Taoist and Buddhist participant social characteristics.

As for empirical evidence, we have ample proof that the Catholics' other-worldly orientation, their conception of labour as a curse and a corollary of original sin; traits which are incidentally participant and quietist, make them less achievement-motivated than the Protestants (McClelland, 1961:51). This places them a considerable distance from the separant extreme of our space continuum.

On the participant extreme of our continuum, we have placed Hinayana Buddhism, of the Southern Theravada school. The Hinayana is the 'small vehicle', as condescendingly labelled by the Mahayana Buddhists, who called themselves the 'great vehicle'. The Hinayana rejects temporal existence as a burden, because all action and interaction is irritation, friction and suffering (Dukkha) (Humphreys, 1952:81). Second, the Samsara, the cycle of growth, fruition and decay, which is the essence of the individual's separate condition, produces disharmony and desire, the harbingers of evil. Third, plurality is an illusion generated by the perception of the separate self. Nirvana, therefore, is achieved by the annihilation of the individual self and 'awakening', into the blissful reality of unity (Humphreys, 1952:88-89). We may identify in the Hinayana doctrine at least four out of our five main patterns of the participant social character: quietist inaction, rejection of temporality, self-effacement and the belief in the omnipresence of unity behind the veil of plurality. Although Hindu yoga is near to the participant pole, it is somewhat removed from the extreme position of the Hinayana. For yoga, for instance, the temporal world is, to be sure, vile and full of suffering and pain, but it is nevertheless real and not illusory (Eliade, 1969:9). Further, the aim of yoga, although quiestist in essence, is not to annihilate the separate self, but to separate spirit (Purusha) and matter (Prakrti) (Eliade, 1969:8). Mahayana, the northern school of Buddhism, has even more separant traits and is, therefore, further removed from the participant pole. Suzuki, expounding this doctrine, says: 'In Mahayana Buddhism, each soul is not only related as such to the highest reality, but also to one another in the most perfect network of infinite mutual relationship' (Humphreys, 1952:87). Relationship with outside objects is thus real and possible and so separant action and interaction are generated. Mahayana also lessened the Hinayana emphasis on Dukkha, the pain of interaction, and preached with a zeal becoming of a Calvin: 'Work out your salvation with diligence' (Humphreys, 1952:49). Zen Buddhism, which evolved from Mahayana doctrine, is even more separant. It seems that Zen influenced the rise of the business class in nineteenth-century Japan. 'Zen discipline', says Suzuki, 'is simple, direct, self-reliant', and Satori (individual enlightenment) is attained not by ritual but by 'one's inner life' (Watts, 1960:108). This, to be sure, is similar to the Protestant ethic. Indeed, Zen flourished in its fullest

191

expression in Japan, the most separant culture of the Far East, which cherishes self-reliance, responsiblity, cleanliness, order and energetic performance.

Thus we arrive at the basic assumption for our present study: the German social character is situated on the extreme separant Sisyphean pole of our continuum, whereas the Jewish social character, although not on the extreme pole, is quite close to the participant-Tantalic ideal type.

CLASHES, SYNTHESIS AND DISRUPTIONS

We propose, therefore, to view anti-Semitism, and specifically the Holocaust, as *inter alia*, a manifestation of the dialectical clashes and syntheses between the Tantalic Jewish social character and a chain of extreme Sisyphean social characters, the Germans being the last.

The Jews were probably the first harbingers of abstract monotheism in Europe. As we have already suggested, religion is a prime component of social character, and thus the Jews' primacy in monotheism contributed greatly to their sense of uniqueness. Another basic fact is the Jews' astounding durability over the years, through all the clashes with an ever changing cast of Sisyphean social characters. The Jews' position on the Tantalic participant segment of the continuum was fairly stable until the advent of Zionism and the establishment of the State of Israel. With this, Israeli Jews, in a remarkable transformation, jolted towards the Sisyphean-separant pole of the social character continuum. These facts are linked to two basic events in Jewish history which are relevant to our present study. The first is the clash between the Jewish and the Hellenistic social characters after Alexander's conquest of Palestine in 332 B.C. Before this the Jews were embedded in an oriental and largely Tantalic set of cultures. The Hellenistic conquerors were the first European, Sisyphean culture with which the Jews were confronted. The second is the destruction of Jerusalem and most of Judaea by the Romans (70 B.C.). The subsequent dispersion of the Jews throughout the Roman Empire generated continuous clashes and dialectical syntheses between Jews, as a conspicuous minority, and the dominant majorities. Our starting point is, therefore, that the seeds of the Holocaust were sown in the frontal clash in the fourth century B.C. between Hellenists and Jews.

Reinach, in his compilation of Greek and Roman sources relating to Judaism and Jews, stresses their relevance to the understanding of anti-Semitism. The Jews, he rightly points out, were usually politically subordinate to Greek and later Roman dominion. Hence, the sympathies or antipathies (anti-Semitism) of these dominant cultures towards the Jews determined their well-being, prosperity and sheer survival (Reinach, 1963). The crucial point, however, is not the Jews' political subjugation by other cultures. This had happened periodically many centuries before the conquest of Palestine by Alexander. The Egyptian, Babylonian and Persian empires, under whose political patronage and cultural influence Judaea and Israel found themselves, were more participant-Tantalic and hence close in social character to the Jews. However, the Greek and Roman cultures were diametrically opposed to the Jewish social character. The Greek social character was anchored on the object and its environment. It strived for aesthetics, whereas the Jew turned to his inner self. The participant ideal of non-being is expressly anti-aesthetic. The Jew's shunning of plastic arts is also expressed in the Old Testament's proscription of the graven image of God. The Jew had a tendency to be more abstract in his religion and culture, while the Greek had concrete deities and *Weltanschauung*. Greeks valued harmony in their surroundings and Sisyphean ordering of their possessions according to a preconceived scheme. Jews tolerated total disarray of things and objects, so long as they could be enmeshed into a normative and ethical scheme, which made this world, and especially the ever-after, meaningful. The Jew focused on transcendence, whereas for the Sisyphean Greek everything important was in the here-and-now , the away and beyond being an illusion. For the Greeks, even myths and hell were part of objective reality. The Jews were monotheistic, reflecting their quest for participant unity, whereas the Greeks were polytheistic and projected onto transcendence, the separant plurality which they perceived in the objective world. The Jew longed for salvation through a divine Messiah, who would deliver him from his temporal vicissitudes into the boundless eternity of the Divine Presence. For the Greek, everything one was able to achieve in this life was through manipulation and cunning.

The Judeo-Hellenistic clash was so fateful to the history of Europe and its culture that some scholars, notably Heinrich Graetz, have exaggerated its importance. Graetz claimed that these two nations moulded the foundations of European civilisation. Even before the destruction of the Second Temple, there was a sizable Jewish diaspora in the Roman Empire. Whatever the veracity of this claim, there is no doubt that the extreme polarities between the Hellenistic and Jewish cultures resulted in the widest possible range of conflicts and the broadest variety of cultural syntheses. Only the Jews amongst all the cultures subjugated by Alexander and his Hellenistic heirs, consistently resisted the imposition of the Greek normative religious code (Graetz, 1853. Vol.1:20-21). This in itself made the Jewish-Hellenistic clash *sui generis* in its violence and in the magnitude of its subsequent cultural syntheses.

One of the most conspicuous outcomes of these polarities was that the self-effacing Tantalic Jewish social character periodically lost its political independence to more carnivorous and action-bound Sisyphean cultures. However, intellectual independence and innovation continued. This is apparent in the flourishing of learning, immediately after the destruction of the Temple, in Jabneh under the leadership of Rabbi Johanan Ben Zakkai. This scholarship continued, with a few interruptions, notably the revolt of Bar Kochba (132 A.D.), which was bloodily suppressed by Hadrian until 351 A.D., when the seats of learning in Tiberias, Sepphoris and Lydda were destroyed by the Emperor Constantius the Second. The pursuit of learning continued however in full force in Mesopotamia, where centres of learning already existed in the second century. These achieved widespread recognition in the third century and were epitomised by the Babylonian Talmud, the most important spiritual core of Judaism to this day. After the Moslems conquered the Middle East, North Africa and later Spain, Jewish spiritual life continued to flourish due to the relative tolerance of the Moslem khaliphas, sultans, and pashas. In Mesopotamia, Jewish exilarchs and *geonim* continued to foster the spiritual excellence of the centres of learning. In Moslem Spain, such figures as Hasdai-ibn-Shaprut (915-970) and Samuel-ibn-Nagdela (993-1063) used their influence with the caliphates to help the Spanish Jews materially, but mainly in furtherance of scholarship, medicine and languages, and in the pursuit of poetic excellence. The most towering figure of the Jewish diaspora in Moslem North Africa of the twelfth century was Maimonides. He was both court physician to Saladin and the author of the Mishneh Torah, which systemised Judaic principles of religion and ethics, and after the Talmud, remains the most important document of Jewish religious philosophy. In Christian Europe too, the Jews pursued spiritual excellence, motivated by their participant-Tantalic social character. The *talmid hakham* enjoyed the highest prestige. He was the Talmudic Scholar who studied most of his waking hours in the *beit-midrash* or in the *yeshiva*. His intellectual studies were mostly an end in themselves, and the repetitious immersion in the Talmud, the primary interest of his life. The *talmid hakham* flourished in a medieval Europe whose Christian population was mostly illiterate, and in the shadow of virulent Crusades. This tradition of holding learning in high esteem lasted until the end of the nineteenth century. In the Jewish *shtetl* of central and eastern Europe, the *gevir*, the *gabai* and the *balebossim*, the prominent members of the community, aspired to be *talmidei hakhamim* themselves. If they could not, they tried to secure a *talmid hakham* as a son-in-law. After the emancipation, the pursuit of spiritual excellence manifested itself in an influx of Jews into prominent positions in the arts, humanities and sciences, far beyond their relative numbers in the population. This led anti-Semites of the nineteenth and twentieth centuries, and especially the Nazis, to

194

regard the pursuit of culture as a Jewish trait. Characteristically, Hans Johst, the Nazi *Arbiter-elegantiarum*, was heard to exclaim that when he heard the word 'culture' he reached for his gun.

In the beginning, Christianity was a Jewish sect, but with the strengthening of its separant components i.e., the deification of Jesus, the dogma of the Trinity in Unity and the foregoing of circumcision and the rules of observance, it became unacceptable to the Jews. The rejection of Christianity by the Jews took place in a typical participant-Tantalic manner by self-segregation and self-effacing resignation. St. Paul, however, was indeed foresighted when he realised that proselitising Gentiles to the new creed was more promising than trying to convert the reluctant Jews. The newly-converted pagans utilised the crucifixion of Christ to persecute the Jews. Typical of separant-activist social characters is this tendency to behave in a militant manner, even in apparently other-worldly religious matters. Moreover, the participant, repressive guilt-laden component in Christianity, contributed by Judaism, curbed the free expression of passions and aggression to which the former Sisyhean pagans had been accustomed. This also fuelled a subconscious feeling of hatred towards the Jews, who were 'responsible' for the displacement and repression of the pagan-separant traits, by Christianity.

The Jews rejected the Greek polytheistic separant religion because they held their own abstract monotheism to be superior. They also dismissed Greek philosophy as inferior to the doctrines and thought of Judaism (Wolson, 1968:85). In a similar vein, the Jews rejected Christianity, amongst other reasons, because of its separant objectification of a man as God and its introduction of the plurality of a Trinity into the uniqueness of monotheism. The Greeks and Romans, on the other hand, accepted Christianity when their religions were in their declining phase, in what Gilbert Murray denoted 'the failure of nerve' (Murray, 1955. Chapter V). Hellenistic and Roman cultures were also exposed for considerable periods to oriental cultural and religious influences, which tempered them with participant components and thus made them more amenable to embracing Chrisitianity.

The German tribes, on the other hand, were in their separant prime of growth, vigour and expansion when they were converted, quite often by coercion, to Christianity. Hence, the fact that Christianity was an artificial graft was especially evident in those Germanic cultures which had not been assimilated by Latinised societies. The German Holy Roman emperors always tried to shirk the yoke of the popes, no doubt mainly for secular, political reasons. However, the conflict was exacerbated by the contrast between a separant force-orientated emperor and a pope whose aim was to impose on the world Judaeo-Christian participant morals, and the notion of universal guilt.

The first massive rebellion against the participant elements in Christianity, and especially its overt Judaic components, was launched by Luther and his German Protestant followers. This again shows that the participant Judaeo-Christian elements were not organically absorbed and integrated into the German separant social character. Finally, when the Jews, after the Emancipation, tried to integrate into German art and culture, they did so through the perspectives and *Weltanschauungen* of their participant background and social character. Hence, quite a considerable segment of the culture and art generated by German Jewry was a synthesis between German separant patterns of culture, utilised as raw material, and the processing contributed by the participant Jewish artists and scientists. This synthetic product was not really accepted or even understood (Sholem, 1975:114-117) by the vast majority of Germans outside the confines of the main urban centres. However, the normative restraints of the participant elements in Christianity kept the German social character in a precarious balance. When this was disrupted by the Nazi rejection of Christianity as a Jewish imposition on the freedom of the Germanic spirit, all hell broke loose. The *Furor Teutonicus* exploded in a frenzy after centuries of confinement within the bounds of participant laws, morals and idealistic transcendence. When the explosion occurred, it erupted violently in all directions, especially against the Jews, who symbolised the former participant restraints in morals, religion and art. Indeed, if legal and moral restraints belonged to the despicable Jewish heritage, which had to be rejected, then everything was possible. The Nazis, paraphrasing Nietzsche, decreed that if the Judaeo-Christian God was dead, then the Teutonic supermen were now gods. In the new order, with Hitler-Odin as leader, these 'deities' could reshape the world, breed new strains of supermen and exterminate the lowly *Untermenschen*.

Our premise may be summarised by the following dialectic between separant and participant social characters. The first phase was the encounter between Hellenism and Judaism which produced the synthesis of Christianity by the participant Jews, and its adoption by the more separant European cultures. The second phase was the renewed encounter in the 19th century between the Jewish social character, recently emancipated from the ghetto but still largely participant, and the separant Germans. The resultant synthesis of 'Jewish' art and culture was rejected by the German *Völkisch* movement when it came to power with the Nazis. In the third phase, the whole Judaeo-Christian mesh of restraints was shed and the explosion of the Holocaust followed.

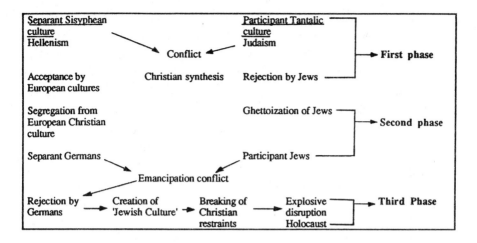

We shall show in this chapter that the Jews rejected the Christian synthesis mainly because of a dynamic we have designated as 'the least interest principle'; (Shoham, 1986:Chapter 10) that is, a mutual rejection of likes and attraction between non-likes. The second phase of segregation will be dealt with in the framework of stigma and scapegoating. The third phase of our model is again amenable to a core dialectics interpretation: the German rejection of the synthesis of 'Jewish' culture and the resultant explosion, were precipitated by the rejection of Christianity, which was the synthesis of our first phase.

This link between the first and third phases of our model makes a cycle in which the removal of the participant restraints, of Christianity (synthesis of first phase), enables the eruption of the Holocaust (third phase) to occur. The violence of the third phase prevents any further viable syntheses. The Jews of Europe were slaughtered, their culture destroyed. The Germans suffered a *Götterdammerung*, their culture was severely maimed and their country divided. Worse still, the rampage of the *Furor Teutonicus*, probably more than any other single factor, set in motion the forces of the Orwellian apocalypse of 1984, which threatened to engulf the world.

THE MURDEROUS FAMILY

One of the main attributes of Judaism is the participant enmeshing of both the here-and-now and the ever-after into a complete legal code. The Torah--the law--is a pulsating unity which engulfs every Jew and the whole Jewish nation. The Torah, as an elaborate system of rules, regulates all the routines of life. Moreover, the duty of every

Jew is to study the Torah, through the Talmud and its interpreters. The *talmid hakham*, the Talmudic scholar, is in essence a law student who imbues his scholastic endeavours with a religious character. These legal and moral rules of behaviour were enforced by the inner controls of conscience and guilt, to which Christianity added mercy and compassion.

The acquisition of morality and a set of norms was denoted by us as the 'Isaac Syndrome', after the biblical myth of Abraham's offering of Isaac. It is a variation on the theme of formal and informal rites of passage. Indeed, most transitions from childhood to adulthood involve the acquisition of the burdens of responsibility by painful rites of passage (Shoham, 1975:114-17). Socialisation involves deprivation and conflict with the normative authority of the family, i.e., the father or his surrogate. The Freudian Oedipal pressures have always been associated with the acquisition of morality and with the social indoctrination of male children. We claim, however, that the process of normative separation is initiated by the father (or his surrogate) by a dynamic which is in fact diametrically opposed to Oedipal pressures. This dynamic involves deprivational pressures on the son by the father and is meant to effect the separation of the adolescent from the family fold and his entry into the loneliness of social responsibility.

Norms are thus imprinted in the adolescent by, as it were, a sacrificial ejection from the permissiveness of the family into the restrictive mesh of laws and morals. Hence, the Nazis' rejection of Judaeo-Christian participant law and morality coincided with the quest to revert back to the German tribal family, where everything was performed with paganistic lack of restraint, where norms were few and almost everything was permitted, if one could get away with it. This might not have been historically true, but it was accepted and adopted by the Nazis through the projection of the amoral and lawless behaviour of the Teutonic family of the *Aesir*. *Odin, Thor, Loki*, and their kin would murder, pillage, rape, and manipulate with the sole factor being the power of the attacker versus the resourcefulness of the opponent. The abrogation by the Nazis of Judaeo-Christian law and morality entailed the rejection of both the norms in the sacrifice of Isaac, as well as the sacrifice of Jesus Christ which signified the ultimate participant morality of achieving grace through victimisation. The quest to return to the previous collective developmental phase of the pagan tribal family is linked to the *Volkisch* ethos of *Blut und Boden*, the return to the blood-kinship of the tribe and the ancestral land of the family.

Tal rightly notes that this stress on the blood element of kinship constitutes the essence of social togetherness and exclusiveness (Tal:114). We may add that Nazi racism is rooted in the idea of the bio-social primacy of the tribal family. The Nazis went further. By rejecting Christian guilt, they abrogated original sin. They thus reverted to Edenic innocence, together with the feeling of omnipotence unrestrained by any participant feeling of guilt. The Nazis' regression to previous developmental phases therefore entailed the amoralisation of the regime of the Third Reich and the adoption of the familial-blood kinship of tribal racism.

When Judaeo-Christian law and morality are foregone and the German finds himself in the bosom of the extended tribal pagan family, he is not subject to collective norms, but as an individual might still find himself subject to morals and compassion. This is why the Nazis intuitively stressed the importance of collectivity: *Ein Volk, Ein Reich, Ein Führer,* which is a variation on the theme of the trinity, or rather, plurality in unity. Indeed, Goebbels highlighted the transformation of the individual German within the collectivity by using the metaphor of the plurality of German worms becoming a dragon within the group. To this end, the Nazi rallies, especially in Nüremberg, served to create a unified, heaving and growling carnivore out of a motley assortment of peasants, artisans, clerks and intellectuals. The uniformed, goose-stepping Nazis felt themselves elevated to the Germanic mythological *Asgaard* and every cowering butcher, salesman and teacher hearing the magic voice of the Fuehrer could feel himself transformed into a demi-god of the *Aesir.* The individual German lost his separate self within the 'dragon', *Sieg Heil* booming in unison, sung to the command of: *Eins, Zwei, Drei: Ein Lied* under Albert Speer's 'Cathedral of Ice' with synchronised spotlights piercing the sky. Such collective regression to a former developmental phase which is the pure participant goal of man, but is impossible to realise, both on the personal and group levels, was thus dragged down to reality by pagan rites.

The Nazis induced the German people to reenact in real life the Teutonic myths, replete with their competitive cruelty and religion of war. This, as we will later elaborate, inevitably led to *Götterdämmerung,* ordained by the Eddic myths and acted out by the Nazis, and through them by the German people as a self-fulfilling prophecy. Myths are projections of longings, quests and collective experiences. But, when someone insists on using mythology as a blueprint for actual existence, it inevitably leads to disaster.

Some sources recount an event after the Wannsee Conference, in which the Final Solution was decided upon, which has not, however, been fully verified. The participants got drunk and danced a Germanic tribal dance on the tables. If true, this is a symbolic ritual signifying that the foreign Jews have no place in the blood (*Blut*) and racially pure tribal family of the *Aesir.* In the Darwinistic struggle of the pagan tribe whose violence is not restrained by law, morals and mercy, Jews are the normative

Wiedergeist, the sinister counter-power of the Wise Men of Zion, who must be exterminated. The wandering Jew has no place in the land-rootedness (*Boden*) of the pastoral *Aesir*. Indeed, the polytheistic deities, both Greek and Teutonic, which are a projection of the separant Greek and Germanic social character, are family-centred, cruel, arbitrary and amoral; yet are subject to the fateful order of things imposed by *moira* (one's lot in life) and *ananke* (divine arbitrary coercion). This lawlessness and amorality correspond to the normlessness and irresponsibility of the pre-rites-of-passage family fold, before the adolescent has been brought into the limits and bonds of normative responsibility by a symbolic sacrifice: the Isaac (or for girls, the *Iphygenia*) syndrome.

The Greek gods are rarely gracious and kind. The Judaeo-Christian conception of a just God, or for that matter, just deserts, is entirely foreign to the Olympian gods. Greek tragedies often depict the arbitrary cruelty of the gods. Moreover, many tragic heroes are incited by the gods to commit acts that will lead these same gods to punish them. The best known example is, of course, the case of Oedipus. It had been predicted by the gods that Oedipus would slay his father and wed his mother. This was ordained so that he could be punished (Ranulf, 1933.Vol.1:42). No reasons of blame, guilt or moral turpitude were given. The condemnation of Oedipus by the gods was surely arbitrary. Oedipus is only one of many cases in Greek tragedy of victims suffering atrocious torture and punishment without being guilty of any sin or crime; in which they are forced by the gods to commit these infractions, and hence are not morally culpable. If we fulminate with righteous indignation against this abomination, we may find the following answer given by Drachmann:

Our first question, when the immediate effect of the magnificent drama has subsided, is this:

> But what has he done? --Done? answers the Greek in astonishment. He has not done anything. That is just the point; it has all happened unknown to him. Well, but then it is all the most outrageous injustice.--I do not understand you, says the Greek: Do you mean to deny that such things can happen to you, any day, nay any moment? Or are you even for an instant safe from the invasion of the most appalling horror that your mind can grasp? If you are, you had best realise what human life is. This is what Sophocles' drama should help you to do (Drachmann, 1911).

The *Aesir* and the *Vanir*, the families of the Teutonic tribal gods, are even more given to xenophobia, cruelty, fornication and infantile practical jokes (MacCulloch,

1964). In contrast, the sacrifice of Isaac and the self-willed victimisation of Christ signify the imposition on man of law, morals, guilt, and the duty of compassion toward other men. Thus, our model decrees that at each developmental stage, both the individual and the collective seek to revert back to an earlier stage. The Germans longed to shed the normative constraints of Judaeo-Christian law and morals, and to return to the amoral irresponsibility of their paganism. They resented the Jews, who symbolised to them the imposition of restraints on their hedonistic paganism.

Some observers have noted the extremities of the German social character and the contradictory fluctuations of the Nazis (Shirer, 1961:434-35). Our thesis also states that the base of the German social character was shaky because its two core vectors were not integrated. When the centre did not hold, it was possible for the Nazis to subdue, or even neutralise, its restraining participant components, so that the separant core frenzy of the *Furor Teutonicus* could reign in full force. The regression to the tribal pagan ethos facilitated the acceptance of the authority of an absolute leader. The Judaeo-Christian concepts of justice and morals imply the weighing of the pros and cons of a given situation, and emphasise restraint, rather than the arbitrary use of power. When this sense of law and justice is rejected, the tribal chieftain reigns supreme. Thus, the separant power of Odin knew no limits; and consequently, the omnipotence of Adolf Hitler, *der Fuehrer*, recognised no boundaries of law, morality or mercy.

LIVING MYTHS AND MYTH-PLAYING

We use myths not only as illustrations for our theoretical premises, but as their empirical anchors. Students of myths have always regarded them as reliable records of events before written history in *ille tempore*. Bachofen says: 'The mythical tradition may be taken as a faithful reflection of the life in those times in which historical antiquity is rooted. It is a manifestation of primordial thinking, an immediate historical revelation and consequently, a highly reliable source' (Bachofen, 1967:73). Eliade further claims that because myths reflect the occurrence of events on a high level of abstraction, they also reveal the principles or designs underlying events. He writes:

> ... the myth disclosed the eventful creation of the world and of man, and at the
> same time, the principles which govern the cosmic process and human existence
> ... the myths succeed each other and articulate themselves into a sacred history
> which is continuously recovered in the life of the community, as well as in the

existence of each individual ... What happened in the beginning describes, at once, both the original perfection and the destiny of each individual (Eliade, 1954:43).

This brings us to Jung, who regards myths not only as the archetypal contents of the 'collective human unconsciousness', but also as a means for individual psychic expression (Jung, 1944:616). Our stance is even more extreme: in *Salvation Through The Gutters*, (Shoham, 1979) we stated:

...our methodological anchor is the conception of myths as projections of personal history. The individual is aware of his personality as the sole existential entity in his cognition. This awareness of existence is the only epistemological reality. Myths cannot, therefore, be divorced from the human personality. Whatever happened to us in the amnestic years, and even later, is projected onto our theory of the creation of the universe, magic and other human beings. The events that happened in the highly receptive amnestic years have been recorded and stored by the human brain. Events that happened after the amnestic years may be recalled cognitively, but whatever happened within these first years of life is recalled *inter alia* by myths of cosmogony. Myths as personal history may, therefore, be regarded as the account of some crucial developmental stages in the formative years. Moreover, human development in the early formative years passes in an accelerated manner through the whole evolutionary phases of the species.

Hence, myths are also a projection of the development of the species, as it is reflected in the development of the individual. It is interesting to note that this conception of myths as a projection of personal history may be inferred from the Apocalypse of Baruch which states that 'every man is the Adam of his own soul' (Shoham, 1979. Introduction). Every human being experiences original sin as a stage of development, so that the myth of the Fall is a projection of individual, yet also universal, human developmental experience. However, myths become archetypal projections of human experience only when they are widespread. The more common a developmental experience, the greater its chances of becoming a mythical projection. The inverse is also valid: the more widespread a myth, the higher the chance that it is a projection of a widespread, or even universal, phase of human development. The universality of the myth of the Fall, for instance, points to the fact that the corresponding developmental phase, the separation of the individual self from the unified whole of early orality, is indeed experienced by every human being.

202

Myths have many layers. The Lurianic Kabbala, for instance, utilizes the myth of the breaking of the vessels to depict cosmogony, yet vestiges of the same myth may be interpreted as a projection of the experience of the 'thrownness', or state of being ejected from the womb, of birth--the ejection of the neonate from the womb into the world, with all the associated trauma. In a similar vein, the myth of the Fall may be taken as a projection of the crystallisation of the self at early orality, but some of its components may also be linked to the proscriptions of incest and hence to the vicissitudes of sexual desire. Thus, myths may serve as empirical anchors of both core personality dynamics and of the structure and processes of social characters. We denote this method as 'mytho-empiricism'. For all their theoretical differences, Bachofen, Jung, Briffault, Claude Levi-Strauss and Eliade are all mytho-empiricists, because they rely considerably on myths for the empirical validation of their theories.

We may point out, however, that the role of myths, and in our context, the German Eddic Mythology, has not been readily appreciated by all scholars of our subject. Trevor-Roper, for instance, considers the mythical roots of Nazism to be '...bestial Nordic nonsense'. The Teutonic Eddic myths were not nonsense, but the core component of Nazism. We shall show that the Nazis were not only guided by the Germanic myths, but that they actually tried to relive and reenact them, both in their frenzied burst of power and their subsequent decline and fall into *Götterdämmerung*.

The mythology of separant cultures is not about the afterlife, but relates to the here-and-now. In Greek mythology, Tartarus (hell) is just another place within space and time. In a similar vein, the concern of Germanic mythology is just another level of existence in the here-and-now. Thus, soldiers slain in battle are taken by the *Valkyries* to *Valhalla*, where they carry on their earthly existence, but as if on another continent, somewhere in the mountains high above the clouds. Hitler and the Nazis aimed to mould the German Reich into a sacred myth. When this was effected, *der Fuehrer* would slip naturally into the role of the god Odin-Wotan (Jung, 1964:185). The vast majority of Germans embraced this manic mythical existence. They started to rebel against Hitler (July 1944 plot) only when it became clear that the myth of a Thousand Year Reich was the pipe dream of a lunatic and that the Fuehrer could no longer credibly play the role of Odin-Wotan.

The Nazis, as Tal states, turned myth into reality (Tal, 1979:43). According to W.I. Thomas' theorem of social sciences, if a myth is defined as reality, it becomes real in its consequences. But as mythology warns, both Sisyphean and Tantalic goals may be longed for but never fully realised; thus, the living of a myth and the acting out of mythological roles inevitably lead to disaster. This is the macabre saga of a whole nation whose mythology ceased to be just one facet of its collective subconscious and became an actuality, guiding its political, social and personal existence. In the beginning, the Nazis took the world by surprise and most of Europe was swept by their mythological frenzy. But, later on, Hitler-Wotan, Goering-Thor, Goebbels-Loki and Himmler-Henry the Fowler and the German war machine committed such glaring mistakes precisely because they were pursuing mythological goals by a *pot pourri* of realistic and mythical means. They soon started sliding on the steep road to ruin.

Often the Nazis played mythical roles in which reality and play-acting intermingled into a surrealistic haze. At Munich, prior to the Second World War, the French and the British conducted themselves by the rules of diplomacy and international law, according to which *Pacta sunt Servanda*. But Hitler and the Nazis played by rules of the mythical *Aesir*, according to which one could cheat and trick one's opponents without the restraining obstacles of law and morals. The end was what counted, whatever the means. For Himmler, the Reich was a sacred myth. In the spirit of Henry the Fowler, the medieval Saxon king of whom he believed himself to be the reincarnation, he regarded his S.S. divisions, and later the whole of German society, as a tribal unit, which had to enslave or exterminate all those who did not belong to it. Hess flew to England, literally motivated by the mythical vapours in his chaotic brain, on a mission to induce the Germanic brethren to stop fighting and to rejoin the Germans in the family fold of the *Aesir*. Hitler frantically planned megalomanic monuments fit for the abode of the chief deity of *Asgaard* and his court. Even on the verge of defeat, he was still contemplating the construction of his Great Domed Hall, larger than St. Peter's and the Arch of Triumph (Trevor-Roper, 1962:55). This mythological role-playing induced Hitler to make his worst tactical error, which probably sealed his fate even at that early stage of the war. After the collapse of France, he behaved towards the British like one *Niebelungen* knight to his brethren.

He did not attack the retreating British forces at Dunkirk, nor did he launch a massive attack against the British Isles. He thus allowed Britain to reorganise its army. As he regarded the British as members of his mythical *Aesir,* he waited for peace overtures from England which never came; nor could he have expected them to come, had he assessed the situation realistically and not through the prism of a mythological tribal chieftain.

The Nazis followed the blueprint drafted for them by Eddic mythology to the hilt, replete with the Grand Finale of The Twilight of the Gods (*Götterdämmerung*). In August 1944, Hitler realised that Germany would surely lose the war. He therefore decided to make good his statement of 27 November 1941, that if the German nation was not strong enough to make the sacrifices necessary to its existence, it should perish. Consequently, he carried out a series of campaigns destined to destroy

Germany (Speer, 1971:72,97,193-94). These included the suicidal German attack in the Ardennes on 16 December 1944 which squandered Germany's last military reserves; the catastrophic decisions with regard to the Eastern front, which left the German army exposed to the vengeance of the Russians, whereas his resolve to resist more ardently on the Western front curbed the advance of the less destructive Western Allies. On 18 March, 1945, Field Marshal Keitel issued a Fuehrer-order to evacuate the entire German populace in the face of the advancing Western Allies. As no organised transportation was available, this evacuation would have amounted to a death march. On 19 March 1945, Hitler issued another order which amounted to a total 'scorched earth' policy to destroy the industrial, communications and supply resources of the Third Reich. Speer writes that this order, if implemented, would have resulted in Hitler's plan to drag the German Nation to Valhalla, and was equivalent to the Final Solution of the Jewish problem. The rationale of this might have been that the Nazis used the contrast with the inferior Jews to reinforce their own sense of superiority and worth. Hence, if the Germans were doomed to perdition, their *Wiedergeist* definers should also go down with them, as an inseparable appendage in both glory and doom.

Furthermore, if the Jews signified for the pagan Nazis the restraining, participant element in European culture, they had to be combated more ferociously. This could explain why, as German military losses increased, so too did the quantity of scarce supplies and logistic means given over to the destruction of the Jews. Thus, destruction of the two went hand in glove, and were to accelerate together.

SYMBIOSIS

Another component in our dialectical model is the fact that prior to the Holocaust, the Jews developed a spectacular symbiosis with German culture. After the Emancipation, *fin-de-siècle* Austria and Germany witnessed an inrush of Jews whose ancestors had just left the ghettoes and were acquiring an ever-growing hold on Austrian, and later German, culture, science and fine arts. People like Einstein, Freud, Marx, Heine, Mahler, Ehrlich, Boaz, Mendelsohn, Hofmanstahl, Schnitzler, Strauss, Zweig, Lasker-Schiller, Wassermann, Schoenberg, Weil, Liebermann, Reinhart, Klemperer, Von-Sternberg, Weittgensten, Toller, and Tucholsky, who were leaders and innovators in German and Austrian science, art, and philosophy, were either Jews, or of Jewish descent. The Jews made their contribution on a German cultural base, but their creativity was filtered through their participant background and social character. This cultural synthesis was largely not understood and basically not accepted by the German hosts. However, with the German *Götterdämmerung* and the Jewish Holocaust, both victim and tormentor suffered severely. Germany and Austria experienced a scientific and cultural decline after the Second World War, from which, in some areas, they have not yet recovered. After the Holocaust, European Jews went into almost total cultural and creative eclipse, and Israel, which absorbed a large proportion of Holocaust survivors, has not reached, in comparative terms, the cultural excellence of Jews in *fin-de-siècle* Vienna or of Germany at the beginning of the present century.

THE SACRIFICIAL VICTIM

We have already pointed out that the collective Jewish adoption of the Torah was a manifestation of the Isaac Syndrome extended to the entire people of Israel. Christianity, which stressed the universal values of love, mercy, and grace, was initiated by the Jew, Jesus Christ, who was the archetypal participant victim. However, this Christ was adopted by the separant Crusaders, the rapacious feudal lords and the martial medieval church, and used as a weapon to bully Christ's old compatriots. The glaring paradox here was that Christ, the self-effacing participant and willing victim--'God's own sacrificial lamb'--was used to further victimise the participant European Jews. The Jews sang while being burned at the *auto-da-fe, 'Lechu Nerannena L'Adonai* i.e., ('Let us sing to the Lord'). This further enraged the bullies who took this readiness to be sacrificed as a diabolical affront. This *dance macabre* of Jewish martyrdom exploded to monstrous proportions with the Holocaust. The fatal encounter of the Jews with a cannibalistic separant horde stripped of the restraining Judaeo-Christian checks of law and mercy, claimed six million non-resurrected Isaacs and Jesuses. The Warsaw Ghetto even provided another archetypal victim, a direct descendant of Isaac and Christ. This was Janusz Korczak, who refused the Nazis' offer of freedom if he agreed to abandon his 200 orphans. He dressed all of them in their best clothes, as befitting *Agni dei*, and climbed with them onto the cattle trucks destined for the crematoria at Treblinka. Unlike Christians, Jews need no passion play to reinforce their faith. Their role as perpetual participant victims has been ingrained in them by torrents of blood. It has been projected onto them in the form of myths and metaphysical symbols, highlighted by the hallowed trinity of Isaac, Christ and Korczak.

There might be some validity in the contention that the younger culture and religion is antagonistic to the older culture and religion in an Oedipal manner. In our context, however, the paternal Jewish participant culture is bullied and slaughtered by a maternal, separant pagan culture. A corollary to this is that the victim himself is to blame for his plight. 'It serves them right, the Elders of Zion and their kin, if we let them have it, for trying to subjugate the world' (Tal, *Structures of German Political Theology in the Nazi Era*, 43). If the victim is 'guilty', then the bully can attack him with impunity. Hence, the Jews were an ideal victim. Their symbolic power and danger justified their being bullied; yet their real powerlessness made such an assault a 'safe' and hazardless venture. This is one of the main reasons why the history of the Jews in Europe is that of an almost continuous martyrdom. A Jungian analyst comments thus: The Jews are the perennial archetypal victim for the last two thousand years. Israel for some years became a heroic nation. This was against the archetype. However, after the Yom Kippur War, Israel became a victim again and thus reverted back to the Jewish archetype. The chosen people were thus chosen to suffer and to be victimised. Ezekiel said (16:6) ... 'and when I passed by thee, and saw thee polluted in thine own blood, I said unto thee, when thou wast in thy blood, live'. Such victimization serves to reinforce the normative excellence of the Jews. The sacrifice of Isaac, which signified the choice of the Jews to accept the legal authority of the paternal God, is constantly reenacted in blood. By his submission to victimisation, the Jew fortifies his normative righteousness before God. His constant affirmation of the Law thus becomes sealed in his own blood.

This might well be the subconscious complicity of the Jewish victim in the carnivorous assaults on him by the separant bully.

THE MACABRE DYAD

Hitler had warned the Jews often but they failed to take him seriously, among other reasons because he spoke bad German. Hitler never gave a written order for the Final Solution. In all probability, it was given orally to Himmler. The roving units of the S.S., the *Einsatzgruppen*, were entrusted in April 1941 with the '*Endziel*', i.e., the 'final goal', Nazi jargon for the killing of all undesirable elements on the Eastern front. On 31 July 1941, the 'total solution' of the Jewish problem was extended to all areas under German dominion. On 29 January 1942, the Wannsee Conference was held to co-ordinate the various ministries and services engaged in the Final Solution. All these murderous preparations were taken with the separant order and Teutonic meticulousness typical of the Nazis. As for the victims, many students of the Holocaust, foremost amongst them Gerald Reitlinger (Reitlinger, 1961) and Raul Hilberg, (Hilberg, 1973) have pointed out the meagre resistance of the Jews to their extermination, as they went like 'sheep to the slaughter'. On the other hand, recent studies showed that the Jews resisted the Nazis more often and in more ways than was previously realised (Bauer, 1979). However, the main reason given for this lack of resistance of the Jews was that no country was eager to receive Jewish refugees; all Nazi plans to deport Jews, including the Madagascar Plan, failed. The Nazis thus launched a full-fledged extermination campaign. Passive acceptance of the genocide of the Jews was shown by the great majority of nations under Nazi dominion; the heroic resistance to the deportation of the Jews by the Danes being a glaring exception. The Nazis utilised techniques of secrecy, deception, and degradation very effectively to break the self-respect of their victims. They gave power and executive functions to the Jewish *Judenrats* and police so that collaboration in the deportation to the death camps was inevitable. The Jews had a long history of bargaining with their oppressor, and during the centuries they had developed a technique of gaining time. This is characterised by the story of the *paritz* (the feudal lord) and his dog. Once, a particularly cruel *paritz* ordered a Rabbi to teach his dog to talk; if not, he would kill all the Jews in the Rabbi's community. The Rabbi agreed to perform this task within five years. When he returned home, his congregation worriedly asked him how he could fulfil such an impossible promise. 'In five years' time', answered the Rabbi, 'the *paritz* may die, or the dog may die'. And so the Jews tried to gain time with the Nazis by complying with their demands, by bargaining with them as much as they could, hoping something would materialise which would save them as it had in the past. It was useless to resist the Nazis, because this would provoke them to accelerate the deportations and exterminations. Some Jews did not believe, or did not want to believe, in the death camps; and others still believed in the compassion and humanity of the Germans.

We, however, claim that whatever the resistance of the Jews to their extermination, and whatever the reasons for helping the Nazis to carry out their task, the opposition of the Jews to their slaughter would have been greater and the task of the Nazis more difficult if there was not a subconscious tendency among the Jews to make victims of themselves. The participant social character, which aims, as a core-goal, the annihilation of itself into non-being, is predisposed in a dyadic situation to assume the role of victim. This macabre symbiosis between oppressor and victim means that persecution of the oppressed reinforces the latter's normative suffering, and hence his sacrificial righteousness. Moreover, in Jungian psychology, the aggressor and his victim are the two complementary components of a single archetype. Through victimisation, the Jew reinforces his unique participation, his moral ascendancy, and his choice of suffering as a sign of transcendental excellence. The Nazis, on the other hand, tried to get rid of their own participant components by projecting them on the Jew and making a scapegoat of him, presumably cleansing themselves of their despised restraining norms and morals. The notion of *kiddush hashem*, the sanctification of God by a willing, dignified self-sacrifice, also includes disdain for the oppressor and moral superiority over him; it is the sign of Jewish participant martyrs from Jesus Christ to Janusc Korczak. We summarise the dialectical component of our model in graphic form as follows:

The Dialectical Component Model

Separant Persecutor	*Participant Victim*
Germany Arise (*Deutchland Erwache*)	Judah Perish (*Juden Verecke*)
The murderous Pagan family	The Isaac Syndrome, Judaeo-Christian, legal and moral restraints
Blood and Earth (*Blut und Boden*)	Participant guilt
Racist tribalism; rejection of Judeo-Christian sacrificial normative restraints. One Nation, One State, One Leader (Ein Volk, Ein Reich, Ein Führer)	
Living Myths (*Götterdämmerung*) The Twilight of the Gods	
Bully	Sacrificial Victim

Symbiosis

↓

The Macabre Dyad

THE SINISTER SIDE

With the present section we start our initial survey of the second group of preconditions for the Holocaust. These relate to the self-definition of the Nazis as worthy and superior to the vile Jews. In Nazi Germany, an authoritarian state where ambiguity could not be tolerated, the Jew was portrayed as the antithesis of the Teutonic superman. Actually, the Jew was much more; he was an essential part of Nazi ideology. Thesis and antithesis, the ideal and its negation, were generally voiced together. In a typical speech, Hitler ranted, 'Everything beautiful we see around us today is only the creation of the Aryan, his spirit and industry; only the bad things are the heritage of the Jew' (Heiden, 1944). This was the basis of the declaration of Von Schonerer, the founder of modern political anti-Semitism, some decades before Hitler,

'We pan-Germans regard anti-Semitism as the mainstay of our national ideology' (Arendt, 1958:229).

Tannenbaum, who wrote one of the most penetrating analyses of Nazi racism, has stated:

> In general, it seems that there could be no 'true Aryan' without a Jew somewhere in the background. This may sound like a paradox, yet it can be easily explained. German racists needed both an 'Aryan' and a 'Semite' race to balance each other out. As in a cable-car mechanism, the two pulleys are needed to compensate each other: down goes the Jew, up goes the Nordic. The superiority of the Aryan is predicated on the inferiority of the Semite (Tannenbaum, 1938).

Pulzer's study of the genesis of anti-Semitism in Germany and Austria concludes, after a rigorous statistical analysis, that it drew its strength mainly from the proliferating new class of white-collar workers, rather than from the lower classes. 'Economically, the members of the new *Mittelstand*...were almost indistinguishable from the proletariat ...In social status, however, they were distinct from the working class and in a society as rigidly hierarchic as the German, they were strongly endowed with consciousness of class superiority. Their (preoccupation was) to keep their distance from those below' (Pulzer, 1964). The more they could stigmatise, degrade, and oppress those below them, the higher became their own relative status. This is why they were so eager to scorn and degrade the Jews, once the government offered them as scapegoats. There was no objective point or level from which status and class could be measured. If one could not climb the tower, one could deepen the abyss.

In *The Mark of Cain* (Shoham-Rahav, 1982), we presented a model of stigmatisation; most of the components of which are relevant for our present premises. We envisaged the tagging process as a projection of undesirable features and an outlet for the aggression of the stigmatiser. The stigmatised were conceived by us as a scapegoat; somebody to look down upon. The object of stigma was characterised by conspicuousness, symbolic threat, and lack of real power. All these components apply to the relationships between Jew and Nazi, or for that matter, between Jew and all anti-Semites.

The conspicuousness and separateness of the Jews was pointed out by one of the earliest anti-Semites. 'And Haman said unto King Ahasuerus: There is a certain people scattered abroad and dispersed among the people in all the provinces of thy kingdom; and their laws are diverse from all people; neither keep they the King's laws; therefore, it is not for the King's profit to suffer them' (Esther 3:8). The separateness of the

Jews arose more than anything else because of their monotheism. Jews were glaringly conspicuous in a polytheistic milieu with a pagan tolerance for a plurality of gods. This led to a social separation and an ethnocentric self-segregation by the Jews. This, in its turn, was balanced with a counter-segregation by their socio-religious environment.

Later, in Christian Europe, the segregation of the Jews was even more conspicuous; their refusal to accept Christianity led to their ghettoisation, their being limited to lowly occupations, and their actual tagging with special signs and attire. Hans Johst defined the excellence of the Aryan race, 'the anti-Jew,' by contrast with the 'degenerate Jew' as follows:

> The uniqueness of the Aryan race is a manifestation of the Volk-spirit. Since this spirit is from and for the Volk by virtue of its elitist essence, 'it cannot be given to everyman to profit' (1 Cor. 12:7). These charismatic gifts are uniquely Aryan. It is enough to look at the Jew and his history of suffering; the Jew who is the very embodiment of moral decay and physical perversion, of spiritual petrification, and aesthetic degeneration, in order to realise that only the counter-Jew, the anti-Jew, is the one on whom the charisma of world leadership, of life, power, and destiny had been bestowed (Tal, 1978:40).

Johst uses, here, the precise terminology of definition by contrast: the Aryan, socially-pure, Nazi, is not defined by his 'positive' attributes, but negatively by his non-Jewish ones. The Jew thus provides the contours and contents of the characteristics of the anti-Jew.

Hence, the Jew in Nazi ideology is the age-old *Wiedergeist*; the sinister side which defines the right side. This vile *Wiedergeist* had to be created out of disparate components because, physically and behaviourally the Jews were heterogenous. This task was entrusted to the anti-Semitic caricature and especially to Streicher's *Stürmer*. The stereotypical *Stürmer* Jew was short, with crooked legs and a pot belly, fat lips below an enormous hooked nose, tiny beady eyes behind thick glasses; his hand fondling money or the helpless, limp figures of Aryan girls. The Aryan stereotype was the positive mirror image of the negative degeneracy of the *Stürmer* Jew. Needless to say, the physically and behaviourally heterogenous Aryans were as remote from their stereotype as the Jews from theirs.

The Jewish stereotype was not invented by Streicher. Seneca and Tacitus had already portrayed the dirty and treacherous Jew. The non-aesthetic Jew was thus contrasted by these early anti-Semites with the Graeco-Roman ideals of beauty. This sterotype of the disgusting Jew was adopted and developed further by the medieval

Christians. It was refined by Luther and inflated to monstrous proportions by Dühring and the *Völkisch* ideologists. Hitler followed a well-trodden path when he claimed in *Mein Kampf* that Jews were dirty, sexually-depraved whoremongers and white slavers. The Jew was racially low--an *Untermensch*, in contrast with the pure-blooded German *Ubermensch*. *Boden und Blut* were also positively contrasted with the homeless wandering Jew. Finally, the Jew was a Marxist; the ideological anathema to Nazism. Dühring thus proclaimed the Jews to be the 'inner Carthage' of Germany; and, like Cato, he demanded their destruction lest they destroy Germany.

The need of the Germans for a scapegoat was fierce. Despite their potential vigour, they lagged behind in most Sisyphean areas. Until the unification of Germany, brought about by Bismark, the country consisted of hundreds of independent principalities, duchies, and counties (over 300 at the end of the eighteenth century). Industrialisation and urbanisation came late. Moreover, The *Deutschland Uber Alles* separant credo suffered a severe blow in World War I. The crack German army was, in the eyes of the Germans, not defeated, but stabbed in the back by the Bolsheviks and the liberals, the puppets of the 'Wise Elders of Zion'. Hence, the participant Jew, 'The Enemy of the People', was the restraining buffer. His curbing of the German Sisyphean force made him an internal saboteur. Yet, if the Jews managed to perform this destructive feat, they must be omnipotent--hence, the Wise Elders of Zion were portrayed by the Nazis as the clandestine rulers of the world. Some of the Nazis sincerely believed in this myth. S.S. General Von Dem Bach Zelewsky, for instance, testified at Nüremberg that only when he saw the Jews helplessly slaughtered with nobody coming to their rescue did he stop believing in the omnipotence of the Elders of Zion. Indeed, the Jews were the ideal scapegoat: a powerless power symbol.

They were also a handy and socially conspicuous enemy of the people. Whenever it was necessary to divert attention from internal problems or to tighten the cohesion of the German people, aggression and hatred were directed toward the bizarre, incomprehensible and hence dangerous, Jew. This scapegoating and rejection of the Jew in Christian Europe during the Middle Ages and in later periods, and the counter-rejection by the Jews of the Gentiles, resulted in Jewish ghettoisation. After the Emancipation, the Jews became frantically *arriviste*, as a reaction to their participant self-effacement in the ghetto. Such achievement-orientation made them ostentatious and conspicuous and thus, once again, prone to scapegoating. This time, however, they could not find solace in Judaism which many of them had left behind in the ghetto. Their frames of reference were German; hence they had no defence in the face of the stigmatising tags. They thus internalised the stigma and sank into *Selbsthaas*, (self-hatred): from the extreme suicidal self-despairing of a Weininger to the stoic self-derogation of a Rathenau, who stated that the Jews were an Asiatic tribe in the midst of Germany.

Consequently, even if the Jews tried to become assimilated, as they eagerly did in Germany, the need for a scapegoat would reidentify them as the despised outsider.

CHURCH, RACE, AND THE NAZI *AESIR*

There is a continuity in the stigmatising of Jews by Christians and Nazis, with some marked differences. The most important of these was that no baptism could save a Jew from Auschwitz. The main segregating criterion of the Nazis was based, not on affiliation, but on blood and race, which cannot be altered. The *deicidal* image of the diabolical *Wiedergeist* branded on the Jew by the Christians was adopted by the Nazis. However, the additional tag of racial pollution added by the Nazis was indelible. The struggle between the pure-blooded Nazis and the racially-polluted Jews could only be resolved by a blood-letting. The seeds of the Holocaust were already sown when the labels of degeneracy, tagged on the Jews, were deemed to be based on unalterable genetic criteria. Furthermore, if the Nazis were the resurrected deities of the *Eddic Aesir* and *Vanir,* they were permitted everything, especially if they were engaged in ridding the German *Herrenrasse*, the Master Race, of genetically-corrupt elements. The task could not be subject to sentiments and morals. The extermination of undesirable elements was viewed as a matter of necessity.

The racial purity of the Nazis was beatified by the transcendence of German mythology, with Hitler-Odin as God incarnate. Race was thus made sacred and the purity of the blood of the German Volk and its excellence ordained by destiny (Geva, 1977:70). One was born into the beauty and wholesomeness of the German Volk. Judaeo-Christian norms did not apply to the separant *Aesir* family in which everything was morally permissible. Moreover, these moral mandates came from a race which anchored itself on anti-aesthetic participant abstractions. Such abstractions stemmed from the proscriptions of graven images by a monotheistic God who did not lend himself to physical, temporal or personal description.

Changes in the self-image of the Nazis and the relabelling of their acts became possible with the shift in their frame of reference from themselves as individuals, to themselves as part of a collectivity. The Nazis' collective fixation on the group whitewashed all their deeds. Morals are for individuals; but a nation, a Reich, cannot be wrong or morally depraved. Hitler, Borman, and Himmler were honest in their personal expenses, (Friedlander, 1971:64), but colossal gangsters in the name of the

213

Reich. The Nazi corporal at Auschwitz, defending himself, claimed that he took part in a collective work; and a collectivity cannot be immoral. Indeed, even Durkheim would have supported him in saying that in a cohesive society like Nazi Germany, being regarded as immoral is a contradiction in terms.

The Nazi revolution, with its radical change of values and abrogation of morals, needed a corresponding change of labels and language. The Nazi 'Newspeak' drew heavily on religion, archaic *Volkisch* sources, Eddic mythology, and *Blut und Boden* terms of speech. 'Language', said Walter Poppelreuther, 'should give free, conscious expression to the primordial impulses of the German man who is bound to a racial stock, and the sound, vital impulses of his natural life, precisely by overcoming the counter-race' (Friedlander, 1971:68). The German language thus became a branding tool in the fight against the Jews.

We may sum up the predisposing labelling and stigmatising factors of Nazi anti-Semitism schematically as follows:

Anti-Semitism as a Stigmatising Process

The Stigmatisers	*The Stigmatised*
An outlet of aggression	Scapegoat, 'Somebody to look down upon'.
Projection of vileness	Conspicuous outsider
Self-definition of worth by contrast with the vile *Wiedergeist*	Powerless power symbol. The stereotype of the racially impure and genetically polluted *Untermensch*

BACKGROUND FACTORS

The two groups of predisposing factors we have posited interacted with the socio-economic background and political processes of German society to effect the eruption of the Holocaust. In the economic sphere, Sombart points out that the Jews, at the beginning of the 20th century, constituted about one per cent of the German population, yet they controlled seven per cent of the national property and were directors of nineteen per cent of commercial and industrial firms. In 1907, 30 out of 52 bankers in Berlin were Jews (Friedlander, 1977:60). This, no doubt, kindled the fires of envy among competitors, particularly among those who were economically hurt, or even ruined, by the war. The severe inflation in Germany of the 1920s, and the economic crisis which ensued shocked the populace and induced them to seek a scapegoat. The economically successful Jews were a target for resentment, especially when their consumption and display of achievement was ostentatious. The press, at that time almost the sole mode of mass communication, was controlled predominantly by Jews. In Berlin, for instance, out of 21 daily newspapers, 13 were owned by Jews and four more controlled by them. The Jews played a central role in the cultural and artistic life in the urban centres, especially in Berlin. An extreme disproportion could be observed in the number of Jewish university students, who constituted around 50 per cent of the student body (Friedlander, 1971:64). This is merely one sign of the frantic Jewish drive for upward social mobility.

Politically, Jews were prominent in the Weimar Republic and occupied a number of positions that made them both politically prominent and vulnerable. Rathenau, for instance, was responsible for meeting the economic and political demands of the victors of the First World War; while Cohn and Zinsheimer were members of the Inquiry Committee which investigated the German defeat and before which such august war heroes as Hindenburg and Ludendorf had to testify (Geva, 77:70). This, we may assume, exacerbated resentment against the Jews.

Anomic processes in Germany were linked to the classic dynamics of social change. In 1871, Germany's population was 69 per cent rural, and 31 per cent urban. Forty years later, the urban population increased to 60 per cent and the rural decreased to 40 per cent (Friedlander, 1971:68). By the beginning of the 20th century, Germany had become the second largest industrial state in the world after the United States, following a relatively short period of industrialisation. This speedy urbanisation and industrialisation was recognised by Durkheim as a potent anomic process. As Jews were prominent in these dynamics of social change, which damaged the social position of the traditionally conservative Germans, they exposed themselves to blame for destroying deep-rooted *Völkisch* values. The 19th century was a time of fierce nationalism in Germany. Complementing this nationalism was a xenophobia directed especially against Jews, 'the outsiders in our midst'.

Defeat in war, the shameful Treaty of Versailles, the masses of disenchanted soldiers returning to a ruined economy, to inflation and unemployment, all fuelled the search for a culprit. The Jews, 'the traitors in our midst', fouled the separantly efficient German war machine, 'stabbing the country in its back'. Otherwise, the German army, the glorious kin of the *Aesir*, could not have lost the war!

Finally, the Jews tended to be democrats, socialists, and Communists because these movements were, outwardly at least, strongly in favour of granting full equality to all minorities, especially to Jews. Moreover, the Jews were conspicuous among the leadership of socialist movements and the Communist revolutionaries in Russia. This again reinforced the *Wiedergeist* image of the Jews in contrast to the predominant

215

Völkisch nationalism of the Germans. These background factors may be roughly classified under four headings: economic, socio-structural, value disintegrating-anomic, and political.

THE MODEL

The interdisciplinary model which we present at the end of this chapter presents the composite interaction of the predisposing and background factors of German anti-Semitism which were triggered by Hitler.

Our approach is composite, dynamic, and multivariate. Any model which tries to explain a social phenomenon solely by one group of factors is untenable. Methodologically, our model is composed of two sets of multivariate factors. It should be stressed that the background factors of our model have been studied and documented by many researchers and scholars. The segregating mechanisms of anti-Semitism have also been researched, but have not previously been structured into the stigma theory which we present. The core dialectics of separation and participation and the mytho-empirical predispositions to anti-Semitism are entirely new, and are the dynamic component of our model.

Core dialectics, as predisposing factors to anti-Semitism, have been adapted from our personality theory to apply to group relationships. When the separant Teutonic social character was seemingly subdued by Judaeo-Christian participant laws and morals, the Germans reacted with an eruption of *Furor Teutonicus* against the scheming, wise Elders of Zion.

The self-definition of the Nazis in contrast to the stigmatising stereotype assigned to the Jews, might overlap the core dialectic factors; but at this stage of our analysis, determinating the nature and extent of the overlap is not crucial. The background factors may also overlap, but this too does not alter the essential structure of our model. It should be noted that both groups of predisposing factors fall within the periphery of the background factors. The triggering of the two parts of our model into the Holocaust by Hitler and the Nazi *Aesir* has not been dealt with by us before; and we shall elaborate on it in the present section.

Scholars of Nazism disagree as to whether Hitler initiated the Nazi movement, or whether it evolved through an accumulation of factors. Our answer is that both views are relevant if considered within a framework of a deterministic model like ours. In our model, the predisposing and background factors are triggered into Nazi anti-Semitism by the person of the Führer. Indeed, Hitler seems to have unified the German people

216

like no other leader before him. He catalysed the process by which, to use Goebbels' metaphor, 'the multitude of German worms became a dragon'. It is irrelevant whether Hitler was sane or not. What counts is that the German people's messianic quests and mythical projections converged on a person who was able, within a given context of place and time, to embody and fulfil them. Hitler became the head of the German dragon, spewing oratorical fire in the 'Cathedral of Ice' built for him by Speer in Nüremberg. Thus he reached for the mythical *Asgaard* in the turgid German heaven. The *Völkisch* nationalist idealogy was free-floating in the German political and social climate. Hitler crystallised it around his person; his leadership embodied the will of the people. He thus provided the Germans with a martial faith in the 'second coming' of Odin, at the head of the Eddic Aesir. 'My will', he declared, 'is your faith'. Hitler regarded himself as a Wagnerian Siegfried, but he was more than Siegfried; he was Odin incarnate (Speer, 1971:72,97,193-94). He was the son of God becoming God in the flesh; the source of faith as well as its symbol; the source of law and justice as well as its enforcer; the source of power as well as its brandisher. The Nazi salute served as, and looked like a benediction; the benediction of the Nazi flags was a communion and a Holy Mass. The Führer provided a magical field force of protection. The Germans believed that the wall on which the portrait of Hitler hung could not be damaged by Allied bombs.

The present work is not value-free. No one can be intellectually neutral toward Auschwitz, especially if the author is a Jew and an Israeli, although the author, being an existentialist, does not believe in regrets or forgiveness. Each act and happening is a unique convergence of events making an indelible mark on the cosmos. Our present chapter therefore seeks explanations that are as intellectually astute as possible; yet in the background there is a muffled shriek of rage. We try unsuccessfully to contain our fury against the monstrosity of man, ever since his Neanderthal forefather was pushed to, or stumbled upon, the path to culture.

Interdisciplinary Model
of
German Anti-Semitism

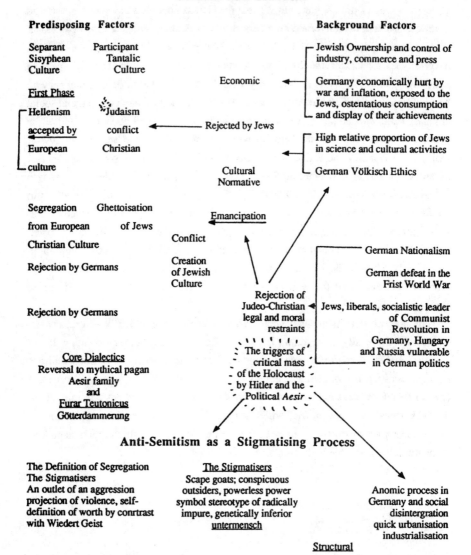

Predisposing Factors

Separant Participant
Sisyphean Tantalic
Culture Culture

First Phase

Hellenism Judaism

accepted by conflict

European Christian

culture

Segregation Ghettoisation

from European of Jews

Christian Culture

Rejection by Germans

Rejection by Germans

Core Dialectics
Reversal to mythical pagan
Aesir family
and
Furar Teutonicus
Götterdammerung

Economic

Rejected by Jews

Cultural
Normative

Emancipation

Conflict

Creation
of Jewish
Culture

Rejection of
Judeo-Christian
legal and moral
restraints

The triggers of
critical mass
of the Holocaust
by Hitler and the
Political *Aesir*

Background Factors

Jewish Ownership and control of
industry, commerce and press

Germany economically hurt by
war and inflation, exposed to the
Jews, ostentatious consumption
and display of their achievements

High relative proportion of Jews
in science and cultural activities

German Völkisch Ethics

German Nationalism

German defeat in the
Frist World War

Jews, liberals, socialistic leader
of Communist
Revolution in
Germany, Hungary
and Russia vulnerable
in German politics

Anti-Semitism as a Stigmatising Process

The Definition of Segregation
The Stigmatisers
An outlet of an aggression
projection of violence, self-
definition of worth by conrtrast
with Wiedert Geist

The Stigmatisers
Scape goats; conspicuous
outsiders, powerless power
symbol stereotype of radically
impure, genetically inferior
untermensch

Anomic process in
Germany and social
disintergration
quick urbanisation
industrialisation

Structural

References

Abraham, Karl (1928), 'Character Formation on the Genital Level of Libido
Development', *Selected Papers of Karl Abraham*, London: Hogarth Press, p.407.

Arendt, H. (1958), *The Origins of Totalitarianism*, Cleveland & New York:The World
Publishing Co., p.7.

Bachofen, J.J. (1967), *Myth, Religion and Mother-Right*, Princeton: Princeton
University Press, p.73.

Bauer, Y. (1979), 'The Holocaust Today: An Attempt at a New Evaluation' I.
Guttman & L.R. Rothkirchen (Eds.),*The Catastrophe of European Jewry*, p.462.

Baynes, H.G.(1941), *Germany Possessed*, London: Jonathan Cape, p.105.

Benedict, Ruth (1934), *Patterns of Culture*, New York: Mentor Books.

Benedict, Ruth, cited by Clyde Kluckhohn (1962),*Culture and Behaviour,* New York:
Free Press, p.26.

Bullock, A. (1962), *Hitler: A Study in Tyranny*, Harmonsworth, Eng: Penguin
Books. pp.313, 397, 474 and 673.

Christmas, Humphreys (1952), *Buddhism*, Harmonsworth, Eng: Penguin, p.81.

Cohn, Norman (1972), *Warrant for Genocide*. Tel Aviv: Am Oved, p.38 (in
Hebrew).

Drachmann, D.B. (1911), *Umdvalate Afhonlinger*, Copenhagen.

Durkeheim, E. (1952), *Suicide,* London: Routledge & Kegan Paul.

Ehrenkranz, J., E. Bliss & M.H. Sheard (1974), 'Plasma Testosterone: Correlation
with Aggressive Behaviour and Social Domininance in Man,' *Psychosom Med.*

Eliade, Mircea (1954), *The Myth of Eternal Return,* New York: Harper & Row,
p.43.

'Jerusalem', Encyclopaedia Judaica: Keter, (1971), Vol.13, p.1390.

Ellingson, R.Y. (1954-55), 'The Incidence of EEG Abnormality Among Patients with
Mental Disorders of Apparently Non-Organic Origin: A Critical Review,' *Amer. J.
Psychiatr.* Vol. 111.

Elliot, F.A. (1978), 'Neurological Aspects of Antisocial Behaviour,' W.H. Reid
(Ed.), *The Psycopath: A Comprehensive Study of Antisocial Disorders and
Behaviours*, New York, New York: Brunner & Mazel.

Erickson, E.H. (1956), 'The Problem of Identity,' *Journal of American Psychological
Association.*

Erickson, E.H., 'Sex Differences in the Play Configuration of Predolescents,'
American Journal of Orthopsychiary 21, Cited in S. Fischer (1951), *The Female
Orgasm*, New York: Basic Books.

Eysenck, H.J. (1967), *The Biological Basis of Personality*, Springfield, Ill: Charles
C. Thomas.

Eysenck, J.J. (1964), *Crime and Personality*, London: Routledge & Kegan Paul Ltd.

Fairburn, W.R.D. (1957), *Psychological Studies of the Personality*, London:
Tavistock.

Falconer, M.A. & E.A. Serafentinides (1963), 'A Follow-up Study of Surgery in
Temporal Lobe Epilepsy,' *J. Neurol Neurosurg. Psychiatry*, Vol. 26.

Fenwick, P., R.Howard & G.F. Fenton (1983), 'Review of Cortical Excitability,
Neurohueral Transmission and the Dyscontrol Syndrome,' M.Parsonage et al,
(Eds), Advances in Epilepotology: 14th Epilepsy International Symposium, New
York: Raven Press.

Fischer, S. (1970), Body Experience in Fantasy and Behaviour, New York:
Appleton-Century Crofts.

Fisher, S. (1973), *The Female Organism*, New York: Basic Books.

Forssman, H. & G. Hambert (1967), 'Chromosomes and Antisocial Behaviour,'
Excerpta Criminologica, Vol.7.

Francis, L.K. Hru (1969),*The Study of Literate Civilizations*, New York: Holt, Rinehart & Winston, p.86.
Frank, A.E. (1992), Violence, the Neurologic Contribution: An Overview, Arch. Neurol.
Friedlander, S. (1971), *Anti-Semitisme Nazi: Histoire d'une Psychose Collective*, Paris: Seuel, p.64.
Fromm, Erich. (1942), *Escape from Freedom*, New York: Farrar & Rinehart, p.277.
Geva, H. (1977). *Theories of Anti-Semitism*, (unpublished M.A.Thesis), Tel Aviv University, p.70.
Gilbert, G.M. (1961), *Nuremberg Diary*, New York: Signet Books, p.17.
Graetz, H. (1853), *Geschichte den Juden Von den Altesten Zeiten bis auf die Gegenwart*, Bd. I, S. XXI.
Haffner, Sebastian (1968), *Der Teufelspakt: 50 Jahre*. Deutschrussische Beziehungen Reimbek, Munchen.
Heiber, H. (1973), *Goebbels* . London: Robert Hale & Co., p.241.
Heiden, K. (1944), *Der Fuehrer*, Boston: Houghton, Mifflin Co.
Hilberg, R.(1973),*The Destruction of the European Jews*, New York: New Viewpoints.
Jung, C.G. (1964), *Wotan in Civilization in Transition*, London: Routeledge, Kegan Paul, Trench & Trubner, p.185.
Jung, C.G.(1944), *Psychological Types*, London: Routledge Kegan Paul, Trench & Trubner, p.616.
Kroeber, A.L. (1963), *Anthropology: Culture Patterns and Processes*, New York: Harcourt, Brace & World, p.101.
Kroeber, A.L. (1952), *The Nature of Culture*, Chicago: University of Chicago Press, pp.23-30.
Levy-Bruhl, L.(1966), *How Natives Think*, New York: Washington Square Press, pp.3-5.
Levi-Strauss, Claude (1966), *The Savage Mind*, Chicago: University of Chicago Press, p.54.
MacCulloch, J.A. (1964), *Eddic Mythology*, New York: Cooper & Square Pub. Inc.
McClelland, D.C.(1961), *The Achieving Society*, Princeton: Van Nostrand, p.51.
Mircea, Yoga (1969), *Immortality and Freedom*, Princeton: Princeton University Press, p.9.
Mosse, G.L. 'The Mystical Origin of National Socialism', *Journal of the History of Ideas*, Vol.22, No.1 (Jan-Mar, 1961), p.81.
Murray, Gilbert (1955), *Five Stages of Greek Religion*, New York: Doubleday/Anchor Books, pp.4-5.
Parkes, James (1963), *Anti-Semitism*. Chicago: Quadrangle Books, pp.35-7.
Pulzer, P.G. (1964), *The Rise of Political Anti-Semitism in Germany and Austria*, New York: John Wiley & Sons Inc.
Ranulf, S. (1933), *The Jealousy of the Gods and Criminal Law at Athens*, Copenhagen: Levin & Munksgaard, Vol 1, p.42.
Reinach, T. (1963), *Textes d'Auteurs Grec et Romains Relatifs au Judaisme*, Ochs: Hildesheim.
Reitlinger, G. (1961), *The Final Solution*, New York: A.S. Barnes & Co.
Riesman, D., N. Glazer & R. Denney (1953), *The Lonely Crowd*, New York: Doubleday/Anchor Books, p.19.
Rosenfeld, S. (1955), *Criminal Case 127: The Greenwald-Hastner Trial*, Tel Aviv: Karni Publishers, p.9 (in Hebrew).
Russell,Bertrand (1947), *History of Western Philosophy*, London: Allen & Unwin, p.383.
Shestov, Lev (1968), *Athens and Jerusalem* , New York: Simon & Schuster, p.61.
Shirer, W.L. (1961), *Berlin Diary*, New York: Popular Library, pp.434-5.
Shoham, S.G. & G. Rahav (1982), *The Mark of Cain*, St Lucia: University of Queensland Press.

Shoham, S.G. (1982), *The Myth of Tantalus*, St Lucia: University of Queensland Press.

Shoham, S.G. (1986), *Rebellion, Creativity and Revelation*, Op. cited, Chapter X.

Shoham, S.G. (1979), *Salvation Through the Gutters*, Washington: Hemisphere Publishing Co.

Sholem, Gershom (1975), *Explications and Implications: Writings on Jewish Heritage and Renaissance*, Tel Aviv: Am Oved, pp.114-117 (in Hebrew).

Speer, A. (1971), *Inside the Third Reich*, London: Sphere Books, Ltd., pp.72, 97, 193-4, 255.

Spengler, Oswald (1954), *The Decline of the West*, London: Allen & Unwin, Vol.1, p.107.

Tal, U. (1979),'Anti Christian Anti-Semitism' I. Guttman & L.R. Rothkirchen, (Eds.), *The Catastrophe of European Jewry*, Jerusalem: Yad Vashem, p. 87.

Tal, U. 'Lebensraum in Nazi Ideology', *Zemanim Historical Quarterly* , October 1979, Vol.1, p.72, (Hebrew).

Tal, U. (1980),'Nazism as a 'Political Faith', *The Jerusalem Quarterly*, No.15 (Spring), p. 70-90.

Tal, U. (June 14, 1978), 'Political Faith of Nazism Prior to the Holocaust'. Jacob M. & Shoshanna Schreiber Annual Lecture, Tel Aviv: Tel Aviv University Press, p.40.

Tal, U. 'Territory and Space (Raum) in the Nazi Ideology', Zemanim. *A Historical Quarterly*, Vol. I (October, 1979), pp.68-75 (in Hebrew).

Tal, Uriel (May,1979), 'Structures of German Political Theology in the Nazi Era', Annual Lecture of the Jacob M. and Shoshanna Schreiber Chair of Contemporary Jewish History, Tel Aviv: Tel Aviv University Press. p.43.

Talmon, J. (1979), 'Mission and Testimony: The Universal Significance of Modern Anti-Semitism', T. Guttman & L.R. Rothkirchen (Eds.), *The Catastrophe of European Jewry*, Jerusalem:Yad Vashem, pp.115 et seq.

Tannenbaum, F. (1938), *Crime and Community*, New York: Columbia University Press.

Tennant, F.R. (1968), *The Sources of the Doctrines of the Fall and Original Sin*, New York: Schocken Press, p.140.

Trevor-Roper, H.R. (1962), *The Last Days of Hitler*, London: Pan Books, p.55.

Watts, W. (1960), *The Way of Zen*, New York: Mentor Books, p.108.

White, L.A. (1949),*The Science of Culture*, New York: Farrar, Strauss & Cudahy, p.25.

Wolfson, H.A. (1968), *Philo*, Vol. 1, Cambridge, MA: Harvard University Press, p.85.

Bibliography

Adams, R.D. (1982), 'The Limbic Lobes and the Neurology of Emotion', *Test book of Neurology*.

Adler, A. (1967), *On Suicide*, P. Friedman (Ed.), NY: International Universities Press.

Allsop, J.F. (1965), In H.J. Eysenck (1967), *The Biological Basis of Personality*, Springfield, Ill: Charles C. Thomas.

Alpers, R.J. (1937), 'Relation of the Hypothalamus to Disorders of Personality', *Arch. Neurol.*, p. 38.

Alvarez, A. (1971), *The Savage God*, London: Weidenfeld & Nicolson.

Amir, M. (1971), 'Forcible Rape', *Sexual Behaviour*, Vol. 1, No. 8.

Andy, O.J. (1970), 'Thalamotomy in Hyperactive and Aggressive Behaviour', *Confin. Neurol.*, Vol. 32.

Arendt, H. (1958), *The Origins of Totalitarianism*, Cleveland & New York: The World Publishing Co.

Arthur, R.G.S. & E.B. Cahoon (1964), 'A Clinical and Electroencephalographic Survey of Psychopathic Personality', *Am. J. of Psychiatry*.

Askenasy, J.J., P. Hackett, S. Ron, D. Hary (1983), 'Violence and Episodic Behavioural Dyscontrol', *Biological Psychiatry*, Vol. 18.

Bach, Rita G., J.R. Lion, C.E. Climent, & F.R. Irvin (1971), 'Episodic Dyscontrol: Study of 130 Violent Patients', *Am. J. of Psychiatry*, Vol. 127.

Bachofen, J.J. (1967), *Myth, Religion and Mother-Right*, Princeton: Princeton University Press.

Bandler, R.J., C.C. Chi & J.P. Flynn (1972), 'Biting Attack Elicited by Stimulation of the Ventral Middlerain Tegmentum of Cats', *Science*, Vol. 177.

Barber, R.N. (1969), 'Prostitution and the Increasing Number of Convictions for Rape in Queensland', *Australian & New Zealand Journal of Criminology*.

Barrat, E.S. (1959), 'Anxiety and Impulsiveness Related to Psychomotor Efficiency', *Perceptual and Motor Skills*, Vol. 4.

Barrat, G.V., C.L. Thornton & P.A. Cabe (1969), 'Relation Between Embedded Figures Test Performance and Simulator Behaviour', *Journal of Applied Psychology*, Vol. 53.

Baur, Y. (1979), 'The Holocaust Today: An Attempt at a New Evaluation', I. Guttman & L.R. Rothkirchen (Eds.), *The Catastrophe of European Jewry*, Jerusalem: Yad Vashem.

Baynes, H.G. (1941), *Germany Possessed*, London: Jonathan Cape.

Bear, D. (1983), 'Hemispheric Specialisation and the Neurology of Emotions', *Archives of Neurology*, Vol. 40.

Benedict, Ruth (1934), *Patterns of Culture*, New York: Mentor Books.

Benedict, Ruth; cited by Clyde Kluckhohn (1962), *Culture and Behaviour*, New York: Free Press.

Berntson, G.G. (1973), 'Attack, Grooming and Threat Elicited by Stimulation of the Pontine Tegmentum in Cats', *Physiol. Behav.*, Vol. 1.

Bingley, T. (1958), 'Mental Symptoms in Temporal Lobe Epilepsy and Temporal Lobe Gliomas', *Acta Phychiatr. Scand.*, Vol. 33 (suppl. 120).

Black, D.J., & A.J. Reiss Jr. (1970), 'Police Control of Juveniles', *American Sociological Review*, Vol. 35.

Block, J. (1977), 'Advancing the Psychology of Personality: Paradigmatic Shift or Improving the Quality of Research'?, D. Magnusson, & N.S. Endler. (Eds.), *Personality at the Crossroads: Current Issues in International Psychology*.

Bonnet, H. (1957), 'La Response Myoclonique a la SLI, en Psychiatrie', *Ann. Med. Psychol.*, Vol. 1.

Brown, G. L. & F.K. Goodwin (1986), 'Human Aggression: A Biological Perspective', W. Reid, D. Dorr, S. L. Walker J.W. Bonner (Eds.), In *Unmasking the Psycopath*, New York: W.W. Norton.

Brownmiller, S. (1975), *Against Our Will: Men, Women and Rape*, New York: Simon & Schuster.

Brutkowski, S., E. Fonberg & E. Mempel (1961), 'Angry Behaviour in Dogs Following Bilateral Lesions in Genual Portion of the Rostral Cingulate', *Acta Brologici Experimentalis*, Vol. 21.

Bullock, A. (1962), *Hitler: A Study in Tyranny*, Hammonsworth, England: Penguin Books.

Burgess, A.W. & I.L. Holmstrom (1974), 'The Rapist's View of Rape', *Rape: Victim of Crisis*, Bowie, MD: Brady.

Burr, E. (1983), 'The Limbic System and Aggression in Humans', *Neuroscience J. Behavioural Reviews*, Vol. 7.

Camus, A. (1956), *The Fall*, NY: Vintage Books.

Casey, M.D. J.C.E. Blank & D. Street (1966), 'YY Chromosomes and Antisocial Behaviour', *Lancet*, Vol. 2.

Cattell, R.B., M.W. Eber & M.M. Tatsuoka (1970), 'Handbook of the 16 Personality Factor Questionnaire', Champaign, Ill. (CAQ), *Institute for Personality and Ability Testing*.

Chappell, D., G. Geis, S. Schafer & L. Siegel (1971), 'Forcible Rape: A Comparison Study of Offenses Known to Police in Boston and Los Angeles', J.M. Henlin (ED.), *Studies in the Sociology of Sex*, New York: Appleton.

Cherno, F.A. (1971), *Avoidance Learning Among Sociopathic, Normal and Neurotic Prisoners under Varied Conditions of Sensory Input*, Unpublished Doctoral thesis, University of Georgia.

Christie, R. & F.L. Geis (1970), *Machiavellianism*, New York: Academic Press.

Christmas, Humphreys (1952), *Buddhism*, Harmonsworth: Penguin Books.

Cleaver, P.T., A.D. Mylonas & W.C. Reckless (1968), 'Gradients in Attitudes Towards Law, Courts and Police', *Social Focus*, Vol. 2 (winter).

Cohen, J. & P. Cohen (1975), *Applied Multiple Regression & Correlation Analysis for the Behavioural Sciences*, Hillsdale, NJ:Erbaum.

Cohen, S. & A.J. Silverman (1963), *Body and Field Perceptual Dimensions and Altered Sensory Environment*, Durham: Duke University Press.

Cohn, Norman (1972), *Warrant for Genocide*, Tel Aviv: Am Oved (in Hebrew).

Cohn, R. & J.E.Nardini (1958-59), 'The Correlation of Bilateral Occipital Slow Activity in the Human EEG with Certain Disorders of Behaviour', *Amer. J. Psychiat*, Vol. 44.

Colquhoun, W.P. & D.W.J. Corocran (1964), 'The Effects of Time of Day and Social Isolation on the Relationship between Temperament and Performance', *British J. Soc. & Clin. Psychol,* Vol. 3.

Crowne, D.P., & D.A. Marlowe (1960), 'New Scale of Social Desirability Independent of Psychopathology', *J. Consult. Psycho,* Vol. 24.

Currie, S.K., W.G. Heathfield, R.A. Hearson & D.F. Scott (1971), 'Clinical Course and Prognosis of Temporal Lobe Epilepsy,' *Brain,* Vol. 94.

Diamond, M. (1975), 'A Critical Evaluation of the Ontogeny of Human Sexual Behaviour', *Quarterly Review of Biology.*

Doering, C.H., H.K.H. Brodie, H.C. Dramer, R.H. Moos, H.B. Becker & D.A. Hamburg (1975), 'Negative Affect and Plasma Testosterone: A Longitudinal Human Study', *Psychosom. Med.*

Drachmann, D.B. (1911), 'Umdvalate Afhonlinger'; Selected Topics, Copenhagen.

Durkheim, E. (1952), *Suicide,* London, Routledge, Kegan Paul Ltd.

Ehrenkranz, J. E., Bliss, & M.H Sheard (1974), 'Plasma Testosterone: Correlation with Aggressive Behaviour and Social Dominance in Man', *Psychosom Med.*

Eichelman, B., G.R. Elliot & J.D. Barchas (1981), 'Biochemical Pharmacological and Genetic Aspects of Aggression', D.A. Hamburg & M.B. Touderau, (Eds.), *Biobehavioural Aspects of Aggression,* New York.

Eliade, Mircea (1954), *The Myth of Eternal Return,* New York: Harper & Row.

Ellingson, R.Y. (1954-55), 'The Incidence of EEG Abnormality Among Patients with Mental Disorders of Apparently Non-Organic Origin: A Critical Review', *Amer. J. Psychiatr,* Vol. 111.

Elliot, F.A. (1978), 'Neurological Aspects of Antisocial Behaviour', W.H. Reid (Ed.), *The Psychopath: A Comprehensive Study of Antisocial Disorders and Behaviours,* New York: Brunner & Mazel.

Encyclopedia Judaica (1971), Jerusalem: Keter, Vol. 13.

Erickson, E.H. (1956), 'The Problem of Identity', *Journal of American Psychological Association.*

Erickson, E.H. (1951), 'Sex Differences in the Play Configuration of Preadolescents', *American Journal of Orthopsychiatry,* Vol. 21, cited in S. Fischer (1951), *The Female Orgasm,* New York: Basic Books.

Eysenck. H.J. (1967), *The Biological Basis of Personality,* Springfield, Ill: Charles C Thomas.

Eysenck, J.J. (1964), *Crime and Personality,* London: Routledge & Kegan Paul Ltd.

Eysenck, H.J. (1977), *Crime and Personality,* (2nd Ed.) London: Routledge & Kegan Paul Ltd.

Fairbairn, W.R.D. (1957), *Psychoanalytic Studies of the Personality,* London: Tavistock.

Falconer, M.A. & E.A. Serafentinides (1963), 'A Follow-up Study of Surgery in Temporal Lobe Epilepsy', *J. Neurol Neurosurg. Psychiatry,* Vol. 26.

Fenwick, P., R. Howard & G.F. Fenton (1983), 'Review of Cortical Excitability, Neurohueral Transmission and the Dyscontrol Syndrome', M. Parsonage et al. (Eds.), *Advances in Epilepotology: 14th Epilepsy International Symposium,* New York: Raven Press.

Fisher, S. (1970), *Body Experience in Fantasy and Behaviour,* New York: Appleton-Century Crofts.

Fisher, S. (1973), *The Female Orgasm,* New York: Basic Books.

Forssman, H. & G. Hambert (1967), 'Chromosomes and Antisocial Behaviour', *Excerpta Criminologica,* Vol. 7.

Francis, L.K. Hru (1969), *The Study of Literate Civilizations,* New York: Holt, Rinehart, & Winston.

Frank, A.E. (1992), 'Violence: The Neurologic Contribution: An Overview,' *Arch. Neurol.,* Vol. 49.

Freud, S. (1964), 'Mourning and Melancholia' in James Strachey et al. (Eds.), *Complete Psychological Works,* Vol. 14, London: The Hogarth Press.

Friedlander, S. (1971), *Anti-Semitism Nazi: Histoirie d'une Psychose Collective,* Paris: Seul.

Friedman. R., R.M. Richart, R.M. Wiele, & R.L. Vande (Eds.), (1974), *Sex Differences in Behaviour*, New York: John Wiley & Sons.

Fromm, Erich (1942), *Escape from Freeedom*, New York: Farrar & Rinehart.

Gagnon, J.H. (1977), Review of J.M. MacDonald's 'Rape Offenders and Their Victims', D.Chappell, R.Geis, & G.Geis (Eds.), (1977), *Forcible Rape: The Crime, the Victim, and the Offender*, New York: Columbia University Press.

Gebhard, P.H. (1965), *Sex Offenders*, New York: Columbia University Press.

Genet, J. (1964), *Our Lady of the Flowers*, New York: Bantam Books.

Geva, H. (1977), *Theories of Anti-Semitism*, (Unpublished M.A. thesis), Tel Aviv University.

Gibbens, T.C. N., C. Way & K.L. Soothill (1977), 'Behavioural Types of Rape', *British Journal of Psychiatry*, Vol. 130.

Gibbs, F.A., B.K. Bagchi & W. Bloomberg (1945), 'Electroencephalo-Graphic Study, of Criminals', *A. J. Psychiat.*, Vol. 102.

Gibson, H.B. (1961), *Manual of the Gibson Spiral Mars,* (2nd. Ed.), Dunton Green: Kent, Britain: Hodder and Stoughton.

Gilbert, G.M. (1961), *Nuremberg Diary*, New York: Signet Books.

Goffman, E. (1967), *Interaction Ritual: Essays in Face-to-Face Behaviour*, Chicago: Aldine.

Goldberg, S. & M. Lewis (1969), 'Play Behaviour in the Year-Old Infant: Early Sex Differences', *Child Developing*, Vol. 40.

Goldzieher, J.W., T.S. Dozier, K.D. Smith & E. Steinberger (1976), 'Improving the Diagnostic Reliability of Rapidly Fluctuating Plasma Hormone Levels by Optimized Multiple-Sampling Techniques', *J. Clin Endocrinol Metab*, Vol. 43.

Goodman, R.M., W.S. Smith & C.J. Migeon (1967), 'Sex Chromosome Abnormalities', *Nature*.

Gove, J.R.W. & R.H. Crutchield (1982), 'The Family and Juvenile Delinquency', *The Sociological Quarterly*, Vol. 23.

Graetz, H. (1853), *Geschichte den Juden Vonm den Altesten Zeiten bis auf die Gegenwart*, Bd. 1, S. 21.

Graves, R. (1955), *The Greek Myths*, Vol. 2, Harmonsworth, England: Penguin Books.

Grossman, C. (1954), 'Laminar Cortical Blocking and its Relation to Episodic Aggressive Outbursts', *Arch. Neurol. Psychiatr.*

Gunn, J.C. (1969), 'The Prevalence of Epilepsy Among Prisoners', *Proc. Ro. Soc. Med.*

Haffner, Sebastian (1968), 'Der Teufelspakt: 50 Jahre', *Deutschrussische Beziehungen Reimbek*, Munchen.

Halleck, S.L. (1971), *Psychiatry and the Dilemmas of Crime*, Los Angeles: University of California.

Hare, R.D. & D. Schallin (1978), *Psychopathic Behaviour: Approaches to Research*, Chichester: John Wiley & Sons.

Heath, R.G. (1963), 'Electrical Self-stimulation of the Brain in Man', *American Journal of Psychiatry*.

Heath, R.G. & W.A. Mickle (1960), 'Evaluation of Seven Years' Experience with Depth Electrode Studies in Human Patients', E.R. Ramey & D. O'Doherty, (Eds.), *Electrical Studies of the Unanesthetized Brain*, New York: Paul B. Hoeber.

Heiber, H. (1973), *Goebbels*, London: Robert Hale & Co.

Heiden, K. (1944), *Der Fuerher*, Boston: Houghton, Mifflin Co.

Henderson, D.K. (1939), *Psychopathic States*, New York: Morton.

Henn, F.A., M. Herjanic & R.H. Vaderpearl (1976), 'Forensic Psychiatry: Profiles of Two Types of Sex Offenders', *American Journal of Sex Offenders*.

Herrmann, W.M. & R.C. Beach (1976), 'Psychotropic Effects of Androgens: A Review of Clinical Observations and New Human Experimental Findings', *Pharmakopsych*, Vol. 9.

Hilberg, Raul (1973), *The Destruction of the European Jews*, New York: New Viewpoints.

Hill, D. & W.W. Sargent (1943), 'A Case of Matricide', *Lancet*, Vol. 1.

Hill, D. (1944), 'Cerebral Dysthymia: its Significance in Aggressive Behaviour', *Proc. Roy. Soc. Med.*, Vol. 37.

Hill, D. (1950), 'Encephalography as an Instrument in Research in Psychiatry,' D. Lewis (Ed.), *Perspectives in Neuropsychiatry*, London: Lewis.

Hill, D. (1952), 'EEG in Epistopic Psychiatric and Psychpathic Behaviour', *Electroenceph. Clin. Neurophysiol,* Vol. 4.

Hirschi, T. (1969), *Causes of Delinquency,* Berkeley: University of California Press.

Hitchcock, E. & V. Cainus (1973), 'Amygdalectomy', *Postgrad. Med. J.*, Vol. 49.

Irwin, J. & D. Cressey (1962), 'Convicts and the Inmate Culture', *Social Problems.*

Irwin, J. (1970), *The Felon,* Englewood, NJ: Prentice-Hall.

Jacobs, P.A., M. Branton, & M. Melville (1965), 'Aggressive Behaviour, Mental Subnormality and XYY Male', *Nature.*

Johnson, S.C. (1967), 'Hierarchical Clustering Schemes', *Psychometrika*, Vol. 32, No. 3.

Jung, C.G. (1964), *Wotan in Civilization in Transition*, London: Routledge & Kegan Paul Ltd.

Jung, C.G. (1944), *Psychological Types*, London: Kegan Paul, Trench, Trubner.

Itri, A. & W. Collino (1964), 'Personality and Depersonalization Under Sensory Deprivation Percepts', *Motor Skills.*

Kagan, J., B. Rosman, D. Day, J. Albert & W. Phillips (1974), 'Information Processing in the Child's Significance of Analytic and Reflective Attitudes', *Psychological Monographs.*

Keating, L.F. (1961), 'Epilepsy and Behaviour Disorders in School Children', *J. Ment. Sci.*

Kelly, S., R. Almy & M. Barnard (1967), 'Another XYY Phenotype', *Nature.*

Kennard, M.A. (1965), 'Effects of Bilateral Ablation of Cingulate Area on Behaviour of Cats', *Journal of Neurophysiology,* Vol. 18.

Kim, Y.K. & W. Umbach (1973), 'Combined Stereotaxic Lesions for Treatment of Behavioural Disorders and Severe Pain', L. Laitman and K.E. Livingstone, (Eds.), *Surgical Approaches in Psychiatry,* Baltimore: Baltimore University Park Press.

Klein, S.G. & H.J. Schlesinger (1950), 'Perceptual Attitudes of Form-Boundedness and Form-Liability', in *Rorschach Responses, Abstract, Am. Psychol.*, Vol.5.

Kling, A. (1975), 'Testosterone and Aggressive Behaviour in Man and Non-Human Primates'. B.E. Eleftheriou and R.L. Sprott, (Eds.), *Hormonal Correlates of Behaviour, A Lifespan View,* Vol. 1, New York: Plenum Press.

Kluver, H. & P.C. Bucy (1938), 'An Analysis of Certain Effects of Ilateral Temporal Lobectomy in the Rhesus Monkey with Special Reference to Psychic Blindness', *J. Psychol.*, Vol. 5.

Kornhauser, R. (1978), *Social Sources of Delinquency: Appraisal of Analytic Models,* Chicago University Press.

Kreuz, L.E. & R.M. Rose (1972), 'Assessment of Aggressive Behaviour and Plasma Testosterone in a Young Criminal Population', *Psychosom. Med.*, Vol. 34.

Kroeber, A.L. (1944), *Psychological Types*, London: Kegan Paul, Trench & Trubner.

Kroeber, A. L. (1963), *Anthropology: Culture Patterns and Processes,* New York: Harcourt, Brace & World.

Lairy, G.C. (1964), 'Quelques Remarques sur le Probleme EEG', *Psychologie du Comportement EEG Clin Neuropshysiol .*

Lane, P.J. (1978), 'Annotated Bibliography of the Overcontrolled-Undercontrolled Assaultive Personality Literature and the Overcontrolled-Hostility (0-4) scale of the MMPI', *JSAS Catalog of Selected Documents in Psychology* (JSAS ms. No. 1790).

Leslie, W. (1940), 'Cyst of the Cavum Vergae', *Can. Med. Assoc. J.*

Levenson, H. (1973), 'Perceived Parental Antecedents of Internal Powerful Others and Chance Locus of Control Orientation', *Developmental Psychology,* Vol. 9.

Levi-Strauss, Claude (1966), *The Savage Mind*, Chicago: University of Chicago Press.

Levine, R.A. (1969), 'Gusu Sex Offenses: A Study in Social Control', *American Anthopologist* .

Levy-Bruhl, L. (1966), *How Natives Think*, New York: Washington Square Press.

Levy, S. (1952), 'A Study of the Electroencephalogram as Related to Personality Structure in a Group of Inmates of a State Penitentiary', *Electro-Enceph. Clin. Neurophysiol*, Vol. 4.

Levy, S. & M.A. Kennard (1953), 'A Study of the Electro-Encephalo-Graph as Related to a Group of Inmates of a State Penitentiary', *American Journal of Psychiatry*.

Linnoila, A.M., M. Virkunen, M. Scheinin, A. Nuntile, A. Rimon, F. Goodwin. Lorne, T. Yeudall, Delee Fromm-Auch, M.A. & Priscilla Davies, B.A. (1970), *Neuropsychological impairment of Persistent Delinquency*.

MacCulloch, J.A. (1964), *Eddic Mythology*, New York: Cooper & Square Pub. Inc.

MacIver, R. (1964), 'Subjective Meaning in Social Situations', L. Coser & B. Rosenberg, (Eds.), *Sociological Theory*, 2nd Ed., New York: Macmillan.

Macfarlene, A. (1977), *The Psychology of Childbirth*, Cambridge, Mass: Harvard University Press.

Mackeller, J. (1975), *Rape! The Bait and the Trap,* New York: Crown Books.

Maclean, P.D. & J. Delgado (1953), 'Electrical and Chemical Stimulation of Fronto-Temporal Portion of Limbic System in Waking Animal', *Electroencephalography and Clinical Neurophysiology* .

Malamud, N. (1967), 'Psychiatric Disorder with Intracranial Tumors of Limbic Systems', *Arch. Neurol.*

Maletzky, B.M. (1973), 'The Episodic Dyscontrol Syndrome', *Dis. Nerv. Syst.*

Mark, V.H. & F.R. Ervin (1970), *Violence and the Brain,* New York: Harper & Row.

Mark, V., H. Sweet & F.R. Ervin (1975), 'Deep Temporal Lobe Stimulation and Destructive lesions in Episodically Violent Temporal Lobe Epileptics', W.S. Fields and W.H. Sweet (Eds.), *Neural Basis of Violence and Aggression,* St. Somis: Warren H. Green.

Marlowe,W.B., E.J. Mancall & J.J. Thomas (1975), 'Complete Kluver Bucy Syndrome in Man', *Cortex*.

Martin, M.K. & B.Voorhies (1975), *Female of the Species*, New York: Columbia University Press.

McClelland, D.C. (1961), *The Achieving Society,* Princeton: Van Nostrand.

McClelland, D.C. (1964), 'Wanted: A New Self-Image for Women', R.J. Lifton (Ed.), *The Women in America*, Boston: Houghton-Mifflin.

McCord, J. (1970), 'Some Child Rearing Antecedents of Criminal Behaviour in Adult Men', *Journal of Personality and Social Psychology*.

McTwin, R.C. & F. Helmer (1965), 'The Symptoms of Temporal Lobe Contusion', *J. Neurology* .

Mednick, S. & K.O. Christiansen (1977), *Biosocial Basis of Criminal Behaviour*, New York: Gardner Press.

Megargee, E.I. (1966), 'Undercontrolled and Overcontrolled Personality Types in Extreme Antisocial Aggression', *Psychological Monographs*, Vol. 3.

Megargee, E.I. (1982), 'Psychological Determinants and Correlates of Criminal Violence', M.E.Wolfgang, and N.A.Weiner (Eds.), *Criminal Violence,* Beverly Hills: Sage Publications.

Memple, E. (1971), 'Influence of Partial Amygdalectomy on Emotional Disorders and Epileptic Seizures', *Neurochir. Pol.*

Meyer-Bahlburg, H.F., B.A. Boon, M. Sharma & J.A. Edwards (1974), 'Aggressiveness and Testosterone Measures in Man', *Psychosom. Med.*

Michelmore, S. (1964), *Sexual Reproduction,* New York: Natural History Press.

Money, J. & A. A. Ehrhardt (1972), *Man and Woman, Boy and Girl*, Baltimore: John Hopkins University Press.

Monroe, R. (1970), *Episodic Behavioural Disorders: A Psychodynamic and Neurophysiologic Analysis,* Cambridge: Harvard Univ. Press.

Monti, P.M, W.A. Brown. & J.D.P. Corriveau (1977), 'Testosterone and
Components of Aggressive and Sexual Behaviour in Men', *Amer. J. Psychiat.*
Vol. 134.

Mosse, G.L. 'The Mystical Origin of National Socialism', *J. of the History of Ideas,*
Vol. 22, No. 1 (Jan-Mar, 1961).

Murray, G. (1955), *Five Stages of Greek Religion,* New York: Doubleday/Anchor
Books.

Murray, M.A. (1938), *Explorations in Personality,* New York: Oxford University
Press.

Narabayashi, H.T, Y. Nagao, M. Saito, Yoshuda & M. Nagohatta (1963),
'Stereotaxic Amygdalectomy for Behaviour Disorders', *Arch. Neurol J.*

Nuffield, E.J. (1969), 'Neurophysiology and Behaviour Disorders in Epileptic
Children', *J. Ment. Sci.*

Ounsted, C. (1969), 'Aggression and Epilepsy: Rage in Children with Temporal
Lobe Epilepsy,' *J. Psychosom. Res.,* Vol. 13.

Parkes, J. (1963), *Anti-Semitism,* Chicago: Quadrangle Books.

Parsons, T. (1947), 'Certain Primary Sources of Patterns and Aggression in the
Social Structure of the Western World', *Psychiatry ,* Vol. 2.

Persky, H, K.D.Smith & J.G.K. Basu (1971), 'Relation of Psychologic Measures
of Aggression and Hostility to Testosterone Production in Man', *Psychosom.
Med.*

Persky, H, C.P. O'Brien, E. Fine, W.J. Howard, M.A. Khan & R.W. Beck (1977),
'The Effect of Alcohol and Smoking on Testosterone Function and
Aggression in Chronic Alcoholics', *Amer. J. Psychiat.*

Person, T. (1967), 'An XYY Man and his Relatives', *Journal of Mental Deficiency
Research.*

Petrie, A., W. Collins & P. Solomon (1960), 'The Tolerance for Pain and for
Sensory Deprivations', *Am. J. Psychol.*

Petrie, A. (1967), *Individuality in Pain and Suffering: The Reducer and
Augmenter ,* Chicago: University of Chicago Press.

Petrie, A. (1980), 'The Tolerance of Pain and Sensory Deprivation,' *A.J. Psych.* Vol.
1-3, No. 1.

Pillien, G. (1967), 'The Kluver-Bucy Syndrome in Man', *Psychistr. Neurol.*

Pincees, J.H. (1980), 'Can Violence be a Manifestation of Epilepsy?', *Neurology,*

Pitcher, E.G. & E. Prelinger (1972), *Children Tell Stories-An Analysis of Fantasy,*
New York: International University Press.

Poeck, K. (1969), 'Pathophysiology of Emotional Disorders Associated with Brain
Damage', P.J. Du Vinken & G. Bruyen (Eds.), *Handbook of Clinical Neurology*
Vol. 3, Amsterdam, Holland: Elsevier Science Publisher.

Pulzer, P.G. (1964), *The Rise of Political Anti-Semitism in Germany and Austria,*
New York: John Wiley & Sons.

Quay, H.C. (1965), 'Psychopathic Personality as Stimulation Seeking', *American
Journal of Psychiatry.*

Rada, R.T., D.R. Laws & R. Kellner (1976), 'Plasma Testosterone Levels in the
Rapist', *Psychosom. Med.*

Rahav, G. (1983), 'Models of Delinquency', *International Journal of Group
Tensions.*

Ranulf, S. (1933), *The Jealousy of the Gods and Criminal Law at Athens,* Vol. 1,
Copenhagen: Levin & Munksgaard.

Raven, S.C., *Standard Progressive Matrices Sets, A,B,C,D,E,* London: H.K.
Lewis.

Reeves, A.G. & F. Plum (1969), 'Hyperphagia, Rage and Dementia Accompanying a
Ventro Medial Hypothalamic Neoplasm', *Arch. Neurol,* Vol. 20.

Reinach, T. (1963), *Textes d'Auteurs Grec et Romains Relatifs au Judaisme,* Ochs:
Hildesheim.

Reitlinger, G. (1961), *The Final Solution,* New York: A.S. Barnes & Co.

Riesman, D., N. Glazer & R. Denney (1953), *The Lonely Crowd,* New York:
Doubleday/Anchor Books.

Romamuk, A. (1965), 'Representation of Aggression and Flight Reactions in the Hypothalamus of the Cat', *Acta Biologicae Experimentalis Sinica*, Vol. 25, Warsaw.

Rose, R.M., T.P. Gordon, & I.S. Bernstein (1972), 'Plasma Testosterone Levels in the Male Rhesus: Influences of Sexual and Social Stimuli', *Science*, Vol. 178.

Rose, R.M. (1975), 'Testosterone, Aggression, and Homosexuality: A Review of the Literature and Implications for Future Research', E.J. Sachar (Ed.), *Topics in Psychoendocrinology*, New York: Grune and Stratton.

Rosen, L. (1970), 'The Broken Home and Male Delinquency', M.E.Wolfang, E. Savitz & N. Johnson (Eds.), *The Sociology of Crime and Delinquency*, New York: John Wiley & Sons.

Rosenfeld, S. (1955), *Criminal Case 127: The Greenwald-Kastner Trial*, Tel Aviv: Karni Publishers.

Rosenzweig, S. (1965), Note of Correction for Schwartz, Cohen and Pavlik's 'The Effects of Subject and Experimenter Induced Defensive Response Sets on Picture-Frustration Test Reactions', *J. Proj. Tech. & Pers. Assess.*, Vol. 29.

Rotter, J.B, M. Seeman, & S. Liverant (1962), 'Internal V. External Controls of Reinforcements, A Major Variable in Behaviour Theory', N.F. Washburne (Ed.), *Decisions, Values and Groups*, Vol. 2, London: Pergamon Press.

Roy, K.K. 'Feelings and Attitudes of Raped Women of Bangladesh Toward Military Personnel of Pakistan'. In E. Viano (Ed.), *Victimology: A New Focus*, Vol. 5, Lexington, Mass: Lexington Books.

Ruff, C.R., D.L. Templer & J.L. Ayers (1976),'The Intelligence of Rapists', *Archives of Sexual Behaviour*, Vol. 5.

Russell, Bertrand (1947), *History of Western Philosophy*, London: Allen & Unwin.

Sadlier, R. (1967), *The Ecology of Reproduction in Wild and Domestic Mammals*, London: Methuen.

Sano, K., Y. Mayaanagi, H.E. Agashiwa & B. Ishyima (1970), 'Results of Stimulation and Destruction of the Posterior Hypothalamus in Man', *Journal of Neurosurgery*.

Saul, L., J.H. Dans & P.A. David (1949), 'Psychologic Corrections with the Electroencephalogram', *Psychosom. Med. J.*, Vol. 361.

Schalling, D, & R.D. Hare (Eds.), (1978), *Psychopathic Behaviour: Approach to Research*, Chichester: John Wiley & Sons.

Schneidman, E. (1975), 'Classification of Suicidal Phenomena', S. Dinitz, Dynes & Clerke, (Eds.), *Deviance*, N.Y: Oxford University Press.

Schreiner, L. & A. Kling. (1953), 'Behavioural Change Following Encephalic Injury in Cats', *Journal of Neuropsychology*, Vol. 16.

Schulsinger, F. (1964), *The Premenstrual Syndrome*, Springfield, Ill: Charles C. Thomas Publishers.

Sellin, T. & M.E. Wolfgang (1964), *The Measurement of Delinquency*, New York: John Wiley & Sons.

Shah, S.A, & L.H. Roth (1974), 'Biological and Psychophysiological Factors in Criminality', in *Handbook of Criminology*, D. Glaser (Ed.), New York: Rand McNally.

Shealy, C. & T. Peele (1957), 'Studies on Amygdaloid Nucleus of Cat', *Journal of Neurophysiology*, Vol. 20.

Shestov, Lev (1968), *Athens and Jerusalem*, New York: Simon & Schuster.

Shinar, D. (1978), *Psychology on the Road: The Human Factor in Traffic Safety*, New York: John Wiley Inc.

Shirer, W.L. (1961), *Berlin Diary*, New York: Popular Library.

Shoham, S.G. (1964), 'Conflict Situations and Delinquent Solutions', *Journal of Social Psychology*, The Journal Press.

Shoham, S.G., Z. Schwartzman, G. Rahav, R. Markowski, F. Chard & A. Adelstein (1967), 'An Instrument to Diagnose Personality Types According to the Personality Theory of Shoham', *Medicine and Law*, Vol. 6.

Shoham, S.G. (1968), 'Points of No Return: Some Situational Aspects of Violence', *The Prison Journal*. Vol. 48, No. 2.

Shoham, S.G., R. Banitt, S. Katznelson & S. Streit (1970), 'The Situational Aspects of Violence', S.G. Shoham (Ed.), *Israel Studies in Criminology*, Tel Aviv: Gomeh.

Shoham, S.G., G. Rahav & L. Guttman (1970), 'A Two Dimensional Space for Classifying Legal Offences', *Israel Studies in Criminology*, Vol. 1.

Shoham, S.G. (1975), *Traffic Offenders' Behaviour, Judgement and Punishment*, Tel Aviv University, Report to the Ministry of Transportation.

Shoham, S.G, G. Nehemia, R. Markowski & N. Kaplinsky (1976), 'Internalisation of Norms, Risk-Perceptions and Anxiety as Related to Driving Offences', *British J. of Criminology*.

Shoham, S.G., G. Rahav, J. Blau, N. Kaplinsky, R. Markovski, Y. Shaked, Y. Stein, L. Weissbrod & B. Wolf (1977), *The Reckless and Anxious Drivers: Some Initial Parameters*, Tel Aviv University, Report to the Ministry of Transportation.

Shoham, S.G., L. Weissbod, B. Gruber & Y. Stein (1978), 'Personality Core Dynamics and Predisposition Towards Homosexuality', *British Journal of Medical Psychology*, Vol. 51.

Shoham, S.G. (1979), *The Myth of Tantalus*, St. Lucia: University of Queensland Press.

Shoham, S.G. (1979), *Salvation through the Gutters*, Washington: Hemisphere Publishing Co.

Shoham, S.G., Y. Esformse, G. Rahav, R. Markovsky, N. Kaplinsky & B. Wolf (1980), 'Separant and Participant Personality Types of Suicides', *The Irish Jurist*, Vol. 15.

Shoham, S.G. & G. Rahav (1982), *The Mark of Cain*, St. Lucia: University of Queensland Press.

Shoham, S.G, G. Rahav, R. Markowsky, & F. Chard (1985), *Reckless and Anxious Deviant Behaviour Drivers*, International Conference of Changes and Innovations in Road Safety, Tel Aviv University, 1956.

Shoham, S.G. (1988), *The Violence of Silence: The Impossibility of Dialogue*, London: Science Review Ltd.

Sholem, Gershom (1975), *Explication and Implications: Wrtings on Jewish Heritage and Renaissance*, Tel Aviv: Am Oved (In Hebrew).

Siegel, A. & H.M. Edinger (1983), 'Role of the Limbic System in Hypothalamically Elicited Attack Behaviour', *Nervose. & Behav. Rev.*, Vol. 7.

Singer, J.L. (1971), 'The Psychological Study of Aggression', *The Control of Aggression and Violence*, New York & London: Academic Press.

Speer, A. (1970), *Inside the Third Reich*, London: Weidenfeld & Nicholson.

Spengler, Oswald (1954), *The Decline of the West*, Vol. 1, London: Allen & Unwin.

Stacey, W. & A. Shupe (1983), *The Family Secret: Domestic Violence in America*, Boston Mass: Beacon Press.

Stafford, D.Clark, D. Pond & J.W.L. Doust (1951), 'The Psychopath in Prison: A Preliminary Report of a Cooperative Research', *Br. J. Delinq.* Vol. 2.

Stafford, D. Clark (1959), 'The Foundations of Research in Psychiatry', *Brit. Med. J.* Vol. 2.

Stein, I. (1977), *Traffic Offenders and Criminal Offenders*, Unpublished Master's thesis, Tel Aviv University: Institute of Criminology and Criminal Justice.

Stevens, J.R. & B. Hermann (1981), 'Temporal Lobe Epilepsy, Psychopathology and Violence: The State of Evidence', *Neurology*, Vol. 31, New York.

Stumpf, W.E. & M. Sar (1976), 'Steroid Hormone Target Sites in the Brain: The Differential Distribution of Estrogen, Progestin, Androgen and Glucocorticosteroid', *J. Steroid Biochem*, Vol. 7.

Sutherland, E.H. & D.R.Cressey (1960), *Criminology*, Philadelphia: Lippincott.

Svalastoga, K. (1962), 'Rape and Social Structure', *Pacific Sociological Review*, Vol. 5, No. 19.

Sweet, W.H., F.R. Erin & V.H. Mark (1969), 'The Relationship of Violent Behaviour to Focal Cerebral Disease', *Aggressive Behaviour*, S. Garattini & E.B. Sigg (Eds.), Amsterdam Excerpta Medica Foundation.

Tal, U. (1978), 'Political Faith of Nazism Prior to the Holocaust', M. Jacob &
Shoshanna Schreiber Annual Lecture, Tel Aviv: Tel Aviv University Press.
Tal, U. 'Nazism as a Political Faith', *The Jerusalem Quarterly*, No. 15 (Spring).
Tal, U. (1979), 'Territory and Space (Raum) in the Nazi Ideology', *A Historical
Quarterly*, Vol. 1.
Tal, U. (1979), 'Anti-Christian Anti-Semitism', I. Guttman & L.R. Rothkirchen
(Eds.), *The Catastrophe of European Jewry*, Jerusalem: Yad Vashem.
Tal, U. (May, 1979),'Structures of German Political Theology in the Nazi Era',
Annual Lecture of the M. Jacob and Shoshanna Schreiber Chair of Contemporary
Jewish History, Tel Aviv: Tel Aviv University Press.
Talmon, J. (1979), 'Mission and Testimony: The Universal Significance of Modern
Anti-Semitism' in T. Guttman & L.R. Rothkirchen (Ed.), *The Catastrophe of
European Jewry*. Jerusalem: Yad Vashem.
Tannenbaum, F. (1938), *Crime and Community*, New York: Columbia University
Press.
Tellegen, A., D.T. Lykken, T.J. Bouchard, K.J.Wilcox & S. Rich Segal (1988),
'Personality Similarity in Twins Reared Apart and Together', *J. Pers. Soc.
Psychol.*, Vol. 54.
Tennant, F.R. (1968), *The Sources of the Doctrines of the Fall and Original Sin*,
New York: Schocken Press.
Thibaut, J.W. & H.H. Kelly (1959), *The Social Psychology of Groups*, N.Y: John
Wiley & Sons.
Trevor-Roper, H.R. (1962), *The Last Days of Hitler*, London: Pan Books.
Trimble, M.R. (1988), *Biological Psychiatry*, New York: John Wiley & Sons Inc.
Trivers, R.L. (1972), *Parental Investment and Sexual Selection*, Chicago: Aldine.
Verdeaux, G. (1970), 'Encephalography in Criminology', *Medicine legale et
Dommage Corporel.*, Vol. 6.
Viets, H.R. (1926), 'A Case of Hydrophobia with Negri Bodies in the Brain', *Arch.
Neurol. Psychiatry*, Vol. 15.
Walker, D. (1968), 'Rights in Conflict', *Reports Submitted by the Chicago Study
Team of the National Commission on the Causes and Prevention of Violence.*
Wasman, M. & J.P. Flynn (1962), 'Directed Attack Elicited from Hypothalamus',
Arch. Neurol, Vol. 6.
Watson, R.E, H.M. Edinger & A. Siegel (1983), 'An Analysis of the Mechanism for
Underlying Hippacompal Control of Hypothalamically-Elicited Aggression in the
Cat', *Brain Res.*, Vol. 269.
Watts, W. (1960), *The Way of Zen*, New York: Mentor Books.
Weitz, S. (1977), *Sex Roles*, New York: Oxford Univesrity Press.
West, D.J., C. Ray & F.L. Nichols (1978), *Understanding Sexual Attacks*, London:
Heineman.
White, L.A. (1949), *The Science of Culture*, New York: Farrar, Strauss & Cudahy.
Wieser, H.G. (1983), 'Depth Recorded Limbic Seizures and Psychopathology',
Neuroscience S. Biobehavioural Reviews, Vol. 7.
Wilkinson, K. (1974), 'The Broken Family and Juvenile Delinquency: Scientific
Explanation or Ideology'?, *Social Problems*, Vol. 21 (June).
Willett, T.C. (1964), *Criminals on the Road: A Sudy of Serious Motoring Offences
and Those Who Commit Them*, London: Tavistock.
Williams, D.P. (1941), 'The Significance of an Abnormal Electroencephalogram', *J.
Neurol. Psychiat.*, Vol. 4.
Williams, D. (1972), 'Neural Factors Related to Habitual Aggression', *Brain*.
Wilson, E.O. (1976), *Sociobiology*, Cambridge, Mass: Harvard Univ. Press.
Witkin, H.A., H.F. Faterson, D.R. Dyk, D.R. Goodenough & S.A. Karp (1962),
Psychological Differentiation, N.Y: John Wiley & Sons.
Wolfgang, M.E. (1967), *Studies in Homicide*, New York: Harper & Row.
Wolfson, H.A. (1968), *Philo*. Vol.1, Cambridge, Mass: Harvard University Press.
Yarzura-Tobias, J.A. & F.A. Neziroglu (1975), 'Violent Behaviour, Brain
Dystrophy, Trauma and Glucose Dysfunction: A New Syndrome', *J.
Psychiatry*, Vol. 4.

231

Yasukochi, G. (1960), 'Emotional Responses Elicited by Electrical Stimulation of the Hypothalamus in Cats', *Folio. Psychiatr. Neurol,* Vol. 14, Japan.

Zeman, W. & F.A. King (1958), 'Tumours of the Septum Pellucidum and Adjacent Structures with Abnormal Affective Behaviour: An Anterior or Midline Structure Syndrome', *J. Nerv. Ment. Dis.*

Zimmerman, I.D. & K. Isaacs (1975), 'A Possible Effect of Testosterone on the Adenosine 3-5 Cyclic Monophosphate Levels in Rat Cerebral Cortex: A Brief Note', *Mechanisms of Aging and Development,* Vol. 4.

Zuckerman, M., E.A. Kolin & I. Zoob (1964), 'Development of Sensation Seeking Scale', *Journal of Consulting Psychology,* Vol. 28, No. 61.

Zuckerman, M., A.N. Bone, R. Neary, D. Mangelsdorff, & B. Brustman (1972), 'What is the Sensation Seeker? Personality Trait and Experience Correlates of the Sensation Seeking Scales', *Journal of Consulting Psychology,* Vol. 39.

Index

group performers, 67
guilt, 39, 42-3, 45, 53, 55
Gunn, J.C., 15
Gurdieff circle, 81

Hambert, G., 15
Hare, R.D., 25
Henn, F.A., 148
Himmler, E., 179, 202, 204, 210
Hitler, A., 176, 178, 180-81, 195-6,
    199-203, 204, 206, 209-13, 215
Holmstrom, I.L., 127
Hsu, F., 183
hypochondria, 93-4

impunitive; parents, 85, 92
impulsiveness, 1, 4, 8-10, 24-5, 28-9,
    43, 44, 53, 60,
independent variables, 83, 85-7, 89-
    90, 92-3
internalisation of norms, 151-3, 155-7
internalisation of traffic norms, 152-6,
    157-9
intolerance of objective ambiguity, 55,
    67
intropunitive type, 6, 66
Introversion, characteristics of, 3. *See
    also* Violence, possible predispos-
    ing factors towards
introvert, 4-5, 44, 60, 67, 163-4
Irwin, J., 8
Isaac, 176, 195, 197, 203-4, 206
Isaacs, K., 18
Isaac Syndrome. *See* Sacrificial vic-
    tims

Jacobs, P.A., 15
Jesus Christ, 176, 206
Jews: buying of time against oppres-
    sors, 205-7, 209-10, 215; victim-
    ization, self-conscious tendency
    towards, 207-9; emancipation, 215,
Johst, H., 191, 208
Judaism, description of 189-93
Jung, Karl, 59-60, 184, 199-200,
    204-5

Kagan's Matching Familiar Figures
    Test, 37, 43
Kant, I., 60, 177
Keating, L.F., 13
Kelly, S., 6
Kennard, M.A., 14
Kim, Y.K., 11, 30
Klein, Melanie, 64
Klein, S.G., 5, 6
Klinefelter's Syndrome, 46; xxy
    chromosomes, 15
Kling, A, 17

Kluckhohn, C., 182
Kluver, H., 11
Korczak, Janusz., 174, 203, 206
Kornhauser, R., 7
Kreuz, L.E., 16
Kroeber, A.L., 181

Lane, P.J., 3
Lairy, G.C., 12, 30
Levenson scale, 37
Levi-Strauss, C., 182-6, 200
Levy-Bruhl, L. 183
Levy, S., 14
Limbic system; 9-11, 26; imbalance in,
    26; *see also* cortical areas; *see also*
    Violence, neurobiology of
low risk taker, 4, 65
Lurianic Kabbala, 199
luteinising hormone (LH), 19, 35,102,
    109
Luther, M., 213

Macfarlene, A., 134
Macro violence, 174
Maletzky, B.M., 10
Mark, V., 10
Marlowe, D.A., 163
Marlowe, W.B., 11
Marxist ideology, 130
Masculine protest, 7
McClelland, D.C., 141-2
Mean Buss-Durkee Hostility
    Inventory, 18
Mednick, S., 16
Megargee, I.E., 3
Mein Kampf, 204
Memple, E., 11
Mens Rea, 114
Meyer-Balburg, H.F., 17
Mickle, W.A., 16
Money, J., 134
monotheism, 186, 189, 204
Monroe, R., 10, 31
Monti, P.M., 18
moral orientation, 6, 67
motive aggressiveness murders, 15
MPI, *see* stimulus aversion-hunger
Murray, G., 185, 189
Mylonas, A.D., 8
myth-playing, 187, 192-6

Narabayasi, H.T., 10-1
Nardini, J.E., 15
Nazi Regime: Judaeo-Christian moral-
    ity and, 200 et seq.; macro-
    criminological context of, 215-7, 221-
    3. myth-playing, Teutonic lore and,
    198-9
neural pathways, 147

neurobiology, 8; neurobiologic, 11
neurosurgery, 11
Niebelungen, 198
non-conformity, 67, 73
nonsynchronic, 15
normative dimension, 4
norms, internalisation of, 6
nuclear famliy, 6-7
Nuffield, E.J., 13
Nüremberg trials, 176

Object inclusion of the separant, 5;
    object exclusion of the participant,
    5; occipital cortex, 15, 30
Oedipal Complex, 98
Ontological Dimension, 4-5
Orientation; inner, outer, sanction, 67;
    time/timeless, 73
Ounsted, C., 13
Outward aggression, commitment,
    105, 167
Overcrowding in prisons, 8, 51, 58

Pain, Amygdalar region, 31;
    Conformist (non-conformist), 166;
    Emotional liability, 166;
    Extra(intra) punitiveness, 166;
    External/internal control, 166; Field
    (independence) dependence, 166;
    Group performer, 166;
    Resentment, 166; High (low) risk
    taking, 166; High/low sensitivity,
    166; Sanction (moral) orientation,
    166; Stimulus hunger
    (aversion),166; Tolerance
    (intolerance) of ideational ambigu-
    ity and objective ambiguity, 166
paranoia, 40, 42
parietal lobes, 27
Parson, T., 7, 16
Participant, 4, 183; Constancy, qui-
    etism, individual, resignation, self-
    manipulation, stability, intuition an-
    choring on the self, 69; unity, 183
periodic dyscontrol, syndrome of, 26
Persky, H., 17-8
Personality types,dimensions and
    traits: 4, 67, 182; augmenter, 161;
    conformist, 161; extrapunitive, 4,
    6, 7, 74, 83, 182; field depen-
    dence, 4, 7, 74-5, 83, 88, 182;
    field independence, 4, 7, 74-5, 83,
    161, 182; field performer, 161;
    group performer, 161; high risk
    takers 4, 161, 174-6; high sensi-
    tivity to pain, 161; inner castiga-
    tion, 161; inner controls, 161; in-
    ner-directed, 161; intolerant of ob-
    jective ambiguity and of ideational

ambiguity, 161; intrapunitve, 4, 7,
74, 88, 182; intropunitive, 161;
isolate performer, 161; low risk
takers , 4, 161, 182; low sensitivity to pain, 161; low vulnerability
to sensory deprivation, 161; moral
orientation 4, 7, 161; non-conformist, 161; normative, 4, 182;
object-inclusion, 161; ontological,
4, 6-7, 182; 'other-directed', 161;
outer control 5; quietist, 161; reducer, 161; sanction, 161; self-exclusion, 161; sensory deprivation,
161; stimulus aversion, 161; stimulus hunger, 161; tolerance of objective ambiguity, 161; traits 161
Personality types: participant, 4; sepa-
    rant 5; *see also* Shoham's
    Personality Theory
Petit-mal patients, 13
Petrie, A., 5, 163
phenothiasines, 31
photic drive, 14, 18-9, 30
PIF secretion, 31
Pillien, G., 11
plannedness, 24
Plum, F., 10
Poeck, K., 10
predisposition to violence, 2
prisoners' attitude of violence, 8
prolactin, 18, 31, 94
prolactive hormone, 89
provoking communication, 101
psychasthemia, 39
psychological parameter, 8
psychopath, 2
pubertal eroticism, hormones, mor-
    phology, 147

Quay, H.C., 4
quietist participation, 5

Rada, R.T., 18
Rahav, G., 7
Rape, 128, 145-65; aetiological hierar-
    chy of, 161-4; aggressive aim, 132;
    'blitz' rape, 132; 'confidence' rape,
    132; combined aim 132; feminist
    ideology concerning, 141-5;
    misogynist theory of 146-7; neuro-
    biology of, 12; personality theory
    concerning, 148-61; typology of,
    132
Raven Intelligence Test, 37
'reckless' driver, 161
Reckless, W.C., 8
Reducers, 4-5, 78
Reeves, A.G., 10
Reinach, T., 189

sponse, 3; Inner Directed, 159; neurobiology of, 8, 11, 100; planned, 43; possible predisposing factors towards, 102, 113-4; provocative behaviour 114-7; relationship structures, 114-8; risks, tendency to take, 2; social and cultural factors, 3; testosterone and cortisol levels, 3, 17
Violence prone, 11
Violent prisoners; dependent variables of, 42; distinguished from non-violent prisoners, 44-7; impulsive violence, 28-9; independent variables of, 39, 48; overcrowding, 48
Von Dem Bach Zelewsky, 209
vulnerability to sensory deprivation, 67

wakefulness, 12

warmhearted, 41
Warsaw Ghetto, 203
Wasman, M., 9
Watson, R.E., 9
Way, C., 130
Weak ego, 45
West, D.J., 145
Wieser, H.G., 30
Wilkinson, K., 6
Williams, D., 12, 14, 30
Wilson, E.O., 143
Wise Men of Zion, 196-7
Witkin, H.A., 2, 5, 37, 43; *See also* field dependence
Wolfgang, M.E., 25, 99

Xyy chromosome theory, 99, 147

Zeman, W., 10
Zimmermann, I.D., 17
Zuckerman's Sensation Seeking Scale, 2, 40, 151, 154